The Mogul

Other Books by Rich Westcott

The Phillies Encyclopedia (with Frank Bilovsky)
Diamond Greats
Phillies '93: An Incredible Season
Masters of the Diamond
Mike Schmidt
Philadelphia's Old Ballparks
No-Hitters: The 225 Games, 1893–1999 (with Allen Lewis)
Splendor on the Diamond
Great Home Runs of the 20th Century
A Century of Philadelphia Sports
Winningest Pitchers: Baseball's 300-Game Winners
Tales from the Phillies Dugout
Native Sons: Philadelphia Baseball Players Who Made the Major Leagues
Mickey Vernon: The Gentleman First Baseman
Veterans Stadium: Field of Memories
Phillies Essential
Remarkable Phillies Stories: Some Never Told Before

The Mogul

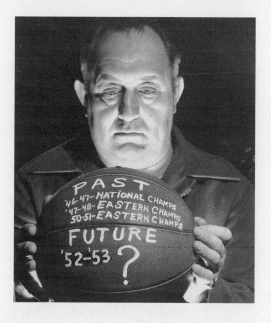

Eddie Gottlieb, Philadelphia Sports Legend
and Pro Basketball Pioneer

RICH WESTCOTT

Foreword by Paul Arizin

TEMPLE UNIVERSITY PRESS
Philadelphia

To Paul Arizin —

April 9, 1928–December 12, 2006

A great basketball player,

but an even greater human being

AND

To Ralph Bernstein and Frank Dolson

Good friends and sportswriting legends

Temple University Press
1601 North Broad Street
Philadelphia, PA 19122
www.temple.edu/tempress

Copyright © 2008 by Rich Westcott
All rights reserved
Published 2008
Printed in the United States of America

Text design by Kate Nichols

♾ The paper used in this publication meets the requirements of the American National Standard for Information Sciences—Permanence of Paper for Printed Library Materials, ANSI Z39.48-1992

Library of Congress Cataloging-in-Publication Data

Westcott, Rich.
The Mogul : Eddie Gottlieb, Philadelphia sports legend
and pro basketball pioneer / Rich Westcott ; foreword by Paul Arizin.
p.   cm.
Includes index.
ISBN-13: 978-1-59213-655-1 (cloth : alk. paper)
1. Gottlieb, Eddie, 1898–1979. 2. Basketball coaches—Pennsylvania—
Philadelphia—Biography. 3. Basketball team owners—Pennsylvania—
Philadelphia—Biography. 4. Jews—Pennsylvania—Philadelphia—Biography.
5. Professional sports—Pennsylvania—Philadelphia—History—
20th century. I. Title.
GV884.G68W47 2008
796.323092—dc22
[B]
2008001843

2 4 6 8 9 7 5 3 1

Contents

Foreword

Paul Arizin

At long last, there is now a book about an extraordinary person, Eddie Gottlieb. *The Mogul: Eddie Gottlieb, Philadelphia Sports Legend and Pro Basketball Pioneer* is a fascinating look at a man who ranks as one of the foremost sports figures in Philadelphia history.

Rich Westcott has written 18 previous sports books, but this one ranks right up there as one of his best. He has carefully researched every aspect of Eddie's life, interviewed numerous people who knew him, and come up with a masterfully written book that provides an authoritative and thoroughly engaging portrait of this highly prominent man.

It is a book that takes the reader from Eddie's early life through his years with the SPHAS (South Philadelphia Hebrew Association), with the Philadelphia Stars, and as a master promoter and booking agent. It continues through the years when Gotty reached the pinnacle of his career as coach and later owner of the Philadelphia Warriors and was at the same time one of the most important people ever connected with the National Basketball Association (NBA). Ending with Gottlieb's sale of the Warriors and his final years, the book is one that covers every aspect of the man's amazing life.

From a personal standpoint, Eddie Gottlieb was one of the most important people in my life. My first meeting with him occurred in June 1950. I was a first-round territorial draft choice of the Warriors. Our meeting was in Eddie's office on the second floor of Keith's Theater on Chestnut Street in Center City Philadelphia.

I really hadn't given the idea of playing professional basketball much thought. But when he asked what I expected in salary, I pulled a figure of $10,000 out of the air, probably because it was a nice round figure. I had no idea what salaries were in the NBA.

Gottlieb was shocked. He said the figure was ridiculously high. I started to leave, but as I did, he told me he would sweeten the pot a bit. He asked whether I had seen the movie currently playing at Keith's. I hadn't, I told him. Eddie knew the manager and got me a free ticket.

I spent that summer in the Catskills. Eddie and I met again in September. It was not important to me that I play in the NBA. I was a college graduate, waiting to be drafted for Korea. Gotty must have sensed my disinterest, and after much conversation, he agreed to the figure I had given him back in June. He told me that it would probably bankrupt the Philadelphia team.

At the time, The Mogul's only title was coach. But he was much more than that. The team, part of the Arena Corporation, was owned by Triangle Publications. Pete Tyrrell was the president and general manager of the company. But Eddie was "the man." He did everything. In addition to coaching, he handled administrative duties, scheduling, transportation, hotels—all the tasks that are performed today by an army of people.

Gottlieb and I seemed to hit it off right from the start when we began training in Hershey. I learned to respect Eddie's honesty, enthusiasm, knowledge, and love of the game, although he was not above a good tongue-lashing when needed. I think he respected the fact that I played hard and came to play every game. In the beginning of my career, I was the other forward with Joe Fulks, although I'm still not certain I deserved that spot initially. We had some very good forwards who were certainly capable of starting, including Vern Gardner, an All-American at Utah and a very, very good player.

In 1950–51, the Warriors won the Eastern Division regular-season title, but were knocked out in the first round of the playoffs by Syracuse. I have never seen Eddie so low as after that final game. He became even lower when Rochester beat the great Minneapolis team with George Mikan in the semifinal. We had handled Rochester all year.

By then, I had become more familiar with Gotty's ways, and my admiration for him continued to increase. His strong character and intelligence were impressive. And a few years later when he became the owner, his hands-on methods and his operation of the team made him even more admirable.

I looked upon Gotty not only as an employer and coach, but as a true friend, maybe even sort of a surrogate uncle. I was very fortunate that he took a liking to me. It helped my career tremendously that he played me right from the start.

In an era in which little TV revenue existed and top ticket prices were $2.50 and $3.00, Gotty had to struggle to exist. But somehow, he made it all work. I can't imagine anybody doing as good a job as Eddie did.

In whatever company Eddie found himself, he was the boss, and his presence was always conspicuous. Without Gottlieb, there would be no NBA team in Philadelphia today, and quite possibly no NBA. Players, fans, and everybody connected with the NBA are all in his debt, and his passing in 1979 was a loss for those of us who knew him.

Fortunately, Rich Westcott has written a book that not only tells the story but preserves the memory of this great man and the many-faceted life he lived. I for one, and I'm sure many, many others, are thrilled that such a book has finally been published.

To take it one step further, any reader interested in early basketball, Negro League baseball, or pro basketball as it once was will find this book well worth reading. And if your interest is in the history of the SPHAS, the Stars, the Warriors, or numerous other Philadelphia sports activities of the past, this is a book that simply must be read.

So read and enjoy. I know you will find Eddie Gottlieb to be a man unlike anyone you've ever read about before.

November 2006

Introduction

In the long and storied history of Philadelphia sports, there have been many participants whose work had a lasting effect on the games with which they were associated. Some were prominent on a local level, while others enjoyed a national reputation.

Most of them, of course, were players. A few, however, were nonuniformed participants who did not perform on the playing field. In this category, no one was more influential than Eddie Gottlieb.

Unquestionably, Gottlieb ranks as one of the most powerful nonplaying sports figures ever to operate in Philadelphia. But his success wasn't restricted to that city. He had an enormous impact at a national level, too. In fact, as one of the pioneers of professional basketball, Gottlieb is unquestionably the single most important reason the sport has reached its current level of success. But, although Gottlieb is most closely associated with basketball, he also attained a high level of prominence in other sports, especially in baseball.

Gottlieb's story is a complex one. Over the course of his life, he wore many hats: owner, general manager, coach, player, entrepreneur, promoter, booking agent, schoolteacher, and sporting goods salesman. He was wise, yet cautious, a stickler for details, loyal, honest, frugal, opinionated, gruff, profane, and cunning. Although he insisted on being the boss—today he might be called a "control freak"—he had legions of friends who included the rare mix of members of his team, opponents, fans, and the media.

Called "The Mogul" by almost everybody, Gottlieb was one of the founders of the Basketball Association of America (BAA), which later formed the basis for the National Basketball Association (NBA). Because of his vital role in that process, Gottlieb has been called "The Father of Pro Basketball." It has often been said that without Gottlieb, there would be no NBA.

He was the coach of the city's first major league basketball team, the Philadelphia Warriors, founded in 1946. He purchased the team for $25,000 in 1952, owning it until 1962, when he sold the franchise to a group from San Francisco for $850,000.

While the Warriors were winning two professional basketball championships, including one in the BAA in its first year of operation, Gottlieb was a dominant figure in the sport. He was chairman of the NBA Rules Committee for 26 years. And he strongly supported the creation of the 24-second clock, while initiating numerous other new rules.

Certainly, the crowning achievement of his career came when he drafted Wilt Chamberlain after almost single-handedly pushing through a rule that allowed teams to draft high school players who played in their areas. For 30 years, he also was responsible for drawing up the NBA schedule, which he did by hand, often making notes on a rumpled sheet of paper that he carried around in his back pocket. When the job was finally switched to a computer, the machine couldn't handle it and the assignment was returned to Gotty.

During his career, Gottlieb always worked out of tiny offices in Center City, handling all of the many duties of a professional sports team with the help of just a few other people. One was the legendary public address announcer Dave Zinkoff, who spent 42 years with Gotty. Another was ticket manager Mike Iannarella, a Gotty associate for 48 years. Harvey Pollack, still active with the 76ers, served as Gottlieb's publicity director, starting in 1946.

Gottlieb was a keen judge of talent. He was also extremely innovative. He disliked excessive dribbling, preferring instead that his players pass the ball. To make his point, he occasionally held drills with a partially deflated ball.

While they existed, the Philadelphia Warriors were one of pro basketball's most colorful—and interesting—teams. They played at both the Arena and Convention Hall (both in West Philadelphia), sometimes taking the court in the second game of a doubleheader in which four different pro teams participated. Symbolic of the unpretentious conditions of early pro basketball, the Warriors also sometimes played games at local high schools.

Believing that it helped to attract fans, Gottlieb usually built the Warriors around local players, a group that over the years included All-Americans such as Chamberlain, Paul Arizin of Villanova, George Senesky of St. Joseph's, Tom Gola of La Salle, Ernie Beck of Penn, and Guy Rodgers of Temple. During their 16 years in Philadelphia, Warriors players Joe Fulks, Neil Johnston, Arizin, and Chamberlain led the league in scoring a combined total of nine times. It was during one of those years (1962) that Chamberlain scored 100 points in one game.

The Mogul, however, was more than the driving force behind the Warriors and the NBA. He helped in the relocation of the Syracuse Nats to Philadelphia where the team became the 76ers. And he was a key figure in Negro League baseball. He was a promoter and booking agent for African American teams dating from the 1920s to the late 1940s, in effect controlling who played where and when in eastern Pennsylvania. In 1933, Gottlieb also became the principal owner and financier of the Philadelphia Stars, a Negro League team with which he was connected until it disbanded in the early 1950s.

Gotty was one of the founders in 1919 of the storied SPHAS (South Philadelphia Hebrew Association), which became Philadelphia's first major pro basketball team and performed in the city for some 35 years. He served two stints as head coach of the Philadelphia Textile School (now Philadelphia University) basketball squad. In 1922, he helped to found the Philadelphia Baseball Association, an organization that eventually included 60 semiprofessional teams. In the 1940s and 1950s, he was the promoter and booking agent for the Harlem Globetrotters during their annual summer tours in Europe.

During his career, Gottlieb was also the commissioner of a local semiprofessional football league and was involved as a promoter of professional wrestling matches. Once, he even attempted—unsuccessfully—to put together a group headed by the well-known Levy family to purchase the Phillies, intending to become general manager and to add to the team star players from the Negro Leagues. Later, in recognition of his vast knowledge of Negro League baseball, he was also named by commissioner Bowie Kuhn to a 10-member committee charged with recommending pre–Jackie Robinson Negro League players for induction into the Baseball Hall of Fame. The work of that group resulted in players such as Satchel Paige, Josh Gibson, and many others getting inducted into the baseball shrine.

Gottlieb's connection with local sports went back to his youth. Born in 1898 in Kiev, Ukraine, he immigrated with his parents to the United States at the age of four. By the time he was 10, Gottlieb was playing on a grade school basketball team. He attended South Philadelphia High School where he played basketball, baseball, and football before graduating in 1916. Gottlieb then attended the School of Pedagogy in Philadelphia, playing basketball for two years and serving as captain in his final year. He graduated in 1918 and soon thereafter launched a career as a teacher.

At the age of 19, Gottlieb joined with former high school teammates Hughie Black and Harry Passon to form an amateur basketball team, which two years later became known as the SPHAS. The SPHAS performed as an independent team and then as a member of the amateur Philadelphia League until joining the semiprofessional Eastern League in 1925. Over the next 22 years, while playing in three different leagues, the SPHAS won 13 league championships, made 18 trips to the playoffs, and became known as the team that held highly popular dances following games at the Broadwood Hotel in Center City.

In those days, basketball was primarily a Jewish man's game and featured low-scoring contests, a leather-covered ball, two-hand set shots, and a center jump after each field goal. Players wore high-top black sneakers, leather kneepads, and sleeveless shirts and were paid between $5 and $30 per game. It was a vastly different game from today's fast-paced version, so much of which is played above the rim.

While he was running the SPHAS, Gottlieb was busy with his Negro League and booking agent duties. He booked as many as 500 amateur baseball games each week. He also booked appearances for entertainers. Gottlieb arranged for the first appearance of fellow South Philadelphia resident Joey Bishop in 1937. He made dates for many years for not only Bishop, but for others such as baseball comedian Max Patkin.

Life was always a big gamble for Gotty, who was never averse to placing a wager at various race tracks and other spots around the city. He took risks. He navigated uncharted waters. And during much of his career, he had an uncanny knack of being able to make things work.

"Eddie was one of the brightest people I've ever been around," said renowned local sportscaster Bill Campbell who broadcast Warriors games in the club's early years. "He was very opinionated, very stubborn, but very honest. He was a very, very interesting guy, and one who was just a brilliant, brilliant person."

Gottlieb had a fascinating and unique life. He was colorful and imaginative, relentless, enthusiastic, and indefatigable. Indeed, there are few sports figures with lives more interesting than Gottlieb's. And he knew virtually everything there was to know, not only about Philadelphia sports, past and present, but about sports on a national level.

Jerry Rullo, who came out of Temple to play with the SPHAS and Warriors, called Gottlieb "a terrific businessman. And his word was as good as his bond. He had a terrific memory. And he was a very honest man."

By virtue of its content, this book serves as a history of two of Philadelphia's legendary basketball teams, the SPHAS and the Warriors. Gottlieb operated both teams during their entire existences, and, to a great extent, his story is the story of these two teams. Because he ran the Stars from their start to their finish—thereby running at one point three pro teams at once—Gotty's story will also serve as a history of that team.

The following pages also include a discussion of the evolution of the Jewish community in Philadelphia and its early passion for the game of basketball. From the 1920s to the mid-1940s, basketball was the preferred sport of Jews, and most of the players were members of that religion.

There is also a look at the African American community in Philadelphia, its relationship to both baseball and basketball, and segregation in those two sports. As a hotbed of black baseball during the first half of the 20th century, Philadelphia has a unique background in this area.

As for Gotty, it was never difficult to find words to describe him. And anyone who tried never had to rely on words that were insipid or ambivalent. Gottlieb was the kind of person who brought out the best in one's vocabulary.

More than 27 years after his passing, Gottlieb continues to inspire provocative comments by those who knew him. In the process of interviewing more than 50 people for this book, and holding conversations with another two dozen or so, virtually everyone had strong opinions about The Mogul. Some were flattering. Some were not. He affected different people in different ways. And descriptions of him sometimes were contradictory. But in all cases, they helped to describe a man who throughout his life was anything but wishy-washy.

"To me, he was in a class by himself," said former Warriors player George Dempsey. "He was a brilliant guy. It was fun to sit down and talk with him because he had more stories than anybody I ever knew. And he knew other sports like baseball and boxing as well as he knew basketball. He was a unique character with a good heart, and it was a joy to be in his presence. He was a competitor like nobody else. He wanted to win in the worst way."

Indeed, Gottlieb was one of a kind, a Damon Runyan kind of character who far surpassed his humble origins. From Russia to South Philadelphia, from dingy gyms to gaudy arenas, from an unknown kid to a nationally prominent sports figure, his life followed an extraordinary path that was crammed with special achievements.

It was a life that could fill a book.

While working on this book, it was obvious to me that the perfect person to write the foreword was Paul Arizin. Paul was a former Villanova All-American, two-time NBA scoring champ, and a man who in 1996 was named one of the top 50 NBA players of all time. An enormously prominent figure in basketball, a star on the last Philadelphia Warriors' NBA championship team, and, like Gottlieb, a member of the Basketball Hall of Fame, Arizin knew Gotty intimately. Gottlieb had signed him to his first pro contract, was his first pro coach, later owned the team, and the two had remained close friends over all the years that followed.

Paul and I had been friends for some years, too. We lived in the same town, and among those interviewed for the book, he was unquestionably my best source. When I approached him with the idea of writing the foreword, he quickly and enthusiastically agreed to do it.

Arizin wrote a wonderful foreword that provides not only special insight, but some interesting personal views and experiences. Unfortunately, shortly after he'd completed the foreword, Paul died suddenly at his home. He was 79 years old.

Paul Arizin was a fine, humble gentleman. And he was a person who, when he was in the local post office or the local library or his local church, would never, never unveil his celebrity status. It was a thrill to have seen him play and then to have gotten to know him, and I am proud and honored that with the consent of his wife, Maureen, who died of an injury about two months after Paul's passing, his foreword appears in this book.

CHAPTER 1

From Russia to South Philly

In 1898, two events took place that would forever shape the game of basketball. Neither commanded much attention at the time, but in the years to come, it would appear to be more than a little ironic that these two seemingly insignificant events occurred in the same year.

Even more ironic was the fact that this pair of unrelated occurrences, which happened on two different continents and in totally different circumstances, would ultimately become indelibly linked. One happened in Russia. One in the United States. Thousands of miles apart. But in their own ways, the two would have a monumental impact not only on a sport but on an entire culture.

It had been seven years since James Naismith, a 30-year-old physical education teacher in Springfield, Massachusetts, had invented the game of basketball. A former rugby and lacrosse player from Canada, Naismith, was an ordained minister who had come to Springfield to learn to be a teacher at the International YMCA Training School. While there, he had helped to form a football team, one of his teammates being the future coaching legend, Amos Alonzo Stagg. After becoming a teacher at nearby Springfield College, Naismith, who later earned a degree in medicine, searched for a game for his students that they could play indoors during the cold winter months. Eventually, he came up with an idea.

Naismith, sharp-minded as always, hung peach baskets 10 feet high on the rails of the balconies at each end of a 35- by 50-foot floor in the basement of his school. Then, he divided his class of 18 boys into two teams. Using a soccer ball, they played a game—the first basketball game ever played. The final score was reportedly 1–0.

Nevertheless, the game caught on quickly. Soon, YMCAs and club teams, mostly in the Northeast, were fielding teams. Philadelphia was at the forefront of the game's rapidly increasing popularity, with teams blossoming all over the city.

By 1895, the first year that backboards were used, many leagues had been formed. They played mostly on courts that were enclosed and in many cases sealed off by steel mesh or chicken wire, with baskets hanging at the far ends of courts that were often as long as 65 feet. The games were rough—controlled mayhem some called it—there were frequent fights, pushing, shoving and slamming shoulders into opponents were the norm, and players were often led off the court bruised and bleeding. There was no out of bounds, one player shot all his team's foul shots, there was a center jump after each field goal and foul shot, two-hand dribbles were permissible, and games lasted 40 minutes.

Basketball also became a popular diversion at schools and colleges. The first college game was played in 1894 with Haverford College defeating Temple University, 6–4, at the Owls' gymnasium at Broad and Berks Streets. That year, while playing in 11 games against college, club, and YMCA teams, Temple outscored its opponents, 59–33.

According to an article written in 1977 in the Philadelphia *Inquirer* by Bill Ordine, a YMCA team from Germantown went unbeaten in 21 games in 1895 and gained the championship of Pennsylvania, New Jersey, and Delaware.

About that time, the first professional teams were assembling. The first pro game occurred in 1896 in Trenton, New Jersey. Trenton defeated Brooklyn YMCA, 16–1, before 700 spectators. That year, Trenton posted a 19–1 record, losing only to Millville, 8–0.

The nation's first professional league, called the National League, made its debut in 1898. It consisted of three teams from Philadelphia—Germantown, the Clover Wheelmen, and the Hancock Athletic Club—and three teams from New Jersey—Millville, Camden, and Trenton, the circuit's first champion. Horace Fogel, then the sports editor of the Philadelphia *Public Ledger* and later the president of the Philadelphia Phillies, served as president of the league, which lasted five years. Players received $2.50 for each home game and $1.25 for away tilts. Referees were paid $3.00 a game.

The formation of the first professional league, which was quickly followed by the start of several other pro leagues, provided the foundation for a movement that over the next three decades saw the emergence of pro teams throughout the country and that eventually grew into a multibillion-dollar operation that now, more than one century later, has become one of the most popular and successful pastimes in the country, if not the entire world.

Coincidentally, but quite appropriately, 1898 was not only the year that gave birth to the first pro basketball league. It was also the year in which Eddie Gottlieb was born.

Records from the Basketball Hall of Fame, as well as early census reports, show that Gottlieb entered the world on September 15, 1898, in Kiev, the capital of Ukraine and one of the oldest cities in northern Europe, dating back to the 5th century. It is entirely possible, however, that Gottlieb was actually not born in the city of Kiev, but—because only the wealthiest and most skilled Jews, such as merchants, craftsmen, retired soldiers, winemakers, and mechanics, were permitted to live in the city itself—may have entered the world in one of the regions that surrounded Kiev (which was not only a city but also an oblast or district).

At the time of Gotty's birth, the Ukraine and the rest of the Russian Empire were in a state of turmoil. Revolts against the czar and his loyalists were becoming increasingly frequent. (Eventually, revolutions would take place in both 1905 and 1917 when Nikolai Lenin and his Marxist regime would take power.)

No group was more subjected to the turmoil than Russia's Jewish population. By the end of the 19th century, some five and one-half million Jews resided in the Russian Empire, which then included Ukraine. Jews had lived in Ukraine for more than 1,000 years; in fact, in the 16th century some 45,000 Jews lived just in the Kiev area. By the late 1890s, the Jewish population in Ukraine had reached two million.

But because of religious and other differences, considerable tension existed between Jews and many of the other residents of the country. Throughout the empire, Jews were severely persecuted and forced by law to live in regions known as Pale of Settlement, isolated villages where only a few clandestine synagogues existed and where most of the residents were either artisans or worked on the estates of wealthy Russians. The settlements were especially vulnerable to roving gangs of Russian thugs, often called Cossacks and sometimes numbering as many as several hundred.

The persecution of Jews in Ukraine, as well as in the rest of western Russia, was widespread. But the pogroms, when whole settlements were waylaid by the criminals on horseback, made conditions for Jews almost unbearable, especially in the late 1800s.

Pogrom was a Jewish word that roughly translated meant devastation or violent attacks. Dating back to the early 1870s, they were frequent and they were condoned by the anti-Semitic czars, Alexander III, then after his assassination in 1881, Nicholas II, each of whom sanctioned the attacks in hopes of bolstering his fading popularity. The mobs that staged the vicious pogroms often murdered—sometimes as many as several hundred innocent people—raped, beat, and plundered the Jewish residents that they attacked, and often captured children who would then be turned into either slaves or soldiers. The perpetrators would then return to their own domains where they received the loud acclamation of their cohorts.

Because of these conditions, frequent anti-Semitic legislation, and the lack of opportunities, large numbers of Jews had started to leave Russia in the 1880s. Of course, some stayed behind, helping to form the rebel Socialist Revolutionary Party in the 1890s. But ultimately, hundreds of thousands of Jews fled the persecution and deplorable conditions of Russia, most of them finding passage to United States.

Most European immigrants landed on Ellis Island in the New York harbor. Between 1892 and 1924, when Congress passed the Johnson-Reed Act, which set quotas on the number of immigrants allowed to enter the United States, 17 million people were processed on the 27-acre island, a large portion of that group being Jews. Others landed at Castle Garden, an early immigration station in New York, as well as at Baltimore, Philadelphia, Boston, New Orleans, and Galveston, Texas.

It was in New York, site of the largest Jewish population in United States, that the four-year-old Eddie Gottlieb and his family—30-year-old parents and a six-year-old sister—arrived in 1902. Presumably, they landed in New York, although no passenger lists are available to verify that claim.

Part of the reason for that may have to do with the family name. Possibly, Gottlieb was not the family name in Russia, or it was spelled differently. As was often the case when immigrants landed, U.S. customs officials arbitrarily gave people new names, ones that were easier to spell, easier to pronounce, more Americanized. Gottlieb was a German name that meant "God's love" or "love of God." It is possible that the family landed under its original name and was then assigned Gottlieb as a new name, but more likely, the name was spelled some other way.

Almost nothing is known about the early life of Gottlieb. No early records exist. When he died in 1979, Gotty had a few relatives living in the area, although their presence was inconspicuous. And the man himself was always tight-lipped about his origins.

As an adult, Gottlieb seldom mentioned his birthplace. In fact, some newspaper and magazine articles about him attributed his birthplace to New York. Even a lengthy feature article by Frank Deford that appeared in a 1968 issue of *Sports Illustrated,* as well as a detailed piece by Gaeton Fonzi in *Greater Philadelphia Magazine* in 1960, claimed that Gotty was born in New York. "I wasn't born, I just grew," Gottlieb once told writer Alan Richman of the Philadelphia *Inquirer.*

Because it was during a period known as the Cold War when relations between the United States and Soviet Union had deteriorated to an untenable level, it is possible that Gottlieb either thought it was expedient to hide his origins or was too embarrassed to admit that he was of Russian descent.

Tom Meschery, an excellent forward with the Philadelphia and San Francisco Warriors, also had a Russian background. His maternal grandfather was a member of the Russian nobility. His father was an officer in the Russian army, a loyalist to the czar who, after the second revolution, was forced to flee across Siberia to Manchuria where Tom was born. Several years later, after the outbreak of World War II, his family wound up in a Japanese internment camp in Tokyo, where they resided until reaching the United States when Meschery was eight years old.

Yet, curiously, despite their similar roots, Gottlieb never mentioned Russia to Meschery, whose original name was Mescheriakoff. "Never said one word the whole time I knew him," said the former player. "I don't know why. I think he was more interested in other things, like making money and having a winning team."

It is known that after their arrival from Russia, the Gottliebs lived in New York where father, Moishe (also known as Morris) Aaron Gottlieb, ran a candy store. Both Moishe and his wife, Chialeah or Charleah (Leah or Lena as she was usually called), who stayed home to manage the household, were born in Russia, as were their parents. The Gottliebs, both born around 1872 and married in 1894, learned to speak some English. The family, including Bella, a sister two years older than Eddie (two other children had died as babies), resided near the corner of 107th Street and Madison Avenue in a heavily populated Jewish section of the city that later became known as Spanish Harlem.

The area was originally a Dutch settlement in the 1600s, and the one from which Peter Stuyvesant governed New York. Later, it was populated by Germans, then Irish and Italians—one of whom was future New York City mayor Fiorella LaGuardia—and finally Jews. The section, which in the late 1800s contained some 65,000 apartments, was mostly Hispanic in the 1930s and 1940s, and then African American after that.

In the early years, the future Mogul's first name was not Edward. It was Isadore. That name was even used in his high school yearbook some years later. By the time he filled out his draft card in 1918, Gottlieb was using the name of Edward. He professed to have no middle name, although on rare occasions over the years he listed himself as Edward I. Gottlieb.

The youngster, unlike the sons of many Jewish immigrants, was not discouraged by his parents from playing sports, and he quickly developed an interest in America's games. Initially, his favorite sport was baseball, and he often hitched rides on ice trucks to Coogan's Bluff where he stood looking down into the Polo Grounds to watch New York Giants games.

He was an avid player, too, holding down a spot as a catcher in kids' games in the neighborhood. "I was just average," he told Deford years later. "Two things wrong with me as a catcher were: I couldn't hit very well and I couldn't throw very well. But, listen, I was an A-1 receiver."

Sometime around 1908, the family moved for unknown reasons to Philadelphia. Morris, Leah, Bella, and Isadore resided in an apartment at 762 South Broad Street in South Philadelphia. According to the 1910 census, six other boarders, all but one a native of Pennsylvania, also lived in the building. Morris gained employment as a "presser" in a nearby tailor shop. Within a few years, however, he had died, leaving the job of raising the family to Leah.

"Leah was a typical Jewish woman," remembered Estelle Litwack, wife of Eddie's lifelong friend, Harry. "She had a Russian accent. Most of the time, she stayed home to take care of the family."

That was especially necessary because Bella—or Belle as she was later known—had various problems. She had an eye ailment that affected her sight. And, described as being "kind of strange," she shadowed her mother virtually everywhere Leah went. In later years, although she worked occasionally as a bookkeeper, Belle spent time at Friends Hospital undergoing treatment for mental illness that plagued her much of her life.

Even when they became adults, Gotty always watched over her, keeping her with him wherever he lived and once giving her a part-time job as a typist with the SPHAS. "I had to take care of her," Gottlieb said years later. In the 1930s, Belle worked briefly as a bookkeeper at Diston Saw Company.

Within a few years after arriving in Philadelphia, where a Jewish colony had existed since the 1730s and which was home to the nation's second-largest Jewish population, the family moved into a first-floor apartment at 114 South Street. Charles and Rosa Delgiorno and their five children lived in the other apartment in the two-story row house.

At the time, South Philly was heavily populated with immigrants. Of the more than 300,000 residents, about 35 percent were foreign-born, most of them Jewish, Polish, Irish, and Italian. Jews by a large margin outnumbered the others. In fact, between 1870 and 1910, the population of South Philadelphia more than doubled, the largest contributors to that increase—at that point totaling about 45,000—being Russian Jews. Many of them landed on ships that regularly brought immigrants from across the ocean, docking at Front and Lombard Streets at a busy port along the Delaware River.

There were so many Jews in South Philly, in fact, that in 1903, four years before the opening of the Market Street subway, a Presbyterian church had to be converted into a synagogue. South Street was the center of the thriving Jewish community, which extended from what was called the Southwark section south to Oregon Avenue and between Broad and Front Streets.

In the early 1900s, the public high schools with the best athletic teams in Philadelphia were Central and South Philadelphia (later commonly called Southern) High Schools. Both schools were well stocked with Jewish immigrants or their sons. Indeed, two people who would soon rank among Gotty's best friends, Hughie Black and Harry Litwack, were Jewish immigrants born in Russia and Austria, respectively. Black, born the same year as Gottlieb, had emigrated with his family from the Russian province of Moldavia, crossing the border at night while holding a little sister in each hand. After the family arrived in Baltimore in 1904, their real name, Schwartz, was translated to the English word Black.

South Philly High, standing at Broad Street and Tasker Avenue, had originally been called Southern Manual Training School when it opened in 1907. It was a vocational school established to teach trades to the scores

South Philadelphia High School, located at Broad Street and Tasker Avenue, as it looked when Gottlieb was a student there. *(Southern High School/Bill Esher)*

of immigrant children living in the area, who at the time were believed to be incapable of grasping academic subjects. Eventually, that notion disappeared, and in 1915, the name of the school was changed to South Philadelphia High School. The school had 14 classrooms and seven laboratories. It was an all-boys school, although a girls school of the same name was located across the street.

Over the years, South Philly High would be the primary source of formal education for some of the city's most famous citizens. Singers Mario Lanza, Eddie Fisher, Frankie Avalon, Fabian, Chubby Checker (Ernest Evans), Marian Anderson, Al Martino, James Darren, Bobby Rydell, Al Alberts, Gloria Mann, Stan Getz, Buddy Greco, and Sunny Gale went there. So did comedians Jack Klugman, Joey Bishop, David Brenner, Larry Fine, and Joey Foreman. And boxing notables Tommy Loughran, Lew Tendler, Angelo Dundee, and Midget Wolgast once sat in SPHS classrooms.

In the early years of the 20th century, there were no junior high schools in Philadelphia. Grammar schools extended through eighth grade, after which students moved directly to high school.

According to the 1916 South Philadelphia High School yearbook, Gottlieb attended Southwark Grammar School, which was—and still is—located at Ninth and Mifflin Streets. Although he had originally attended grade school in New York, it was at Southwark where Gottlieb's love of sports blossomed. He developed an interest in football. He liked baseball even more, and although he knew it was unrealistic, he harbored a burning desire to become a big league player.

Gottlieb, whose family were members of the congregation of B'nai Abraham Synagogue, went from Southwark to South Philadelphia High, arriving with his classmates—all dressed in their finest clothes—at his new school as a ninth grader on September 8, 1912.

Basketball was the school's game of choice. And when Gottlieb entered South Philly High, the sport was already starting to flourish. Ultimately, Southern won the city championship in 1914, 1915, and 1916.

Gotty, though, kept his sports interests varied. He was already attracted to football and, although small for his age, had become a quarterback. "I was the only guy who could remember the signals," Gotty once said.

Gotty (sitting on right) was a member of South Philly High's varsity football team, although he was not a starter. Also on the team was Hughie Black (standing in first row, fourth from left). *(Southern High School/Bill Esher)*

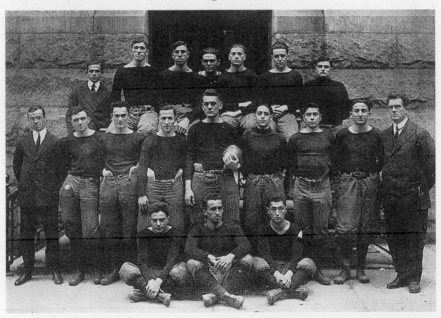

He played on the junior varsity team, then spent two years on the varsity. Although not a starter, he occasionally revealed a desire to someday become a football coach.

He also maintained his allegiance to baseball. Even at the age of 15, perhaps providing an early glimpse of his managerial skills, he ran a sand-lot team stocked with 18 and 19 years olds. A few years later, while still in high school, he was moonlighting as a catcher in a fast-paced industrial league, playing on weekends and in the summer and earning $3 to $5 a game. Perhaps because of his busy sandlot schedule, Gottlieb never played varsity baseball at Southern, although he did play on classroom teams and one year of junior varsity.

All along, though, Gottlieb's focus was turning toward basketball, a sport he had never played until coming to Philadelphia. Although he was only 5 feet, 6 inches tall, Gottlieb held his own on South Philly High teams that featured standout players such as Black, Harry Passon, Moe Ingber, Mockie Bunin, and Charlie Neuman, all Jewish friends from the neighborhood. "I was considered a tough kid," Gotty told Deford.

Eddie Gottlieb played basketball at South Philadelphia High School. Here he is (top row, third from right) on the 1915–16 team. Hughie Black (with ball) was captain of the team and Moish Ingber (top right) was the coach. *(Southern High School/Bill Esher)*

Then known as Isadore Gottlieb, the future Mogul looked dapper in his high school graduation picture. *(Southern High School/ Bill Esher)*

"Not to blow my own horn, but I was also always considered a player with a pretty good noodle."

Gotty was especially known for his ability to deal with numbers, a talent that would serve him well in the years to come. He had a sharp mind and was completely comfortable solving even complicated mathematical problems without the use of paper or pencil. He also had the gift of a tenacious memory. In his later years, he could still recall not only the scores of games, but also the weather, the sizes of the crowds, and the gate receipts of games played many years earlier.

On the basketball court, Gotty played a huge role in channeling the kind of game his team played in a direction that was far different from the norm. "These Jews introduced a different style of play," Harry Litwack, himself a Southern grad, once said. "It was a quick-passing, running game, as opposed to a bullying and fighting way, which was popular other places."

Gottlieb played three years of varsity basketball at Southern, captaining the squad in 1915. Enrolled in the academic course, he also held a spot on the checkers team, was a member of the Play and Dance Committee, and belonged to the Student Senate.

During his high school days, Gottlieb was already being called "Gotty." And, perhaps as a veiled prophesy, the 1916 Southern yearbook offered a descriptive phrase to explain him: "Ask me no questions and I'll tell you no fibs." The yearbook also proclaimed that "We love Gotty," citing as an explanation, "The world loves a lover."

After graduating from South Philly High in 1916, Gottlieb enrolled that fall at the School of Pedagogy in downtown Philadelphia with the hope of becoming a school teacher. The School of Pedagogy was one of the principal institutions in Philadelphia where students learned to become teachers. Offering a two-year course, it was later renamed Philadelphia Normal School before eventually being absorbed by Temple University.

Gottlieb attended classes for the required two years. All the while, he played on the school's basketball team, serving as captain in 1917–18 and in one game scoring a then-staggering total of 26 points in what was an even more staggering 103–19 victory over Philadelphia Trade School. The game attracted national attention, although as Gotty said many years later, "Nobody could believe it." Gottlieb also held down a job as a clerk at Becker, Smith and Page, a wallpaper company located at Water Street and Snyder Avenue.

Soon after graduating, Gottlieb took a position as a physical education teacher at George W. Childs School, a grade school at 17th Street and Tasker Avenue in South Philadelphia, which had been around since 1893. Gotty also took some additional courses at Temple. He still lived with his mother, who by then was operating a grocery store at 1713 S. Eighth Street, and sister, although his 1918 draft registration shows that the family had moved to 419 Porter Street, just two blocks off Oregon Avenue in lower South Philly.

Gottlieb appeared ready for a long career as a teacher. But in an article in the Philadelphia *Inquirer,* Edgar Williams reported that Gotty's teaching career lasted just three years. Something else was pulling him in another direction. It was like a huge magnet attracting a piece of metal. For Gotty, the temptation would be too great to resist.

• • •

CHAPTER 2

A Jewish Man's Game

Unlike some sports in America that lingered on the sidelines for long periods before becoming popular with the masses, basketball was a quick sell with the public. Soon after James Naismith invented the game in 1891, it began to attract widespread attention.

Teams and, shortly thereafter, leagues of all kinds began forming. By the early part of the 20th century, club, college, and even professional teams and leagues battled fiercely for superiority just about anywhere there was room to locate a basketball court.

Nowhere was the game more popular than in the Northeastern cities of the country. It was ideally suited to jammed urban areas. One reason was that because of its limited spatial demands, basketball offered an outlet in the crowded inner cities that was not as easily met by sports such as baseball and football, which required much larger fields of play. Especially for the kids in the neighborhood, all it took for a game of basketball was a peach basket, a couple of nails, a phone pole or the side of a building, and, of course, a ball.

That was certainly how it worked in Philadelphia, which, within a decade of Dr. Naismith's brilliant idea, had become, along with New York, the center of the basketball universe. Teams burst from every locale as males of all ages and sizes tried to outshoot, outrun, and outsmash each other with almost brutal determination.

No area of the city gave more attention to basketball than South Philadelphia. With its narrow streets, endless blocks of thin row houses, and neighborhoods teeming with people, the area was a hotbed of basketball activity. Every schoolyard had at least some kind of basketball court. Nearly every street had a peach basket dangling from a pole. And inner city kids, sometimes as many as 80 of them living in a single block of 54 houses on either side of the street, played the game all hours of the day and night.

The game was especially popular in the Jewish community, one of the largest ethnic groups in South Philly. For the most part, Jewish boys didn't play baseball or football, in some cases simply because the gentile players refused to let them play. Basketball—and, to some extent, boxing—was the preferred game of the sons of the immigrants who had flocked to the city from those faraway places in Europe. The parents were generally poor but trying valiantly to make a living—usually with some kind of manual labor—and raise families under the most difficult of circumstances.

Actually, in its early years—the Jewish Basketball League, where the competition was incredibly intense, was established in the city in 1902—on up through the 1920s and 1930s, and into the 1940s, basketball was to a large extent a Jewish man's game everywhere, whether it was played on playgrounds, in community centers, settlement houses, schools and colleges, or on club or pro teams. In fact, the first Jewish professional player appeared as early as 1900 when a man named Paul (Twister) Steinberg made his debut with Little Falls, New York.(Later, he became the basketball coach at Cornell University.)

Of course, there were black, Irish, and other minority players and teams in some sections of the Northeast. But especially in Philadelphia and New York, the game was ideally suited to Jews, and they dominated the game, not only as participants, but also as spectators. And basketball played an important role in their social and economic activities, too.

Jews were not normally six footers—in fact, the average height of all players at the turn of the century was 5 feet, 8 inches—but some said that was to their advantage because they had better balance and rhythm, more speed, and more dexterity. They were not particularly inclined to be rugged, either. Baseball was thought to require better eyesight and coordination than Jews supposedly had. Football was considered too rough and too dangerous. But basketball was more suitable to the Jewish mind and physique and was viewed as a way to escape the ghetto, and even to get to college. And while parents did not encourage their sons to play sports, mostly demanding that they pursue opportunities to gain suitable employment, they generally placed far fewer restrictions on their sons playing basketball.

Even in the 1920s, future Hall of Fame baseball player Hank Greenberg was initially discouraged by his parents from playing that sport, one reason being that they were too embarrassed to admit that their son participated in what was considered a game that was not only un-Jewish-like but that consistently rejected Jewish players. "Apparently, it was all right to say your son played basketball," stated the great Villanova University and Philadelphia Warriors player Paul Arizin, himself a native of South Philadelphia along with such other basketball standouts as Larry Foust, Earl Monroe, Red Klotz, Chink Scott, and John Chaney. "But after all, the Jews were the first to establish the game."

Jews were at the forefront of the game of basketball for other reasons, too. "Basketball was a city game, and at one time Jews were dominant in the inner city. And they dominated basketball," said Sonny Hill, who grew up playing with Jewish kids and has been a prominent player, coach, administrator, and community leader in Philadelphia for nearly five decades "The game is really about how much you want to put into it. It's also about putting in time and developing your talent. Jewish people and later blacks were willing to do that."

By the 1930s, according to Simcha Gersh, longtime president of the Jewish Basketball League Alumni, 95 percent of the basketball players in South Philadelphia were Jewish. "In the Public League, seven out of 10 players on every team were Jewish," he said. "It was a way to get out of the gutter."

In his masterful book *Ellis Island to Ebbets Field: Sports and the American Jewish Experience*, Peter Levine wrote: "The experience of participating as the majority in an American game carried special meaning for participants and spectators alike, especially for second-generation youth who found in the game opportunities of freedom, mobility, and choice not always available to their fathers and mothers."

Levine added: "A rich part of a second-generation community life, both as experience and symbol, it (basketball) served as a middle ground in which the children of immigrants took advantage of opportunities provided by themselves and by others to determine their own identities as Americans and Jews."

At least one writer took a different approach. "The reason I suspect that basketball appeals to the Hebrew," New York *Daily News* columnist Paul Gallico wrote more than one-half century ago, "is that the game appeals to the temperament of the Jews and places a premium on an alert, scheming mind, flashy trickiness, artful dodging, and general smartaleckness."

Such degrading opinions notwithstanding, the popularity of basketball in the Jewish community extended well into the first half of the 20th century with names such as Red Auerbach, Red Holzman, Dolph Schayes, Max Zaslofsky, Arnie Risen, Harry Litwack, and legions of others playing dominant roles in the game in both the college and professional ranks. And even today, when Larry Brown is one of the last descendents of the pioneers who gave the game its foundation, many fans—especially at the professional level—are Jewish.

Much of the credit for that dates back to a time long ago when Eddie Gottlieb started a basketball team.

Gottlieb had discovered the game of basketball at an early age. After moving from New York to South Philadelphia, the youngster, whose name was then Isadore, became part of a new team called the Combine Club. The team was made up entirely of Jewish boys from South Philly, all about 12 years old.

The stars of the team were Harry Passon and Abe Radel, two boys with whom Gottlieb would have a lifelong connection. Passon and Radel led the team to several championships in a junior Jewish league.

Trying to learn a new game, Gottlieb was at first unsure of himself. He struggled with the nuances of shooting and dribbling. And he was shorter than most of his teammates. Eventually, though, young Izzy gained confidence as well as ability, and by the time he reached his mid-teens he had become established as an agile backcourt performer who not only played well, but who was highly adept at the cerebral part of the game.

At South Philadelphia High School, where he matriculated as a ninth grader, Gottlieb was especially close to Harry Passon and Israel (Hughie) Black, two kids who, like Gotty, lived in the area around Fourth and Reed Streets. Their years together had forged a strong friendship that carried from the neighborhood through school and onto the basketball court.

After graduating from South Philly High, the trio faced one discomforting prospect: as much as they wanted to continue as teammates, they would probably never again play basketball together. There must be some way, they thought, to overcome that dilemma.

In 1917, they found that way, forming a club team known as the DeNeri Juniors. The team, sponsored by the DeNeri Club located at

The School of Pedagogy team included Gottlieb (top right) and Hughie Black (with ball). *(Courtesy of Marvin Black)*

Eighth and Locust Streets and that included Sog Grauley, later the sports editor of the Philadelphia *Inquirer* for 30 years, took on all comers. The Juniors played two or three times a week, most of the time, appearing in the preliminary game before the older, more seasoned DeNeri Club team, a member of the Eastern League, took the court.

It was an era when woolen jerseys, high-top sneakers, knee pads, quilted shorts, and leather-padded eye protectors were part of a player's normal attire. Many games were played in South Philly at St. Martha's Settlement House at Eighth Street and Snyder Avenue where set shots had to be made through the rafters and players were required to duck around radiators. The Juniors, all about 18 years old, played an exciting brand of ball. "Some right pert basketball they played," wrote Cy Peterman in an *Inquirer* article.

As much as they enjoyed playing together, however, the Gottlieb, Black, Passon triumvirate—Gotty and Hughie both went to the School of Pedagogy together—wasn't satisfied with its current status. The boys were already well-known around South Philly, and they harbored the desire for a bigger piece of the action.

Soon, it appeared that they had found a way to get it by persuading the local Young Men's Hebrew Association to sponsor a semiprofessional team. The YMHA would provide the uniforms. Otherwise, the team would be run by the three friends.

But two years after fielding a YMHA team, the organization decided to withdraw its sponsorship. One apparent reason was that organizations such as the YMHA and the YMCA had become disenchanted with the bullying and the often-violent style of play that had become the hallmark of basketball, and because that conflicted with their religious teachings, they wanted no connection with the game.

It was back to the search. Again, it didn't take long to find a solution. It came in the form of a social club located at Fourth and Reed Streets called the South Philadelphia Hebrew Association. It was 1919, and an event was taking place that would leave a basketball legacy for the ages.

The agreement with the new organization called for it to sponsor the team and provide uniforms. But there was one problem. The club wanted players to pay annual dues of $10. The players resisted the request, countering with an offer of their own to play games in the name of the association if they were not charged dues. After some debate, the club agreed to the free memberships.

Uniforms were made with the acronym SPHAS written in Hebrew across the fronts of the shirts and the Mogen David symbol on the backs. The team played at Auditorium Hall at Seventh Street and Snyder Avenue. Gottlieb was the coach, Black the captain, and Harry Passon, his younger brother Chickie, Charlie Neuman, and Mockie Bunin—all Southern graduates—and Lou Schneiderman from Central High School—formed the team. Players were paid $5 a game, and gate receipts were applied mostly to team expenses.

The SPHAS, a somewhat nomadic team that was called "The Wandering Jews" by some, found willing opponents throughout the city. Many were Catholic club teams. Because of the intense rivalry as well as the normally harsh style of play, the games were often brutal affairs with broken noses, bloody lips, and bruised bodies being standard fare.

It didn't take long for the SPHAS to attract a following. And before long, crowds consisting mostly of Jewish fans and numbering several hundred were attending their home games.

Games of that era, played on courts surrounded by chicken wire, had few points and scores such as 11–9 or 17–14 were common. There was lots

The YMHA team that Gottlieb (top right) helped to found played together for two years. Other identifiable members of the team included Lou Schneiderman (top left), Mockie Bunin (top center), Harry Passon (bottom left), and Hughie Black (with ball). *(Courtesy of Marvin Black)*

of faking, two-hand dribbling, passing, and no such call as discontinue in which a player would start a dribble, stop, and then start again. A player with the ball often slammed his shoulder into a defender's side, and the defender would retaliate by throwing his own shoulder right back. Players often smashed each other into the chicken wire, too, the result sometimes being cut hands and faces. Even an early version of the weave was put into play on offense. And the ball, with its hard-leather cover, laced bladder inside, and protruding inflation tube, was larger than today's ball. A good ball in those days would last as long as two years with only minor repairs.

For a while, the letters SPHAS were removed from the fronts of the players' jerseys and replaced by the Hebrew letter equivalents—*samech, pey, hey, aleph*. The colorful uniforms worn by the team were a refreshing change from the drab way most other squads were dressed.

With heavy use, the team's uniforms had started to fray. Gottlieb decided it was time for a change. The only trouble was, the association was not willing to buy replacements.

Never one to let mere hurdles such as that stand in the way, Gottlieb summoned his pals Black and Passon. Together, they came up with an idea. They would form their own sporting goods company and buy uniforms at wholesale prices, then sell them to the team at retail.

They called the new company PGB Sports and in 1920 opened a store at Eighth and Pine Streets. Not only did they supply snappy uniforms with white shirts and blue plaid shorts to the SPHAS, they quickly found other clients. And a business that began with modest ambitions was soon flourishing.

Along with uniforms, PGB began selling sports equipment. Most of its clients were basketball teams, including the SPHAS. But some were even baseball teams. In fact, an entry in the 1921 ledger of the Negro League baseball team the Hilldale Daisies lists the purchase of $20.25 worth of supplies from PGB. Two years later, Hilldale spent $59.25 on supplies. And in 1927, a Hilldale entry showed that a check had been written to PGB in the amount of $526.40 for the purchase of baseballs.

In the late 1920s, the business was moved to larger quarters at 507 Market Street. There, Gottlieb had a second floor office. He remained there for a number of years, even after Harry and Chickie Passon had bought out Black and Gotty and launched a full-scale operation. Called Passon's Sporting Goods, it stood for a number of decades as one of the major sporting goods businesses in the Philadelphia area and continues to this day as a mail order business.

In the years immediately following the birth of the SPHAS, Gottlieb had become a teacher at George W. Childs School at 17th Street and Tasker Avenue. Gotty, however, did not consider the job terribly rewarding. Beside, he had other things on his mind. Eddie was possessed with an overpowering urge to make basketball the main focus of his life.

After three years at Childs, Gottlieb's future was put in perspective. As the story goes, Gotty had called in sick to work so he could take the SPHAS on a road trip. When somebody at Childs saw a picture in a newspaper of him leaving town with the team, the truth was exposed. Soon afterward, Gotty was fired from his job.

Gottlieb hardly skipped a beat. His dismissal freed him to spend his boundless energy full time in the sport he had grown to love. And he plunged even deeper into the process of playing for, coaching, and running the SPHAS. He also found the time to develop some of the other activities, which would help to elevate him to a position as one of Philadelphia's leading sports figures. A few years later, perhaps because he still needed a steady income, Gotty briefly returned to teaching, working as a gym instructor at George G. Thomas Junior High School at Ninth Street and Oregon Avenue.

Back in the 1920s, when a kid's school lunch sometimes consisted of three graham crackers bought at a cost of one penny and a small carton of milk that sold for five cents, Bernie Slatko was a student at Thomas in Gottlieb's seventh grade gym class. "He was just an ordinary guy, always laughing," the 95-year-old Slatko said. "We had lots of fun with him. He would line us up on the side of the basketball court and everybody shot baskets. Then we'd go to the other side of the court and shoot from there. That was our gym class. Everybody got an A."

All the while, the SPHAS' popularity and reputation continued on the rise. Tiny Auditorium Hall was proving to be far too small. "We didn't even have a cage because the hall was too small to put up a cage and then get spectators in, too," Gottlieb told the *Inquirer*'s John Dell. "We only had one row of seats around the court. The rest of the people had to squeeze in and stand behind the chairs."

In the early 1920s, the team moved into more spacious quarters at Musical Fund Hall at Eighth and Locust Streets. But even that wasn't big enough for long. A few years later, the SPHAS again relocated, this time to the Palace Royale, where there was both a basketball court and the Olympia boxing arena at Broad and Bainbridge Streets.

"We were always growing," Gottlieb said. "Our following increased and the game, I believe, became more interesting."

By then, there was no more recognizable team in Philadelphia basketball than the SPHAS. True, the college game had become pretty big, too. At the University of Pennsylvania, coach Lon Jourdet, having developed what was thought to be the game's first zone defense, was en route to leading the Quakers to six Eastern Intercollegiate League championships, at one point between 1917 and 1920 compiling a 56–4 record. Temple had been fielding solid teams for more than two decades, and in 1923 would even launch its first women's team. Villanova was on the verge of starting a team. And a number of smaller local colleges were fielding their own quintets.

But as far as basketball was concerned, the SPHAS were the big name in town. They had the records—they seldom lost while playing as many as 80 games a year—and the crowds to prove it. In a hall that normally held 600 spectators, the team often drew 1,200 or even more. One night against the St. Peter's Catholic Club, 1,700 fans jammed Auditorium Hall. "Half of those people never saw the game," Gottlieb told Dell. "They were standing on the long stairway leading down to the street. All they got for their money was a relay of the score handed down from mouth to mouth."

The SPHAS had players, who, if they weren't already, became friends on and off the court and in many cases for the rest of their lives. "Every Jewish kid in South Philadelphia played basketball," said Harry Litwack some years later. "And every Jewish kid dreamed of playing for the SPHAS."

While the same players who had been with the original team were still the mainstays of the squad, and Gottlieb continued to man a guard post as well as coach and run the team, frequent additions were being made to the roster. Big Babe Klotz (no relation to Red) out of Girard College joined the team. So did Manny Davidson, a South Philly pal of the Passons'.

The biggest change, though, came before the start of the 1921 season when the *Inquirer* sports editor William Scheffer suggested that the team join the Philadelphia League, a circuit made up of teams from various parts of the city, and not so coincidentally a circuit of which he was founder and president. Since nearly the start of the century, Scheffer had been involved in local basketball leagues and had his fingers spread throughout the local world of sports.

Some of the teams in the Philadelphia League had religious affiliations. Holy Name, St. Peter's, and St. Henry's represented the Catholics. Other teams such as Shanahan, Kayoula, and Tri-Council came from neighborhood organizations. Home courts were scattered throughout the city. Wherever the game, though, a packed house was sure to occur.

At the time, the SPHAS were traveling throughout the tri-state area, driving by car to places such as Scranton or North Jersey, and usually stopping along the way for games at Wilkes-Barre, Hazleton, Pittston, Honesdale, Carbondale, Nanticoke, or Tunkhannock. As cited by Bill Ordine in the *Inquirer*, when the SPHAS rode into town in those places, the locals were always half-crazed in anticipation of seeing the home boys give the "Jew boys from the big city" a thrashing. It rarely happened.

Eventually, though, it seemed like a good idea to settle down a bit, dump the vagabond sneakers that roamed far from home, and join a league where the games would be close and the competition stiff.

Gottlieb agreed. And at the start of the 1921–22 season, the SPHAS became members of their first organized league. Over the next three decades, it would not be their only league. But it would be the start of a run that would see the SPHAS become one of the best and most prominent basketball teams in the country.

• • •

CHAPTER 3

Kings of the Court

L ong before multimillion dollar salaries, corporate-sponsored arenas, and seven-foot-tall players; long before scholarships, worldwide recruiting, and six-man coaching staffs; long before slam dunks, behind-the-back dribbles, and three-point field goals; long before dancing girls, exploding scoreboards, and screaming public address announcers, basketball ranked as one of America's most important sports.

It placed far ahead of football and ice hockey. Track and rowing had small followings. And golf and tennis were sports played mostly by the idle rich. Only baseball, a sport for the masses, and boxing, a sport for the manly, had more widespread appeal.

Beginning at the end of the 19th century, basketball had started its climb up the popularity charts in America. By the early part of the 20th century, it was impossible not to find a place to play the sport somewhere, especially in the inner cities where kids as well as adults found basketball to be their preferred choice of games.

Some adults even played the game for money.

While the first professional league—the National Basketball League, composed of teams from Philadelphia and New Jersey—had begun in 1898, it was soon followed by other leagues. Most of their games were played in dingy gyms or decayed dance halls, none having much room for either the court or the spectators. Many of the leagues had strong Philadelphia connections.

A circuit called the American League was formed in 1901. Lasting until 1903, it consisted of two teams from Philadelphia and one each from Chester, Norristown, Camden, Wilmington, Burlington, and Trenton.

Another league of only slightly less quality and known as the Philadelphia League began in 1902 and included club and neighborhood teams called Columbia, Jasper AC, St. John, Greystock, Xavier, Covenant, St. Simeon, and East Falls. Before folding in 1909, the league had admitted teams from Germantown, Conshohocken, Manayunk, Gray's Ferry, Bridesburg, North Wales, and a team called the North Philadelphia Phillies.

As the Philadelphia League was ceasing operations—it would eventually return and run from 1918 to 1925—a new league, both bigger and bolder, was starting. The Eastern League (EL) began in 1909 and—other than suspending its schedule for World War I in 1918–19—existed until 1923. Originally, teams came from Germantown, Kensington, the DeNeri Club in South Philadelphia, Reading, and New Jersey teams from Trenton, Elizabeth, and Patterson. Eventually, the league, which returned for one season in 1925–26, then again from 1929 to 1933, included teams from Coatesville, Camden, Harrisburg, Scranton, Wilkes-Barre, Wilmington, Atlantic City, Newark, Bridgeton, and various clubs from Philadelphia such as the Jasper Jewels, the Greystock Grays, and the Philadelphia Moose.

Although most of the leagues were quasi-professional and centered in the Northeast, it was not uncommon to find circuits elsewhere. In fact, at least 10 pro leagues, some on the other side of the Appalachians, existed at various times before World War I.

The American Basketball League (ABL) was formed in 1925 by Joe Carr, George Halas, and Preston Marshall, of whom the latter two were future owners of football's Chicago Bears and Washington Redskins, respectively. The ABL experienced several folds and restarts, then lasted until 1946, and was considered the top pro league in the country. Under President Carr, who also served as the first president of the National Football League (NFL) and later ran minor league baseball for many years, the league in its first year had teams from Brooklyn, Rochester, Buffalo, Boston, Washington, Cleveland, Ft. Wayne, Detroit, and Chicago. Later, a number of other cities were represented, including Philadelphia, Wilmington, and Baltimore. The ABL was one of the foundations on which the

National Basketball Association (NBA) (originally the Basketball Association of America) would later be built.

Another midwestern pro league emerged in 1929. Also called the National Basketball League (NBL), it, too, would play a key role in the formation of the NBA. The founding teams came from the Ohio cities of Toledo, Canton, Columbus, and Dayton, and Detroit and Pontiac, Michigan. Although the league in its original form lasted just one year, it returned for one season in 1932–33, then resumed play in 1937. With new teams added to the league from places such as Sheboygan, Rochester, Minneapolis, Ft. Wayne, Oshkosh, Cleveland, Chicago, Anderson, and Tri-Cities, it lasted until 1949. Future Philadelphia Phillies baseball players Howie Schultz and Frankie Baumholtz played in the NBL.

The professional teams, which in the early days played three 15-minute periods, depended entirely on gate receipts. The crowds, however, were small, often consisting of relatives and friends of the players along with people from the neighborhood. Players' pay seldom exceeded $5 for a game. Naturally, the men in uniform had full-time jobs elsewhere. Over the years, SPHAS players were teachers, lawyers, mailmen, and salesmen; one was even a violinist.

Crowds, no matter how small, were often raucous. It was not unusual to hear taunts and insults screamed at opposing players or items hurled from the stands into the wire mesh that surrounded the courts or onto the playing areas in cases where they were not enclosed. Many fans drank heavily. And it was common practice to bet on games. The stands and areas outside the gyms were often heavily populated with small-time gamblers, some of whom were not opposed to trying to get players to throw games.

The increasingly popular world of pro basketball welcomed the SPHAS in 1921 when they joined the Philadelphia League. Over the next 22 seasons, the SPHAS under Eddie Gottlieb won 13 titles while playing in 18 championship series in three different leagues. The SPHAS were beyond dispute not only the crown jewel of Philadelphia basketball but a team that ranked among the very best in the nation.

With the SPHAS, Gottlieb not only played but coached the team while running the entire operation, paying the players, booking games, counting the money, and even designing the uniforms. The team emphasized, as it did for many years, strategy, cleverness, discipline, quickness, and rugged defense. More than anything, though, the SPHAS were known as "a thinking man's team."

Players on the original SPHAS team in 1919 included (top row from left) Charlie Neuman, Mockie Bunin, Hughie Black, Chickie Passon, and Gottlieb (bottom from left) and Harry Passon and Lou Schneiderman. Standing is team manager Bobby Seitchict. *(Philadelphia Jewish Sports Hall of Fame, Adolph and Rose Levis Museum)*

"We have no set style," said Gottlieb in an *Inquirer* article. "The fast break is used a good deal, as with most teams, but generally our boys meet the situation as it arises. Keep moving the ball and run. If you do that, you'll run the other team right off the floor. And if you come down to the last five minutes with the score tied or only a few points behind, your youth and stamina will win the game."

Gottlieb's strategy called for lots of layups, high, arching two-hand set shots, and no jump shots. The fast break and the deft shot were the SPHAS' biggest strengths. "Rarely will you see a man who's out of position shoot for the basket," Gotty said of his players. Of course, defense, in which a player would not hesitate to bang his opponent into a wall or wire mesh, was also a key part of the team's game.

"The customers demand action," Gottlieb said, "and we try to see that they get it. The professional basketball follower is hard to fool. They know the game and what to expect from the players."

Even to most of their early local opponents, the SPHAS were no strangers, having already played independently against them as well as some of the best teams on the East Coast. Although the SPHAS were all in their early 20s, not that far removed from high school, the team commanded the kind of respect often reserved for veteran clubs.

Initially, the team played its home games at Auditorium Hall. The tallest player on the squad was 5-foot, 10-inch Charlie Neuman. A young kid named Harry Litwack, who lived just a few blocks from the court, had a job setting up chairs for 25¢ a game plus free admission.

Hughie Black and Gottlieb—called a "stationary guard," meaning he was wholly unlike the mobile, playmakers of today—formed the team's backcourt with Mockie Bunin and Lou Schneiderman alternating at forward and center, Neuman and Chickie Passon also playing forward, and Harry Passon rotating between guard and forward. Gottlieb, who had grown to 5 feet, 8 inches, was a very good player. He was strong and very athletic. And like everybody else on the team, he was not timid. "Eddie was a tough little guy as a player," recalled Red Klotz. "He had learned the game mostly on the playgrounds. He knew the fundamentals, too."

Like all other teams of the era, the SPHAS played rough. They were frequently involved in fights. "They were all tough guys," remembered Hughie Black's son, Marvin. "They were like today's hockey players— very physical. And there were never many fouls called. When there were, the referees would make very loud, dramatic calls. That was all part of the game."

In their first season in the Philadelphia League, the SPHAS won 32 of their 36 games, and the team soon earned the nickname, "Gotty's Goal Gatherers." But a championship was not part of the picture.

That had to wait another year. And in 1922–23 with the team having brought in 5-foot, 6-inch sharpshooter Davey Banks, the best player in New York City and a future member of the Original Celtics, the SPHAS captured the league championship. They repeated in 1923–24 and then, continuing to improve, won again in 1924–25.

The 1924–25 season was especially noteworthy as the SPHAS won their first 11 games and cruised to the first half championship. But with injuries to Neuman and Chickie Passon, the team could only manage the runner-up spot in the second half.

In the first round of the playoffs, Gottlieb's team defeated Kingston in the opener, 25–22. But during a victory celebration afterward, Banks broke his arm and was lost for the remainder of the season. Nevertheless, even without their ace scorer, the SPHAS won Game Two, 35–32, to clinch the series.

The SPHAS met a Philadelphia team known as Tri-Council in the final. Tri-Council, winners of the second half crown, featured a powerful lineup led by rugged 6-foot, 1-inch Tom Barlow, Jimmy (Soup) Campbell, a Camden native, and George Glasco, all top-level veterans.

The teams split the first two games of the best-of-three series, each overcoming a large halftime deficit. As the deciding game approached, Tri-Council's Barlow, Glasco, and Lew Sugarman said they would be unable to play unless the league changed the date because they had agreed to play in an exhibition game elsewhere. With a heavy advance ticket sales, the league refused to make the change, hoping instead to persuade the trio to forgo the exhibition. When they refused, the final game was canceled, and the championship was awarded to the SPHAS.

Unfortunately, the league was unable to survive the fiasco, and it folded shortly thereafter. And Gottlieb's SPHAS were forced to become a team without a league.

The original SPHAS teams were made up entirely of Jewish players, many of whom became good friends for life. Although they played out of a love for the game, they also regarded basketball as a way to improve their standing in society. By establishing a reputation in basketball, a young Jew could not only develop a following, he could provide himself with a possible escape from the ghetto, likely reaching a point where he might even get a better job. Indeed, many future high-ranking professionals in the work force played basketball in their early years.

Within a few years after the SPHAS entered the Philadelphia League, however, Charles Tettemer, a Gentile from Trenton, and Girard College alumnus Babe Klotz (no relation to Red) joined the team. Klotz was said to be of Polish descent, although most people at the time thought he was Jewish.

But even the presence on the team of a few non-Jews did nothing to diminish the anti-Semitic behavior demonstrated by many spectators. The SPHAS, who made no attempt to hide their Jewish heritage, were subjected to numerous kinds of abuse, not only in local gyms but especially when they played on the road. It was a condition that badgered the team throughout its existence, although, ironically, the SPHAS played many of their early games in churches.

"We represented the Jewish community," Gottlieb was quoted as saying in an article penned by Robert Strauss in a 1989 edition of *Philly Sport.* "It was a togetherness thing."

When the hostile crowds—and often the referees, too, some of whom deliberately made calls that went against the SPHAS—reached their highest levels of abuse, it was a signal for the team to raise its own level of intensity. Gottlieb insisted that the best way to answer the bigots was to play the best basketball it possibly could play.

"When people in the crowd said, 'Get those Jews' or 'Kill those Jews,'" Litwack once told Steve Cohen in an article in the *Jewish Exponent,* "we played extra hard. We had to stick together, and we had to fight to defend our people.

"Fans followed the game like it was a religion," Litwack added. "We were the best around, and we were all Jewish. It was an amazing combination."

That was not always so easy. Along with their treatment as second-class citizens, the SPHAS had to endure racial slurs, which included spectators calling the players "Christ killers" and "kikes," and men sitting in the front rows touching players' legs with lighted cigarettes or cigars. Wet newspapers and beer bottles were thrown at the players. Fistfights—even all-out brawls with spectators—were common.

Once while playing in Jersey City, Litwack was smacked in the head with a Coke bottle as he chased a loose ball out of bounds. Bleeding profusely, Litwack was taken to a nearby hospital while his teammates stormed into the stands after the culprit, setting off a wild melee. With 14 stitches in his head, Litwack returned to the game soon afterward.

Another time in Wilmington, players were pelted with wet newspapers, an act that again instigated a nasty fight. And in Scranton, miners attended games still wearing the hard hats with lamps that they used underground. The miners used the hot light from the lamps to heat pennies, which they then threw at SPHAS players.

"I remember the team getting off the train once in a little town in Ohio and a group of people was standing there staring at us," Shikey Gotthoffer said in an article by Ron Avery in the *Jewish Exponent.* "They looked like they had never seen Jews before."

The abuse of the SPHAS was at its worst at Prospect Hall, where the Brooklyn Visitation team played. Whenever something happened that they didn't like, occupants of a balcony that hung above the court frequently fired beer bottles and partially eaten sandwiches down on the players. And a lady in the front row was fond of jabbing a hat pin into players' legs.

The Brooklyn arena also had another kind of fan. "The seats in the front row were always occupied by Murder, Inc.," Gottlieb told Frank Dolson for his column in the *Inquirer.* "If trouble started, they'd be the first guys out because they knew the cops would go after them."

In Brooklyn, Gottlieb said half jokingly, "They made the fans check their guns at the door." Then turning serious, he added: "Half of the fans would come to see the Jews killed. The other half came to see our boys win."

Of course, the bigotry increased considerably with the emergence of Hitler and Nazism. Particularly fans of German extraction were merciless in their treatment of Jewish players. And an organization called the German-American Bund wore Nazi uniforms and sometimes paraded outside SPHAS games.

"There was so much anti-Semitism," former SPHAS player Gil Fitch said, "that Eddie wanted to jam it down everyone's throat and let the world know that his team was Jewish and a Jewish team could hold its own."

And hold its own it did. Despite the persecution and bigotry to which they and their fellow Jews were subjected, the SPHAS kept getting better and better. And their status among the basketball powers of the country kept getting higher and higher.

In the spring of 1925, Gottlieb, having retired as a player because of a foot injury, faced an unpleasant dilemma. The Philadelphia League had disbanded, which meant that the SPHAS were without a league.

By all reasonable estimates, they had grown too good for the league, anyway. It was really time for the SPHAS to move on, to raise their sights, to climb to a higher calling. It was time to find a new league.

In a timely coincidence, the upcoming 1925–26 season was one in which the Eastern League was attempting a comeback. Having been in limbo for two seasons, but now having an interest in improving its quality of play and stretching its geographic scope, the league was primed for a return to the basketball scene. And the SPHAS, the recipients of invitations to join both the EL and the newly formed American League, accepted the overture from the former.

The SPHAS, who sometimes went by the name "Hebrews," were joined in the new EL by two other highly prominent teams, the Original Celtics from New York and the Harlem Renaissance, or Rens as they were most commonly called. With this trio, the EL could boast that it had three of the top professional basketball squads in the country.

The Celtics were a team from New York made up of Irish and Jewish players, including Joe Lapchick, a brilliant player who was later head coach at St. John's University. The team, which often played before crowds numbering as many as 12,000, especially after Madison Square Garden opened in 1922, traveled to away games in a seven-passenger Pierce Arrow.

The Rens, on the other hand, were the first all-black team, formed in 1922 and sponsored by a Harlem casino and ballroom. Between 1912 and 1936, they were said to have posted a 497–58 record, at one point winning 88 games in a row and in one season 120 out of 128 games. Playing mostly on the road in their early years, the Rens claimed to have traveled as much as 38,000 miles per season.

Gottlieb's club had a particularly potent offense that made it the highest-scoring quintet of the era. The SPHAS still featured not only most of the team's original members, including Chickie Passon, who had emerged as a standout player and was often portrayed as "a real tough cookie." "There were men who thought they could beat the hell out of you," Passon once said, "so you had to know how to protect yourself. I had educated elbows. They found places, sometimes in the eyes, sometimes in the nose. I was no chicken."

Another top player was ace shooter Banks. In one game, the SPHAS crushed a team from Hammonton, which was billed as the New Jersey champions, by a score of 75–11. After the game, the Philadelphia *Public Ledger* reported that the SPHAS "tossed in field goals whenever they pleased, and when they tired of this, showed a passing game that made their opponents dizzy." Another time, the Philly guys copped a 46–9 decision against a team called Wilbar.

The SPHAS' games with the Rens had a particularly unusual twist. Both teams represented minorities, and both faced widespread abuse on the basketball court (as well, of course, as elsewhere).

Their common problem notwithstanding, SPHAS-Rens meetings, which began in the mid-1920s and extended well into the 1940s, were colossal battles that never lacked excitement. Along with games both teams played with the Original Celtics, they were the most captivating clashes of the era.

Among those with heightened biases, SPHAS-Rens games were known as the "Yids" against the "Niggers." And the teams met not just in

Philadelphia and New York, but traveled together to places such as Hartford, Detroit, and Atlantic City where they squared off on Steel Pier.

The Rens' home court was at a casino at 138th Street and Seventh Avenue. Fans jammed into what was considered for the day a rather sophisticated court. The casino held dances before, at halftime, and after games, often featuring the musical talents of Count Basie, Ella Fitzgerald, Earl (Fatha) Hines, and Duke Ellington.

The Rens, coached by future Hall of Famer Bob Douglas, a native of the British West Indies, seldom lost at home, and when they did, it was often at the hands of Gottlieb's SPHAS, one of the few teams that was not reluctant to venture into Harlem. But whether the Rens played at home or on the road, fans always felt as though they got their money's worth.

With no other place to play at the upper levels of basketball—and often no teams to play against—black players from Philadelphia usually appeared on the Rens' roster. Among the more prominent were Zack Clayton, a superb all-around athlete who later became a noted boxing referee, Bill Yancy, a fine Negro League baseball player and later an important scout with the Philadelphia Phillies, and Charles (Tarzan) Cooper, a 6-foot, 6-inch, 280-pounder out of Central High School who stood in front of the basket, looming like a trailer in a doorway.

Although they have been incorrectly labeled as the forerunner of the Harlem Globetrotters (the Globies first fielded a team in 1927 and never played a game in Harlem until 1968), the Rens were considered quick and flashy for that era, but by today's standards were a well-drilled, methodical team featuring quick passes, speed, and relentless defense. The only time they really cut loose was at home late in the game when they had a commanding lead.

"The Rens would have you licked, then in the last three or four minutes of the game they'd start passing the ball around," Gottlieb told Jon Entine. "The crowd would go crazy."

Typically, when they were playing on the road, the Rens, who were often refused lodging and food, let their opponents stay close, ultimately winning by small margins. That way, the home team wouldn't feel bad about losing, and the Rens would be more likely to get invited back.

Games with the SPHAS were usually close anyway. A former Ren, 91-year-old John Isaacs, remembered the admiration he and his teammates had for Gottlieb's club.

"The SPHAS reminded me of the Original Celtics," he said. "They had the same mode of operation. They played together, shared the ball. They were not selfish. They played with their heads. They were intelligent. They didn't waste a lot of time dribbling. They had a lot of movement, gave the good pass, rebounded, played defense, and could shoot. It was always fun playing against them because they knew how to play the game."

Gottlieb's decision to enter the SPHAS in the Eastern League was not a good one. Although highly touted when it was re-established, the EL quickly demonstrated some serious weaknesses once the season began. Money was a problem. But more than that, there were huge differences in the quality of the various teams. Because of the absence of anything even close to parity, the league had little support, and soon after reaching the midway point of its first season, it went out of business. At the time, the SPHAS were undefeated in six games in the second half after having gone 8–6 to place third in the first half.

Ever the innovator, Gottlieb wasted no time plotting his team's activities for the rest of the season. Gotty had developed numerous contacts throughout basketball, and calling on them now, he set up a series of exhibition games with some of the other top teams in the country. That would not only keep the team active—and in the public eye—but just as important, would put a few dollars in Gotty's pocket.

To bolster the SPHAS' lineup, the savvy Gottlieb then made two more moves. With the disintegration of the EL, players became free agents. Gotty quickly signed two talented non-Jews—6-foot, 7-inch Francis (Stretch) Meehan, the tallest player in the EL who began his pro career in 1919, and Tom Barlow, the well-traveled, rough-and-ready forward who scored, rebounded, and defended as well as any player in pro hoops during a career that led him into the Basketball Hall of Fame.

With a powerful team that now included the two new players and Banks, Chickie Passon, and Lew Schneiderman in the starting lineup, the SPHAS met the Brooklyn Arcadians of the ABL in their first outing. The SPHAS came away with a 45–30 victory.

Next, Gotty's club met Patterson (New Jersey) of the tough Metropolitan League and won again, 39–27. The Ft. Wayne Hoosiers of the ABL then fell, 37–26, before the SPHAS' winning streak came to an end with a 36–32 loss to the ABL's premier team, the Cleveland Rosenblums. Then back-to-back 26–25 and 31–26 victories over the Washington Five of the ABL put the SPHAS back in the win column.

Flush with success, Gottlieb was now ready for his next move. Approaching the Original Celtics and the Renaissance, he proposed setting up a series of playoffs designed to crown the best team in the country. Both teams quickly agreed, and two best-of-three series were scheduled with the SPHAS and Celtics, coached by the legendary Nat Holman and at one point winners of all but 11 of 200 games, meeting in the first round.

In the first fracas, before a packed house, the SPHAS were dispatched by the Celtics, 32–24. Banks's field goal with 15 seconds left to play gave the Philadelphia club a 26–25 victory in the second game. In the deciding contest, with Banks playing so well that the Celtics later signed him to a contract for the following season, the SPHAS captured a 36–27 decision to win the round.

Next up were the Rens. In the opener Gottlieb directed the SPHAS to a 36–33 win in overtime. The SPHAS then squeezed out a tense 40–39 triumph in the second battle. To the SPHAS, their fans, and many sportswriters, and plenty of others, the club could now be called the best in the country.

"They are one of the greatest, if not the greatest organizations in basketball history," wrote one scribe. Whether that was actually true was a matter of conjecture, especially because the Rosenblums, certainly a great team in their own right, had not been part of the playoffs. But for the time being, no one rose to dispute the claim.

Once again, though, the SPHAS—as they had been twice in the last year—were without a league. Moreover, Gottlieb's players were leaving the team, most of them to engage in full-time jobs that paid livable wages without the strain of having to fit in side trips to the basketball arena.

With no league and not enough quality players to go into the 1926–27 season, Gottlieb took a drastic step. He disbanded the team that for the better part of a decade had represented the epitome of basketball excellence.

Fortunately for Gottlieb, another opportunity was available. A group from South Philadelphia was planning to assemble a team and enter it in the ABL. The team was initially called the Philadelphia Quakers, and Gotty was hired to be its head coach.

The two principal owners were Jules Aronson and Max (Boo Boo) Hoff, a couple of local boxing promoters. Hoff, who not only staged fights but had a stable of boxers that numbered as many as 16, was said to have ties to the Jewish Mafia, at the time a relatively small group that operated in South Philadelphia.

Then, as later, South Philly had more than its share of crime. It was a haven for crooks and gamblers, including plenty of Jewish ones. "There was always gambling on the streets," Samuel (Leaden) Bernstein told Murray Dubin in his book *South Philadelphia: Mummers, Memories, and the Melrose Diner.* "You had gangsters. Seventh and Porter, all the gangsters hung out there, and they used to bump each other off."

According to local writer and historian Parry Desmond, Hoff, who grew up at Eighth and South Streets, the son of Russian-Jewish immigrants, used boxing as a front for his other activities, which included a loan shark business and numbers and gambling operations he had run since 1917 in today's Society Hill section of Philadelphia. While those ventures had made Hoff a millionaire while still in his 20s, the youthful gangster had also become involved in the manufacture and distribution of liquor after the Volstead Act ushered in prohibition in 1919.

Hoff made another fortune in his bootlegging operation, using banks, a phony investment company, and police bribes to help earn as much as $5 million a year by the late 1920s, working out of an office that had 175 telephones and a weekly payroll of $30,000. While becoming one of the nation's richest mobsters—in 1928 in Atlantic City, he attended a national meeting of underworld leaders that included Al Capone and Lucky Luciano—Hoff, called "The King of Bootleggers," often played host to lavish parties. Many were held in fancy hotels and were attended by his friends in the sports and entertainment worlds, as well as anyone else who cared to show up. Hoff's idea of fun was to shoot guests with small tinfoil pellets fired from a rubber band.

Following the famous heavyweight fight in 1926 at Philadelphia's Sesquicentennial (later called Municipal and JFK) Stadium between Jack Dempsey and Gene Tunney, Hoff had achieved notoriety in another way. He filed a $350,000 lawsuit against the new champ, Tunney, and his manager, Bill Gibson, claiming that he was owed 20 percent of the fighter's earnings after signing an agreement and making a $20,000 loan to the pair. Hoff eventually dropped the suit in 1931.

Often arrested but never jailed, Hoff's luck ran out in 1933 when the Volstead Act was repealed. Within a few years, he was sued for unpaid income taxes by the Internal Revenue Service, had his home in the Cobbs Creek Park area and his car repossessed, and eventually died of a heart ailment in 1941 at the age of 48.

Long before he died, though, Hoff's brief fling with basketball had helped to make an impact on the local sports scene. He and Aronson had been approached by ABL president Joe Carr about running a new team in Philadelphia. Carr said he had been considering putting a team in the city for several years.

"Philadelphia has always been looked on as the main spoke in the basketball wheel," wrote Sog Grauley of the Philadelphia *Inquirer*. "There is no doubt but that this city will welcome the project with open arms. Let this Philadelphia team keep apace of the leaders in the American League next winter and there will be more personal interest taken in this club than any heretofore shown."

After a new team was formed, it was sometimes referred to as the Phillies. But once Gottlieb, who it was occasionally claimed had a passing acquaintance with the Jewish Mafia over the years—probably an unavoidable occurrence for those who lived in South Philly—came on board, the team was called the Warriors, a name that was said to have been suggested by Gordon Mackay, sports editor of the Philadelphia *Record*. In some ways, though, there was still a strong SPHAS flavor.

Gottlieb summoned some of his former players. Chickie Passon answered the call. So did Schneiderman, Meehan, and Barlow. To that group he added Al Kellett, a pitcher who worked in five games in 1923 for the Philadelphia Athletics, Harry Riconda, an infielder who played in 243 games between 1923 and 1930 for five big league teams, including the A's, and Jimmy (Soup) Campbell from Camden. The rest of the team was made up of a miscellaneous cast of players from Philadelphia and elsewhere.

In the book *Luckiest Man: The Life and Death of Lou Gehrig* by Jonathan Eig, it is claimed that the team nearly had one other player, which at the time made big news. New York Yankees first baseman Lou Gehrig had been a skilled basketball player in his younger days, and Gotty gave him a pitch to sign with the Warriors. Gehrig, just a few years into his Hall of Fame career, respectfully declined.

The Warriors played their home games at the Arena at 45th and Market Streets. Built in 1920, the Arena had been intended as an ice hockey venue, but when that idea failed to materialize, the building was used primarily for boxing matches, most of which were promoted by Aronson and Hoff.

In the two years that the league existed, the Warriors won no championships. They finished in the middle of the pack their first year and second in their division behind the eventual league champion Celtics the following season. But the Warriors did fill a void in Philadelphia. They kept professional basketball alive, even though they had only mediocre success at the gate.

The ABL disintegrated after the 1927–28 season, one major reason being that the heavy costs of travel, hotels, and players' salaries, which could be as high as $125 per game, had put the league and most of its teams deeply in debt.

The process was getting a bit tiresome, but once again it was time for Gottlieb to come up with a new plan.

As annoying as it had become, Gottlieb was faced with a familiar predicament. He was a man without a league. That was no way to make a buck, something that one could say was the consuming interest in Gotty's life.

By now, Gottlieb had his hands in an assortment of ventures. But despite his various activities, basketball was still his primary focus. Yet, he had dissolved the SPHAS and the Warriors had ceased operations when the ABL collapsed. There was no pro team on the menu for Gottlieb or for Philadelphia for the 1928–29 season.

Instead, the franchise was shifted to New York where it played without Gottlieb as the Hakoahs, a Jewish team made up mostly of players from that area. The team, however, lasted just one year. In 1929, Gottlieb brought the SPHAS back to life.

All the SPHAS of previous seasons, however, had retired from the game. By then, Gottlieb had bought out his partners Hughie Black and Harry Passon. Black had become a full-time school teacher, eventually spending his entire career at Leeds and Sayre Junior High Schools, and Passon was running his increasingly successful sporting goods business. It was now strictly up to Gottlieb to form and operate a whole new team.

No one in Philadelphia knew more about the city's basketball teams and players than Gottlieb. He constantly attended college and independent league games, looking for talent. He knew where all the good players were. And when he formed the SPHAS, he put that knowledge to use, recruiting some of the best players in the area.

One of the best was Cy Kaselman. A 19-year-old South Philadelphian when he joined the SPHAS, Kaselman was quiet, handsome, and nicknamed "Sundodger" because he was said to sleep all day and play all night. Sometimes described as a lady-killer, Kaselman never went to college, but he was a magnificent player. He was a deadly shooter who once claimed to have made 198 foul shots in 200 attempts during a practice session. Kaselman could put the ball in the basket with such proficiency that later when Gottlieb was coaching the Warriors, he made his former forward the club's shooting coach.

Gottlieb also brought to his new SPHAS team center Louis (Red) Sherr, a student at the Penn law school. Many years later, Red's daughter, Lynn, was a highly visible network television news reporter. Among other newcomers were Jack (Yock) Welsh, later to become a Philadelphia deputy city commissioner, and Babe Liman, a star player at New York University.

When the 1929–30 season dawned, the SPHAS could be found back in the Eastern League which had just come back to life after dissolving during the 1925–26 season.

Along with the SPHAS, the third edition of the EL consisted of teams from Philadelphia, Reading, Camden, Wilmington, and Trenton. The league was not as strong as the old ABL, but as far at Gottlieb was concerned, it was better than nothing.

In their first season, the SPHAS romped to the league title, winning 30 of 37 games during the regular season. They then met the Philadelphia Elks in a best-of-five final that would prove a lot more interesting than most playoff matches.

The Elks were led by a marvelous former Germantown High School athlete named William (Bucky) Walters. Not only was Walters an outstanding basketball player, but he would later become a prominent big league baseball player. While playing third base in the mid-1930s with the Philadelphia Phillies, he was converted to a pitcher, became a three-time 20-game winner, and in 1939 while hurling for the Cincinnati Reds was named the National League's Most Valuable Player.

The SPHAS and the Elks were bitter rivals, and when Gottlieb's club lost two of the first three games in the playoff, the hostility between the two teams heightened considerably.

To make matters worse, Walters was nowhere in sight when the fourth game was about to start.

According to Ordine in his Philadelphia *Inquirer* article, it turned out that Walters had been on his way to Philadelphia from upstate New York, and the train in which he was riding was involved in an accident. Apparently unaware of this development, Elks officials accused Gottlieb of hiring some underworld characters to kidnap the team's star player.

Future Phillies pitcher and National League MVP Bucky Walters caused a major commotion when his basketball team played a series against the SPHAS. *(Courtesy of Rich Westcott)*

As he was often capable of doing, Gottlieb blew his stack. The game was, nevertheless, delayed, leaving 3,000 unhappy fans groaning in the stands. Eventually, Walters showed up and the game began. But with three players injured and unable to play, Gottlieb was forced to put on a uniform.

By now, not only Gottlieb and the fans but the entire SPHAS team was livid. And they took their anger out on the Elks. The SPHAS roared to one-sided victories in the next two games to win the series, three games to two. Not only was it the first of three straight Eastern League championships for Gotty's team but it launched what became the Golden Era of SPHAS basketball.

By the 1930–31 season, Gottlieb had made several major additions to the SPHAS lineup. The two most important ones were 6-foot, 3-inch New Yorker Lou Forman out of Dickinson College and guard Harry Litwack from Temple University.

Forman, a graduate of West Philadelphia High School, was a tough, aggressive center who once suffered a broken jaw after getting punched in the face, but returned to finish the game. He played with unbridled passion and was the team's top rebounder while scoring an average of seven or eight points per game.

Litwack, who had emigrated with his parents from Austria, had gone to South Philadelphia High School before which he had attended George W. Childs School, where one of his gym teachers was Gottlieb. Small at 5 feet, 7 inches, but scrappy, Litwack had made a name for himself as a player at Temple where he was twice selected as the team's most valuable player. After college, he became a teacher while coaching for one year at Simon Gratz High School, then from 1931 through 1951 piloting Temple's freshman basketball team. In 1952, Litwack became the Owls' head basketball coach, and in 21 seasons en route to a place in the Basketball Hall of Fame, compiled a 373–193 record while guiding teams to 13 post-season playoffs and the 1969 National Invitation Tournament championship.

With such a powerful lineup, there were few teams that could stop the SPHAS. Predictably, they won the first half crown with a 17–3 record, placed second in the second half with a 14–6 mark, then roared to another Eastern League title by lacing Camden, three games to one.

By now, the EL had nearly doubled in size. There were more teams from Philadelphia, clubs from Kennett Square and Bridgeton, and even a squad called the Philadelphia WPEN Broadcasters (which won two of 25 games in its only season).

With virtually the same team, the SPHAS won the championship again in 1931–32, posting a 15–5 record, which was good for second place in the first half, placing first in the second half with a 14–4 log, and defeating the Philadelphia Moose in three out of four games in the playoffs.

The SPHAS made another major addition to the squad before the 1932–33 season when they picked up forward Gil Fitch. A graduate of Central High School, Fitch had gone on to become captain of the soccer, basketball, and baseball teams at Temple. Along with being an exceptional athlete, Fitch had another special talent: He was an accomplished musician. In the years that followed, Fitch's musical skills would play a role as important to the SPHAS and their fans as any performance on the basketball court.

But after winning three straight titles, the SPHAS' streak finally came to an end. During the season, the club won the first half (12–6), but

Gil Fitch won special acclaim not just as a basketball player, but also as a bandleader. *(Philadelphia Jewish Sports Hall of Fame, Adolph and Rose Levis Museum)*

finished just third (8–7) in the second half. Even so, the SPHAS qualified for the championship playoff, but lost three games to one to the Trenton Moose.

Despite the loss, it was again time for the SPHAS to move on. The ABL was back in business. And ABL officials, fully aware of the value the astute Gottlieb could bring to their league, wanted the SPHAS as a member. Gotty readily accepted the invitation.

It was a decision that during the next decade would solidify for the SPHAS their place as one of the most storied teams in basketball history.

• • •

CHAPTER 4

They Were the Days

The 1933–34 season marked a special milestone in the legendary history of the SPHAS.

It was a season that ushered the team into an entirely new and different era.

The whole character of SPHAS games underwent some dramatic changes. Basketball was still the main attraction. But it now had company.

Now, an evening at a SPHAS game featured both dribbling and dancing. Field goals and foxtrots. Rebounds and romance.

Now, there were women, lots of them, in the stands. There was Gil Fitch and his band. And there was an entirely new place to play. SPHAS games would never be the same again.

The SPHAS, of course, were still one of the best pro basketball teams in the country. They still had Eddie Gottlieb masterminding the entire operation, attending to every detail from important right on down to the most minute. They still had the attention of Philadelphia's ever-increasing Jewish population.

But the new season introduced a number of significant differences from the past. For one thing, with yet another disintegration of the Eastern League, Gottlieb had moved the team back to the reorganized American Basketball League (ABL). For another, the quality of the team on the court was on the verge of rising to a level higher than it had ever been, and it would remain at this elevated position for the next decade.

The Broadwood Hotel played a major role in the SPHAS' most prominent era as the site of games followed by dances. (*Temple University Libraries, Urban Archives, Philadelphia, Pennsylvania*)

The key factor in this most significant of upheavals, though, was the SPHAS' change of venue.

As they had become increasingly successful and their reputation had expanded, the SPHAS had attracted more fans every year. It had reached the point that the little court at the Palace Royale at Broad and Bainbridge where the SPHAS played could no longer accommodate the team's large following. To Gottlieb, having to turn away paying customers was like throwing away the keys to a new car.

Gottlieb decided to find a bigger venue. He found it at the Broadwood Hotel, so named because it was located at Broad and Wood Streets, just a few blocks north of City Hall.

It cost Gotty $50 a night to rent the place.

Originally, the structure had been built in 1923 at a cost of $4 million by Philadelphia Lodge No. 2 of the Benevolent and Protective Order of Elks. The building served as a hotel and the Elks' clubhouse. Due to a lack of business, the Elks lost the building through foreclosure in 1930. Several owners later, the athletic facilities became the property of the Philadelphia Athletic Club.

Renamed the Broadwood, the hotel's basketball court was on the third floor, which meant that fans had to climb three flights of steps to get there. But the arena, which included a set of upholstered reserve seats and a balcony, could hold up to 3,000 spectators. It was better in every way than the old courts in which the SPHAS had previously played. And in later years, when the crowds were even too big for the Broadwood, Gottlieb sometimes switched the games to Convention Hall, which seated 11,000.

Players, who by now could make as much as $50 a game, dressed in the basement and rode an elevator up to the court. There was always a game on Saturday night with tipoff time at 8 p.m. In those days, a regulation game consisted of three 15-minute periods with few or no timeouts. The team usually played during the week, too. The crowd was almost entirely Jewish.

Seemingly about as important as the games themselves were the dances held afterward. Gottlieb had decided that one way to get more men to attend a game was to have women there, too. A logical way to do that was to hold Saturday night dances. At first, Gotty admitted women at no charge. After a few games, having gotten their attention, he put their admission price at 35¢, while men paid 65¢ to get into a game.

Gil Fitch, an all-around athlete out of Temple, was an aggressive forward who played with the SPHAS from 1932 to 1939. Along with being a fine basketball player, Fitch was a superb saxophone player with aspirations for a career as a musician. Soon after graduating from Temple, he started a band. Knowing a good thing when he saw it, Gottlieb thought the band would be a natural fit at SPHAS games. And the Gil Fitch Band became a featured attraction at the post-game Broadwood dances, earning $50 for the night.

With about 10 minutes to play in the final period, Fitch, who was not a starter, would leave the court, race down to the locker room, get a shower if there was time, dress in a tuxedo, and return to the third floor where he would climb onto the stage and lead his 10-piece band. Usually, the band was accompanied by a singer. Most of the time it was an up-and-coming teenager from South Philly named Kitty Kallen, who would go on to become one of the top pop singers in the country, working with both the Harry James and the Jimmy Dorsey bands. Kallen was only 15 years old when she started with Fitch, and because her mother wouldn't let her come to the Broadwood by herself, the ball-playing bandleader always had to drive her to and from home to the hotel. The young songstress was paid $5 for each performance.

With music and dancing on the court, which had been converted into a ballroom after the bleachers had been pushed back, there was no place a Jewish basketball fan would rather be. Even though it was at the height of the Great Depression and people's disposable incomes were severely limited, it was the highlight of the Jewish social calendar. "It was *the* thing to do on a Saturday night," Gottlieb told Gaeton Fonzi in his *Greater Philadelphia Magazine* article. "About 400 dames would show up. Many a fella met his wife there. Many a fella met somebody else's wife there, too."

Many Jewish families wouldn't allow their daughters to attend dances, except the ones held after SPHAS games. Dances lasted for several hours, usually ending around 11 p.m. "It was a fun place to go," said Estelle Litwack, Harry's wife. "There was always lots of laughter. It was mostly young people. It was a very pleasant evening."

"They were the days," Dave Zinkoff remarked in the Fonzi article. Zinkoff was the team's public address announcer and editor of a highly popular program called *SPHAS Sparks,* the main features of which were his gossip column and a lucky number, which awarded winners items such as $19 suits at Sam Gerson's South Philly clothing store. "Basketball and girls. What a combination," Zink said.

Saturday night games were always sellouts with a big crowd turned away at the gate. Spectators even sat on the stage at the far end of the court. Others stood on the steps leading up to the third floor. Everybody was dressed in his or her finest clothes. Future major league umpire and college basketball referee Johnny Stevens often served as a doorman. And once, even future NBA great George Mikan made an appearance at the Broadwood while playing for the Chicago Gears in a game in 1945.

There were always 50 or 60 gamblers hanging out in the lobby and behind the stands, openly making bets on not only SPHAS games but other league games as well.

Although there is no evidence to suggest that Gottlieb was involved in any basketball betting, he never turned them away, figuring every patron added money to the coffers. "The guy who paid a buck was still paying a buck, no matter what he did," Gotty said.

Zinkoff told Fonzi a story about meeting a man on an elevator at the Broadwood. Very politely, the dapper stranger asked Zinkoff about the condition of each SPHAS player. Later, after giving the man a rundown, the Zink told Gottlieb about his conversation.

"Gee, Mr. Gottlieb," Zinkoff said, "you have some awful nice patrons at the games. Why just tonight, one of the customers was kind enough to inquire about the health and welfare of your whole team."

Immediately, an indignant look crossed Gottlieb's face. Then, after asking for a description of the man, Gotty exploded. "You stupid son-of-a-bitch," he screamed. "That was Big Banana the Thief. The biggest cheating bookie in the East." According to the Zink, Gotty then chewed him out in a nonstop tirade that lasted for several minutes.

Most of the players never cared much for the basketball court at the Broadwood because as a dance floor it was kept waxed and slippery. "You'd slip all over the place," remembered Butch Schwartz, who played from 1941 to 1948 with the SPHAS. "You couldn't give your best. You couldn't cut or change directions very easily. It was very hard to play on that floor."

One season, the slippery floor was such a concern that Gottlieb concocted a special pad with glue on the bottom that the players wore over the soles of their sneakers. It was a creative idea, but not terribly practical.

As hard as the court was to play on, though, the players were not opposed to dancing on it. Most of them hung around for the post-game galas. Nobody wanted to miss out on the action. "It was a social event," recalled Jerry Fleishman, a SPHAS star from 1943 to 1946. "Everybody knew everybody. Most people came every weekend."

"Eddie ran a very nice evening," said Red Klotz, who as a high school youth often played in preliminary games at the Broadwood on a junior SPHAS team. "The crowd was always well-dressed and well-behaved. Everybody always seemed to be very comfortable."

Actually, there were a few misbehavers once in a while. Fights sometimes broke out in the stands. And Ralph Bernstein, a kid at the time who became a highly prominent writer and editor for the Associated Press during a more than 50-year career as a sports journalist, remembers the time he got into a hassle with a female fan.

"A lady wearing a big hat sat down in front of me one time," he recalled. "I tapped her on the shoulder. 'Please remove your hat,' I said. 'I can't see.' She didn't respond. I asked her a second time, and nothing happened. The third time, I said, 'If you don't remove your hat, I will.' And I did. A guy next to her turned around and threw a punch at me. The only trouble was, he missed me and hit the guy sitting next to me. That started a riot. The next day, there was a headline in the paper. It said, 'SPHAS win as fans riot.'"

While SPHAS games at the Broadwood launched a new era in the social fabric of Philadelphia's Jewish community, change was underway for the team itself, too. The SPHAS had moved to the American Basketball League (ABL), which was back in business once again after a two-year hiatus, and this time would operate until 1954.

The ABL now had teams such as the Brooklyn Visitations, the Jersey Reds, the Trenton Tigers, and the New York Jewels, a team made up of players from St. John's University where they were known alternately as "The Wonder Five" or "Four Jews and a Gentile."

The SPHAS, though, were unquestionably the best team in the league. They proved that by winning seven championships over the next 13 years while finishing as the runner-up two other times.

"At best, they were as good as any team in the country," said Maje McDonnell, who formed a backcourt at Villanova with Red Klotz while sometimes playing under an assumed name with a team called the Masked Marvels that sometimes faced the SPHAS. "Certainly, there was no better team in the East," said McDonnell, who spent six decades with the Philadelphia Phillies as a batting practice pitcher, coach, and front-office employee.

In their first season, the SPHAS captured the title over the Trenton Moose in the playoff final, winning four out of six games. Two years later, they beat the Visitations, four games to three for the crown. They won again in 1936–37 over the Jersey Reds, 4–3; in 1939–40 over the Washington Henrichs in a one-game playoff; in 1940–41 over the Brooklyn Celtics, 3–1; in 1942–43 over the Trenton Tigers, 4–3; and in 1944–45 over the Baltimore Bullets, 2–1. They lost in the finals in 1943–44 to the Wilmington Bombers—a team operated by the Carpenter family, new owners of the Phillies baseball club—in seven games, and in 1945–46 to Baltimore in four meetings.

When they joined the ABL in 1933, the SPHAS still had a few holdovers from earlier years. Cy Kaselman, Harry Litwack, Fitch, and Lou Forman were very much in the picture and would continue to be for much of the 1930s (Kaselman played until 1942).

Meanwhile, though, Gottlieb was packing his roster with the best young players he could find. At first, he fielded an all-Jewish lineup of players from Philadelphia and New York. But as the 1930s progressed, an increasing number of non-Jews appeared on the roster on what was usually Gotty's seven-man team.

In 1933, Gotty brought in noncollegians Inky Lautman and Shikey Gotthofer, and Red Wolfe, who had been a star at St. John's. The following season he hired Moe Goldman out of City College of New York (CCNY). Later, he would sign Red Rosan from Temple (1936), Petey Rosenberg, who played one year at St. Joseph's (1938), Ossie Schectman and Butch Schwartz, both from Long Island University (both 1941), Red

At the height of their biggest era, the SPHAS fielded a team that consisted
of (seated) Inky Lautman, Moe Goldman, Red Rosan, and Cy Kaselman, and
(standing, starting third from left) Harry Litwack, Red Wolfe, Gil Fitch, and
Shikey Gotthofer. Club officials Marty Weintraub and Abe Radel are on the upper
left and Gottlieb is on the upper right. *(Philadelphia Jewish Sports Hall of Fame,
Adolph and Rose Levis Museum)*

Klotz from Villanova (1942), Jerry Fleishman from New York University
(1943), Art Hillhouse from Long Island University (1943), Ralph Kaplowitz from New York University (1945), and pro basketball's first 7-footer,
Elmore Morgenthaler from New Mexico (1947).

There was nothing shabby about any of these players. The 6-foot,
3-inch Goldman was an All-American, who played his last college game
on a Saturday night and was in the lineup for the SPHAS the following evening. Rosan was also an All-American. Rosenberg became an ABL
scoring champion. Lautman was a local favorite, a high-scoring, ambi-

dextrous guard out of Central High School. Wolfe, a balding, scrawny defensive wizard, was said to look more like an accountant than a pro basketball player. Morgenthaler had played a few games in the Basketball Association of America (BAA) the previous season.

Schectman, a top performer with the team from 1941 to 1946 and the player who later scored the first field goal in the BAA while playing for the New York Knicks against the Toronto Huskies in the new league's first game on November 1, 1946, remembered how he became a member of the SPHAS. "It was all done verbally," he said. "I didn't have a contract. I saw the team play in New York. I liked the way they played. It was less of an individual approach to the game. I was told I could play with a New York team, but Gotty contacted me and asked if I'd like to play in Philadelphia. I said I'd like to. He said, 'OK. You now belong to me.'"

One of the more colorful SPHAS players was Gotthoffer, whom Gottlieb had secured in a trade with the Jewels for Max Posnack. A rough, tough, rock-solid athlete, Gotthoffer was the SPHAS' most valuable player six times. When he wasn't playing with the SPHAS, he suited up for a team in Nanticoke in the minor Penn State League. As long as his players made it to SPHAS games, Gottlieb never had a problem with them playing elsewhere on off days.

Especially in the 1930s, SPHAS players were held in particularly high esteem by the fans of Philadelphia. The Phillies were in the midst of a 31-year disaster, the Athletics were sliding downhill quickly, and the Eagles were newly formed. The SPHAS were at the top of the heap in local pro sports circles.

"We were the darlings of Philadelphia," Gotthoffer said in Robert Peterson's *Cages to Jump Shots*. "We couldn't go anywhere without being recognized. We were very well-loved."

"It was the pinnacle of athletic achievement just to be able to wear that jersey with those four Hebrew letters on it," Yock Welsh said to Bill Ordine. "The money meant nothing. The goal, the fulfillment, was to play for the greatest basketball team in the world."

By the late 1930s, players earned as little as $1,500 and as much as $3,000 a season. No one ever knew what other players were paid. Gottlieb, whom Klotz described as "fair but tough," compensated each player separately, shelling out the night's wages from the wad of gate receipts that he kept in his pocket. He paid each player in the men's room.

Ralph Kaplowitz, a star guard in the 1945–46 season, told the story of his signing with the SPHAS. "I had no written agreement," he said.

"When he gave his word or his handshake, that was all that was needed. Eddie was sincere and honest, a man of his word. There was no double-talk. He didn't pat you on the back to make you feel good. But I never heard him badmouth anyone."

"Players were paid on a per diem basis," recalled Schectman. "Plus you got $2 or $3 for dinner when we were on the road. Sometimes, you had to fight Gotty for $5 or $10 more a game. He wasn't cheap, but he wanted value. And he made the SPHAS the soundest financial team in the whole league

"I got hurt once, and I really had to sweat that one out," Schectman added. "I had to play because I was afraid that if I didn't, I wouldn't get paid. The next night we had a game in New England. I knew I couldn't play, but I went anyway and sat on the bench. If I'd gone home, I'd have never gotten paid."

Schwartz, a native New Yorker, said that he was paid just $20 for his first game with the team. "Guys today light their cigars with that kind of money," he said. "But Gotty was pretty fair with his players. He was more intimate with the players from Philadelphia, probably because he knew them better than the guys from New York.

"Gotty was 20 years ahead of his time," Schwartz claimed. "Why? Because of the stuff he initiated. He knew the game better than anybody else. He was the only guy in the league who made any money. Everybody in the league liked him. He often loaned money to other owners."

Sometimes they needed it. Fleishman remembered what it was like in Wilkes-Barre. "If it rained and there was a lousy house," he said, "the owner would reduce the players' pay. Gotty never did that. He was the most honorable man in the league. If he promised you $100 a game, no matter what the conditions were, he gave you exactly that. He didn't give money away. But if you dealt with him, you knew he wasn't cheap. He paid our guys more than guys from other teams got."

Once the SPHAS reached the 1940s, Gottlieb peppered their roster with new players with varied backgrounds. Although no new SPHAS were African American—Gottlieb's social consciousness had not yet reached that point—many of them were not Jews. Future Philadelphia Warriors captain George Senesky played for the SPHAS during the 1945–46 season. Another future Warrior, Matt Guokas, Sr., was also a member of that team. Philadelphia Athletics pitcher Bill McCahan, who hurled a no-hitter on September 3, 1947, and had been a standout basketball player at Duke, wore the SPHAS uniform for the 1948–49 season. Eddie Lyons from Temple, later a longtime manager in the Phillies' farm system, played from 1947 to 1949. And Max Patkin, the Clown Prince of Baseball, played for the team in 1949.

Schectman remembered the time Gottlieb brought in baseball player and future actor (most notably on the television show *The Rifleman*) Chuck Connors to play an exhibition game for the SPHAS against the Rens. "At one point," Schectman said, "the Rens started doing figure eights, passing the ball around. Connors got tired of standing around. He stole a Rens' pass and shot it into their basket. Then he started to walk on his hands right on the court. He said, 'You guys want to make us look bad. The hell with this.' He was fed up with the Rens."

"Even though we weren't all Jewish, we found that we were no different from each other," said Klotz, referring to the diverse collection of white players on the team. "And we got to admire each other's abilities. We competed with each other, but we tolerated all the prejudices and overcame them. Gottlieb was part of the reason. He knew how to intertwine us. Eventually, we had all different kinds of people playing with us. It was wonderful, which is the way it should be."

There was never anything ordinary about the SPHAS' playing schedule. The team wandered all over the map. Gottlieb took it to any city, town, or hamlet where he thought there was a chance to attract a crowd—and hence, put money in his and his players' pockets.

If the SPHAS weren't playing league games, they'd play exhibition games. And they'd travel throughout the Northeast and even into the Midwest, playing mostly in armories and taking on all comers. The fact that the SPHAS were one of basketball's most successful and widely known teams was a distinct advantage. They drew big crowds almost everywhere they played.

The SPHAS were nothing if not flashy. Sometimes, when they appeared on the court before a game, they'd be dressed in fancy mackinaws and jackets. Underneath, they wore the spiffy red and gold uniforms that had become a trademark of the club.

"It was like they were putting on a show," recalled Marvin Black. "Not only were their clothes flashy, they did a drill that was as good if not better than the Harlem Globetrotters, passing the ball around. The fans loved it."

Almost every year at Christmas, the SPHAS journeyed to Oshkosh, Wisconsin, where they participated in a tournament with other top teams of the era. Along the way, they played in cities such as Pittsburgh, Akron,

Detroit, Chicago, and Sheboygan. In March 1941, the team also played in Chicago in what was billed as a "world tournament." Among other teams entered were the Harlem Globetrotters and some of the better clubs from the Midwest. The SPHAS lost that year in the quarterfinals to the Oshkosh All-Stars, 38–31.

Getting to those points could be tricky. Sometimes, the team traveled in two Buick Specials piloted by drivers hired by Gottlieb. Once, during a long road trip, one of the drivers fell asleep. Another time, a truck hit one of the cars.

During a trip home from Reading one snowy night, with Gottlieb driving, the car skidded off the road into a ditch. "OK, you're on your own," Gotty advised his players. "I expect to see everyone at the game in Philadelphia tonight." The players had to thumb rides home, but they all made it on time for the game.

On short trips, the team went from town to town in Gottlieb's nine-passenger Ford sedan—with players jammed in, virtually unable to move. When he traveled with the SPHAS, after joining the team in 1935, public address announcer Zinkoff rode lying on the floor of the back seat, players using his prone body as a footrest.

"The travel was tough," said Fleishman, who was usually the designated driver when the team took only one car. "It was winter, and you'd have to go to Scranton or Wilkes-Barre or Hazelton. There'd be snow on the road. There were always a few mishaps.

"Then there were the times we'd play on a Saturday night at the Broadwood," Fleishman added. "You'd go to sleep, get up, and go to Wilmington for a Sunday afternoon game, then race to Trenton for a night game. On Sundays, you'd wear the same uniform for each game and wouldn't shower between games."

Players from New York were often picked up at their homes if the team was headed north. And when the SPHAS were at home, the New Yorkers traveled by train to North Broad Street Station, where they got picked up by a car and taken directly to the Broadwood. After the game, they returned to New York the same way. Because of their travel expenses, Gottlieb gave the out-of-town players slightly higher paychecks.

Once, though, four New York players took the wrong train out of Penn Station. Instead of traveling to a game in Trenton, they went the opposite direction. "When we saw water, we knew we were headed the wrong way," recalled Schectman. "We asked the conductor to let us off in Bristol, Connecticut. He said the next stop was Stamford, and we could get off there, but if we pulled the chain to stop the train before that, we'd go to jail. Needless to say, we missed the game in Trenton."

During the war years, many of the SPHAS players signed up for military service. Some were stationed at West Point, New York. Those players drove to New York City, hopped a train to Philadelphia, played the game, and then returned to their barracks.

On occasion, the SPHAS played games against the House of David, the legendary, bearded barnstorming team that was more noted for its baseball exploits. Other times, Gottlieb scheduled his club against the Globetrotters. One season in the mid-1930s, Gotty booked the team at the Flager Hotel in the Catskills. In exchange for meals and lodging, the team played exhibition games for the guests. Players also got the chance to ski. In 1939, Gottlieb even scheduled a triple-header at Convention Hall with the SPHAS, New York Jewels, Harlem Renaissance, and Oshkosh Stars among the participants.

Promoting his team and booking it into places wherever he could get a game was as important to Gottlieb as anything he did with the SPHAS. It was, after all, his extraordinary gift in this area that played a major role in making the team so successful. Without Gotty's promotional genius, there would've been no chance for the team to occupy such a lofty position in the basketball hierarchy. Gotty, of course, was fully aware of this.

Gottlieb, however, was more than an entrepreneur of the highest magnitude. Among his many other duties, he was a coach. Few in his era were any better.

"He was a very good coach," recalled Fleishman. "He used his head quite a bit. Even if he disliked a player personally, he'd keep him in the game if it was best for the team. He was a very hard loser, though."

By the mid-1930s, Gottlieb, once called "the portly pilot of the Hebrews" in an *Inquirer* article by Bill Dallas, had been coaching for a long time. He'd started back in 1917 and had been the skipper of the SPHAS since then. In all those years, Gotty was the team's only coach. Until the mid-1940s, he never had any assistants.

Gottlieb wasn't the stereotypical coach. He didn't look like a coach. At 5 feet, 8 inches, he was short. By the 1930s, he was a little plump, a little jowly, and beginning to get the bags under his eyes that became one of his most noticeable characteristics. On the bench, he always wore a suit and a large, flowered tie.

"But he was tough," said Red Klotz. "If I went for a hook shot and missed, I'd head for the end of the bench. I knew he'd take me out. And if you didn't play defense, you were in trouble. He knew the game, and he dominated the team."

No one would ever describe Gottlieb as being a master strategist. He knew the game backward and forward. And he often gave out instructions to players, sometimes even donning a uniform in practice to demonstrate a point. But he wasn't big on pre-game plans or diagramming plays. No X and O man was he.

"Coaching was different back then," said Schectman. "You didn't have set plays like you do now. You just went out and did what you knew how to do. Before each game, Gotty would come into the dressing room and look around. If your top was not on straight, he'd straighten it. There was no pre-game pep talk. He'd just say 'give me a period.' He had a broken pinky. He'd wave that hand when he was saying it."

"He just let the players play," remembered Kaplowitz. "When he wanted us to play better, he would plead with us: 'My boys, my boys, give me a period, one period,' he would say."

To a certain extent, Gottlieb coached by intimidation. Yelling at players and at referees was an important part of his style. And he was extremely excitable. He was up and down on the bench like a jackrabbit, prancing back and forth.

"He sits on the bench and suffers," said one newspaper account of Gottlieb's coaching style. "He yanks on his tie. He gazes ceilingward. He smites his brow, buries his face in his hands and makes noises like a she-wolf whose young are threatened. Few enraged bulls can bellow louder than Eddie when an official calls a questionable foul."

During timeouts, he could sometimes be heard screaming and cursing at the players. "He never yelled at me," said Schectman. "But he would often yell at the Philly guys. I guess he respected New York guys more. We had one guy on the team who got married. He took his wife on road trips. Eddie got very upset about that and yelled at him a lot."

Gottlieb once told Edgar Williams in an article in the *Inquirer* that his courtside behavior came naturally. "It's real," Gotty said. "I know I make a jackass out of myself every time we play, but what can I do?"

Kaplowitz claimed that Gotty's players "all loved him." On more than one occasion, though, that feeling was put to a stiff test. "Inky Lautman was having a bad night," he said. "We were in a huddle during a timeout, and Eddie kept hounding him. He said, 'You look sad. You're not get-

Irv Torgoff (center) and Petey
Rosenberg get some words of
wisdom from coach Gottlieb.
*(Philadelphia Jewish Sports Hall
of Fame, Adolph and Rose Levis
Museum)*

ting the ball off the backboards, your passes are
sloppy. What the hell's
the matter with you?' Inky
replied, 'You called me a
horse's ass. You insulted
me.' Eddie said, 'I didn't
insult you. I said you're
playing like a horse's ass.'"

Winning meant everything to Gotty. Once, he even got into a
loud argument with Matt Guokas over which one of them wanted to
win more.

In an article in the *Jewish Exponent* written by Ron Avery, Shikey
Gotthoffer told a story about Gottlieb's antics after the SPHAS had lost
a game he thought they should've won. "Eddie thought we had let him
down," Gotthoffer said. "After the game, he went into a drugstore and
bought a bottle of iodine and poured it all over the back of his shirt.
Later, we're all eating in a restaurant. Gotty stands up, takes off his jacket,
turns around, and says, 'You guys stabbed me in the back.'"

Although they had won nine league championships over a period
that covered 16 years in the Eastern and American Leagues, by
the mid-1940s, the SPHAS were having problems. Ultimately, they would
prove to be insurmountable.

One extremely critical problem was the team's declining fan base. As
the 20th century had moved past its early decades, fields that previously
had been closed to members of the Jewish community were opening. And
as greater opportunities surfaced, Jews became increasingly successful.

One of the by-products of this success was that Jews were developing a
wider circle of interests. These interests were no longer restricted to ones

with a religious connection. They were opportunities that were available to all citizens, no matter what their religious affiliation.

Gottlieb had seen this coming. He had seen how basketball had ceased to be a Jewish man's game. A major reason, according to Peter Levine in his book *Ellis Island to Ebbets Field-Sports and the American Jewish Experience,* was that sports were no longer a priority among newly minted Jewish parents. They wanted their sons to become lawyers, doctors, businessmen, and teachers.

Gotty had also seen how people of all creeds and colors were not only playing the game but watching it, too. To meet this change, he had taken some of the SPHAS games out of the Jewish climate at the Broadwood Hotel and moved them to Convention Hall. And he had brought in Gentiles to play for the team, such as George Senesky, Jerry Rullo, Matt Guokas, and various others. That, Gotty reasoned, would attract non-Jews to the games, thus broadening the SPHAS' appeal to a greater number of potential spectators.

"The Jewish decline in basketball was a metaphor for the Jewish advancement in culture," said Jeffrey Gurock, a professor of history at Yeshiva University.

Along with changes in their interests, Jews were also changing the places where they lived. No longer was Philadelphia's tightly meshed Jewish community residing almost entirely in South Philadelphia. With more income and having become upwardly mobile, Jews were relocating to better neighborhoods. They were moving into West Philadelphia, along Broad Street between Girard and Diamond, into apartments on Rittenhouse Square, and into Northeast Philly, Oak Lane, and Cheltenham Township.

Of course, World War II had also added to the SPHAS' problems, taking away fans who would have otherwise attended games. Adding all their problems together, SPHAS games at the Broadwood Hotel were no longer considered the highlight of the Jewish social calendar.

But there was still one other situation that above all others contributed to the declining popularity of the SPHAS. That was the formation of a new professional basketball league. It was destined to drive the SPHAS into extinction.

When the BAA was formed in 1946, one of its chief architects was Eddie Gottlieb and one of its franchises was placed in Philadelphia. And the coach of the new team was none other than Gottlieb himself.

With this kind of a commitment and the chance to make more money with a league that appeared destined to play on a higher plane, Gottlieb had little time for the SPHAS. Now, the league and the Philadelphia Warriors were more important. Now, the future of the SPHAS was in jeopardy.

As it turned out, the 1945–46 season was the SPHAS' final year at the top level of professional basketball. Following that season, the creation of the BAA would reduce not only the SPHAS but the entire ABL to minor league status.

Gottlieb remained the owner of the team. But he stepped down as coach, and on August 16, 1946, he appointed Harry Litwack, the former SPHAS defensive ace and at the time the freshmen basketball coach at Temple, as his successor.

Under Litwack, the SPHAS played in the watered-down ABL against teams such as Wilmington, Jersey City, Wilkes-Barre, Scranton, Trenton, Paterson, Brooklyn, and Hartford. Each team played only 35 or so games a season. The SPHAS played most of their home games at the Arena, often performing as a preliminary to Warriors games, many times against the Globetrotters. SPHAS fans often left after the first game. Most of the team's road games were played in armories.

Jerry Rullo, who went from the SPHAS to the BAA, then back to the SPHAS, shared his recollections of the games with the Trotters. "We traveled with them on the bus," he said. "Jesse Owens was their announcer. Most of them were very nice guys, although Goose Tatum was not. He was kind of nasty.

"When we were on the road, I was the player-coach because Litwack was a schoolteacher and couldn't get away. I'd call Gottlieb after every game and give him a report.

"I remember that the SPHAS had a few routines of their own," Rullo continued. "Len Weiner would put the ball under his shirt. We had a guy named Bobby McDermott who had played with Ft. Wayne in the old ABL. He had a great set shot. He'd shot one from the foul line. After each shot, he'd step back a few more feet. He'd finally get to the other team's foul line to shoot. All this was during the game. It was quite a show. Elmore Morgenthaler was a 7-footer. He'd put on a pretty good show, too."

SPHAS players were now getting paid from $75 to $125 a game. Most of the team's roster consisted of former high school and a few college stars from Philadelphia such as ex-Public League standouts Stan Brown, signed as a 17-year-old just before his senior year at Southern High

School, and Frank Stanczak from Roxborough High. Few of the SPHAS players were Jewish.

By the late 1940s, there was little interest in the SPHAS in Philadelphia. The team's Jewish fans had either died or were now pursuing other interests. The Warriors and college teams dominated the local basketball scene. There were only a few Jewish players still in the game, and basketball was in the early stages of attracting an increasing number of black players.

Gottlieb was still in control. But in 1949, he pulled the team out of the ABL, turning it into one that played only exhibition games. Up-and-coming baseball funnyman Max Patkin, who had been on the basketball team at West Philadelphia High and Brown Prep in Philadelphia, played and provided comic relief for the SPHAS. And Louis (Red) Klotz was named the team's new coach.

The son of Russian immigrants, Klotz was in the early stages of an epic basketball career. A diminutive (5-foot, 7-inch) guard who had one of the deadliest set shots ever to grace a basketball court, he had been a basketball star at South Philly High, played at Villanova, and in 1942 joined the SPHAS. He put in a stint with the Baltimore Bullets during the 1947–48 season when that team captured the BAA championship, then returned to the SPHAS.

With Klotz as player-coach, the SPHAS became one of the opposing teams that traveled with the Globetrotters (the SPHAS rotated with the Toledo Mercuries, Boston Whirlwinds, and later the Washington Generals). One year, appearing all around the world, the SPHAS met the Globies 106 times.

"I whipped them a couple of times," Klotz recalled. "Abe Saperstein [the Globies' owner] called me in after they beat the [Minneapolis] Lakers in a series of games. He said, 'Look, we're going to move into some big auditoriums, and I'm going to need some tough competition. You're the right guy to form your own organization.' That's when I resigned from the SPHAS job and formed the Washington Generals [originally called Klotz's Komets]. Eddie wasn't too happy about it.

"He wasn't too happy either when we beat the Warriors in an exhibition game. That was my first victory with the Generals. Eddie was terribly upset. He said, 'What the hell are you doing?' I said, 'Well, I have to beat somebody.'"

Klotz, whose teams in those days didn't completely capitulate to the Globies, went on to play for, coach, and own the Generals, later renamed the New York Nationals, during an incredible career that is still going strong. Overall, the now 86-year-old basketball wizard, who still plays nearly every day on a court in Margate, New Jersey, against men one-third his age, has appeared in 117 countries on every continent except Antarctica. While playing professionally for 45 years and against the Globetrotters until he was 68 years old, Klotz appeared in an estimated 16,000 games (his teams winning just six of them, none since 1971). He still owns the four teams that now face the Globetrotters under the names of the Nationals, New Jersey Reds, Atlantic City Seagulls, and Boston Shamrocks.

Meanwhile, Gottlieb continued to make changes with the SPHAS. In 1950, he sold the franchise (but not the name or the players) for an undisclosed amount to a syndicate in Utica, New York, that included Leo Ferris, part owner of the Syracuse Nats. The new team became a member of the ABL.

The reconstituted SPHAS, operating as a farm team for the Warriors, continued to play exhibition games after Klotz left the team in 1952. One of the team's players, Pete Monska from West Chester State, was appointed coach. Other members of the final squad were Rullo, who had gone from the SPHAS to the Warriors, then back to the SPHAS, and future Warriors player George Dempsey.

"I was the last cut of the Warriors in 1951," Dempsey said. "Eddie offered to send me to the SPHAS, and I agreed. I'll never forget him saying, 'If you're smart, you can save money on meal money,' which at the time was $7 or $8 a day."

The 1954 season turned out to be the last one for the SPHAS, just as it was the final year for the baseball Athletics in Philadelphia. The Generals under Klotz were now the full-time traveling companions of the Globetrotters, and there was no place left in basketball for the Philadelphia club.

When Gottlieb folded the team, there was no outcry, no mourning, no somber editorials in the local newspapers. The SPHAS' end attracted virtually no attention, even though for nearly four decades they had been one of the most successful, most celebrated teams in Philadelphia sports history.

CHAPTER 5

A Born Promoter

There may have been times during his life when Eddie Gottlieb simply sat back and relaxed. But if there were, hardly anyone ever noticed them.

Gotty was always on the move. He was always busy, always working on some kind of project. Downtime was a term with which he was not familiar.

Gottlieb had been that way since his early days in sports. Beginning with the SPHAS, he maintained a heavy schedule, seldom slowing down, rarely taking a break. It was that way nearly 12 months of the year for most of Gotty's long career. It has often been said that Gotty probably played in, coached, directed, scheduled, or promoted more athletic events that any person in the history of mankind.

Life was especially hectic for Gottlieb during the decades of the 1920s, 1930s, and 1940s. That was largely because he had his hands in so many different activities. Basketball, baseball, football, wrestling, even entertainment, Gottlieb was not only deeply involved in each of these, he was the guy who more often than not made them happen. He booked 500 baseball games per week. He coached a college basketball team. He began a semipro football league. He scheduled appearances for entertainers. And, at one point in the 1940s, he owned three professional teams at the same time.

That's how he got the nickname The Mogul. A mogul, Gottlieb once explained, "is the top banana." That he was. In Philadelphia sports, Gotty was the main man, the big cheese, the head honcho. No one was more involved in such a broad array of sports than The Mogul.

Gottlieb always had his sights set on ways to make a living off of sports. "There is nothing more satisfying than being involved in sports," he told an interviewer long ago. Ultimately, Gotty would confirm that statement by spending some 60 years in the business.

In the early 1920s, Gottlieb was a schoolteacher, part owner of and salesman at a sporting goods business, and part owner, coach, and player with the SPHAS. For the ordinary person, that would be enough. But it wasn't for the young man in his early 20s from South Philadelphia.

Gotty had yet another calling. He felt that there was a pressing need for someone in Philadelphia to serve as a booking agent and promoter for the city's many sandlot, independent, and semipro baseball, basketball, and football teams and leagues. Finding fields and scheduling games on their own was a virtual impossibility for the hundreds of teams in the area.

Sometimes, four teams would appear at the same time for games on the same field. Sometimes, fields would sit empty because of a flaw in the scheduling process. There were too many teams and not enough fields. The situation was chaos. Gottlieb saw the void and stepped in to fill it.

Gotty was well acquainted with the local sports landscape. From the various roles he already played, he had been both a participant and a close observer. He knew all the angles. He was perfectly equipped for the work. And he saw it as a means not only to expand his own interests and bank account, but also as a way to increase sales for PGB Sports, the sporting goods business that he owned with Harry Passon and Hughie Black.

While managing an amateur baseball team called the Philadelphia Elks, Gottlieb attempted to get a game with the House of David. He called Nat Strong, a powerful New York booking agent. "He told me that he couldn't afford to send the House team down for just one game," Gottlieb said in an article in *The Sporting News*. "If I could line up four games, he'd be willing to talk business. I lined up four games and became a promoter."

Before long, Gottlieb was scheduling more baseball games. He was scheduling basketball games. And football games. "I was a born promoter," he said some years later.

He was also born to be someone who exerted a great amount of power. Gottlieb was named to the board of governors of the Philadelphia Baseball Association, a group that had been around since 1922 and that consisted of some 60 independent semipro teams, some of which were African American. By 1933, Gotty had become president of that organization. A few years later, a headline in the Philadelphia *Ledger* said, "Gottlieb Re-Elected Dictator of Baseball League." Gottlieb also headed another group of teams called the Quaker City Baseball League. Unquestionably, he had maneuvered himself into a position in which he controlled when and where all these teams played.

Especially in the 1920s and 1930s, Philadelphia was a sandlot baseball hotbed. Industrial and neighborhood leagues, a department store league, a bank league, a league of rapid transit workers, even a league of telephone company employees, and many other leagues with outstanding teams and exceptional players performed in every section of the city and suburbs. In a number of cases, top players rejected overtures to play professional baseball because they could make more money working and playing for the companies that sponsored their teams. In some cases, too, major leaguers—Chief Bender, Erskine Mayer, Howard Ehmke, Wid Conroy, and Bris Lord, to name a few—played on the Philly sandlots after their big league careers were over.

As time went on, more and more baseball teams, especially the independent ones, began to use Gottlieb's services. By the 1930s, these teams didn't play unless Gotty booked them. The same was true of out-of-town teams seeking games in Philly. If you didn't go to Gotty, you didn't get a game.

And should a team have the audacity to anger Eddie or, worse yet, not show up for a game, it would be unlikely that they would get any more games, either. "They feared me like they feared the wrath of God," Gottlieb advised Gaeton Fonzi.

That, of course, begged the question: How did he get so powerful? Certainly, Gotty knew people in the right places. He got into the booking game before anyone else. He was a strong personality. He was a salesman. And he drove a hard bargain. "He was a no-nonsense guy," said Marvin Black. "He was tough. You didn't mess around with him. He had his own agenda, and he knew what he wanted to do."

Gottlieb rarely used contracts. And he didn't like to negotiate. His agreements were usually verbal, with both sides accepting each other's word. "I would set a fair price and strike a quick bargain," he once said. "And then I'd settle with a handshake."

The Mogul's duties included assigning umpires to games. Sometimes, he even found players for various teams. Gotty hung out at the Horn and Hardart's at 15th and Market Streets, along with a large contingent of local sports hangers-on. Occasionally, a manager came in saying he needed a pitcher or some other player. "Who's loose tomorrow?" Gottlieb would yell. Shortly, the manager had his player.

Gottlieb also booked Negro League teams and eventually traveling exhibition teams from outside the area. Among these were the House of David, and teams called the Zulu Jungle Giants, the Black Shadows, and the Hillbillies, whose players wore overalls and checkered shirts.

Gottlieb's workload steadily increased. With some 200 adult teams playing on fields throughout the Philadelphia area, including places such as Chester, Norristown, and Camden, just about every one of their games was booked through Gotty. "Eventually, I was staying up until 3 a.m. booking semipro baseball games, 500 of them a week," he told Sandy Grady for an article in the *Evening Bulletin*.

A team usually got its money by passing a hat through the stands during the game. Normally, Gotty charged a service fee of 50¢ a game, plus 5 percent of the take. Most of the time, he had a $3 per game guarantee. And it was not in the teams' best interests to cheat him. If they did, they might as well take up tennis. There'd be no more games booked for them.

Football and basketball also became a regular part of Gottlieb's portfolio. Like baseball, independent (a word often used to describe both amateur and semipro sports) football and basketball teams and leagues operated throughout the city. Gotty found games, playing sites, and referees for virtually all these many teams.

He even found a nonleague rivalry for the SPHAS. The team played an annual game against St. Anne's Church in Kensington. A Jewish team versus a Catholic team. It was a major event. The St. Anne's gym at Memphis Street and Lehigh Avenue was always packed for the game.

Gottlieb did not limit his work to men's teams. In the 1930s, he also booked games for local women's baseball teams, some of which played in a fast-paced industrial league in the city.

One women's team that Gottlieb especially liked to book was sponsored by Fleisher Yarn Company in South Philadelphia. The star of the team was an outstanding all-around athlete named Mary Gilroy. A decade later, her son, Bill Hockenbury, was an infielder in the Philadelphia Athletics' farm system. And the Mary Gilroy Hockenbury Award became an annual honor presented for many years to the city's top woman basketball player by the Philadelphia Old-Timers' Association.

In the 1940s, Gottlieb was also a major promoter of pro wrestling matches at the Arena in West Philadelphia (Gotty's name does not appear on any records as the promoter of boxing matches). He'd rent the venue for a night and stage a series of matches. Among his biggest clients were the Dusek brothers—Rudy, Ernie, Emil, and Joe—from South Philly.

"I heard Gottlieb speak on the phone regularly to Rudy Dusek, going over the scenario for the current show," said Bernie Brown, who served as a water boy for the SPHAS before getting an office job running errands for The Mogul for $7 a week. "They would talk about how the match was going to turn out, who was going to bet on who, and how long the match would be. It was all fixed. Even in those days, pro wrestling was no longer a sport, but was evolving into an entertainment business whose matches were all planned."

Gotty is also credited by Alan Trumper as being the first promoter to book a match for a wrestler known as Gorgeous George, a glitzy grappler who wore gold-plated hairpins in his long, curly, bleached blond locks. The ultra-flamboyant wrestler, whose real name was George Wagner and who was accompanied by music and a valet when he entered the ring, was considered the "sport's" first real showman. "At one time or another," Gottlieb told a writer some years later, "I guess I handled everything."

Everything, perhaps, but college sports. Gottlieb steered clear of them. "I never considered going into college sports," he said. "Why should I? You just couldn't promote in college. A college has alumni and students. They put on a dull show, and nobody gives a goddamn one way or another."

Gottlieb's booking and promotional activities were not limited to sports. At the peak of his career as a booking agent in the 1930s, he was also involved in the entertainment field.

It has been said that he booked circuses and musical events, including performances by various orchestras. The world-renowned violinist Isaac Stern was one of Gotty's close friends, and when he was in town, he could often be seen at Philadelphia Warriors games. As the story goes, Stern

Future Hollywood luminary
Joey Bishop, who grew up in
South Philadelphia, was booked
for his first appearance in 1937
by Gottlieb. (*Temple University
Libraries, Urban Archives,
Philadelphia, Pennsylvania*)

once asked to have the starting time of a Warriors game
moved up so he could per-
form in a concert that night
at the Academy of Music. The
request was rejected.

Gottlieb booked an assortment of entertainers. For 20
years, he scheduled appearances for his friend and briefly
a SPHAS player, Max Patkin. Known as the Clown Prince of Baseball, Pat-
kine eventually performed his comic routine at ballparks throughout the
country.

Gottlieb also arranged comedian Joey Bishop's first appearance in 1937
at a resort called South Mountain Manor in Wernersville, Pennsylvania.

Although born in the Bronx, Bishop moved when he was three
months old to South Philadelphia where his father ran a bicycle shop
for many years. One of an endless number of entertainers from South
Philly, Bishop, whose real name ironically was Joseph Abraham Gottlieb
(no relation to Eddie), launched his career while still a teenager. After
dropping out of South Philly High following his junior year, he began
performing with two friends from the neighborhood. They billed themselves as the Bishop Brothers.

Bishop told the *Inquirer*'s Frank Dolson about a conversation he had
with Gotty leading up to his first professional gig. "He gave me my start,"
Bishop recalled. "He said, 'We'll give you $25.' I thought that meant $25
for each of us, so I said, 'OK.' But he meant $25 altogether. So we got

paid $8 apiece. I went to Gotty and I said, 'I don't think that's fair.' He said, 'I'll tell you what. We'll do your laundry, too.'"

In the years following that exchange, Bishop appeared numerous times in Philadelphia, frequently at Palumbo's in Center City. Whenever Joey came to town, Gottlieb was there to catch his act.

One of Gottlieb's more memorable promotions didn't involve an entertainer, but in its own way was high-level entertainment. It involved Art Shires, a good-hit, no-field first baseman, who enjoyed a brief big league baseball career between 1928 and 1932.

In the winter of 1930, having hit .312 for the Chicago White Sox the previous season, Shires was invited to the annual banquet of the Philadelphia Sports Writers' Association (PSWA). Shires had flattened his manager, Lena Blackburne, twice during one season, and had become a boxer who was short on talent, but a good drawing card. When gangster-boxing promoter Max (Boo Boo) Huff learned that Shires was coming to Philadelphia, he decided to try to arrange a match for him. The night of the banquet, in an attempt to win Shires's favor, he filled the player's bathtub at the Adelphia Hotel full of ice and beer.

Meanwhile, Gottlieb had been told that the PSWA could not pay Shires's expenses. "I've read where Art claims to have played basketball," Gotty told PSWA president Bob Paul. "Ask him if he'll stay over two days. I'll pay him $200 to appear with the SPHAS against the Renaissance. Maybe, he'll sell out the place."

Shires agreed, but at a practice session with the SPHAS missed most of his shots by a foot or more. Gottlieb figured he'd give Shires as little playing time as possible. But during the game, the sell-out crowd chanted "We want Shires," and Gotty complied, instructing his players not to let him touch the ball. Knowing Shires's inability to hit the basket, though, the Rens started passing the ball to him. Shires took shots, but missed them. After a few minutes, Gotty benched Shires. At halftime, he handed him $250. "I promised him $200, but gave him another $50," said Gotty. "Art proved he is no basketball player, but he certainly is a great gate attraction."

Shires returned home without a boxing match, but with enough money to cover his expenses, thanks to another innovative maneuver by Gottlieb. One week later, Shires received a letter from baseball commissioner Kenesaw Mountain Landis that warned him if he engaged in any other boxing matches, he would earn an early retirement from major league baseball.

With all Gottlieb's many ventures, it would be logical to assume that his operation was superbly organized and ran as smoothly as a ship on a calm sea. Surely, the office was without clutter, files were clearly marked and neatly arranged, and a smartly honed assistant or two was there to help keep order.

Nothing could be farther from the truth. Gottlieb's operation was about as close to being a well-oiled machine as an elephant is to being a squirrel. His office looked like a flea market on a bad day. More than a few people said they'd seen better looking dumps.

Gotty, who was extremely well organized himself, couldn't be bothered with such mundane details as keeping a fancy office. After all, he was a guy who kept everything in his head. He had an extraordinary mind. Some called him a genius. And his memory was faultless. He could remember even the most trivial details. Ask him about a particular game, and he would tell you the score, the attendance, and even the weather.

"He had a mind like a trip-hammer," the former Philadelphia 76ers general manager and longtime executive with several other NBA teams Pat Williams said many years later. "He was absolutely brilliant. He could carry endless amounts of information up there in his head. He was amazing."

Because he carried his business in his head and on a few slips of paper that he kept in his pocket, Gottlieb—who rarely discussed his business with anybody else, anyway—didn't need a sophisticated organization. All he really required were a couple of telephones. They provided The Mogul with a way to do business, and they rang constantly.

Like all good entrepreneurs, though, Gottlieb maintained an office of sorts. It was originally located on the second floor of the sporting goods store he ran with Harry Passon and Hughie Black at Eighth and Pine Streets. By the late 1920s when the company had moved to 507 Market Street, Gotty was stationed on the second floor there, too.

In many ways, the office seemed more like the site of a social club than a place of business. It bordered on organized chaos with an assortment of characters always coming in and out, shouting, arguing, joking. "Gotty had a whole entourage," said Brown, who ultimately took a full-time job in the office doing public relations work for Gotty's many enterprises. "Umpires and referees from the independent leagues were always hanging around the office," he added. "Writers and others from sports would stop in. Sports luminaries congregated almost daily."

The regular members of the entourage were, of course, the people who The Mogul employed. Marty Weintraub, the real workhorse and backbone of the organization, according to Brown, served as Gottlieb's chief assistant, confidant, secretary, cashier at games, and original editor of the SPHAS' game program. Abe Radel, an accountant and former basketball star, handled the money end of the business, paying bills and keeping track of the income and expenses. Nathan (Shooey) Sisman, a hunchback, who it was said played a pretty good game of basketball, took care of the equipment and handled odd jobs.

Although he was the only non-Jew, Mike Iannarella was another significant member of the group. A South Philadelphia native, Iannarella originally met Gottlieb in the late 1920s when he was seeking games for his baseball team. The team had no name. Gotty told Mike he needed a colorful nickname. "We had a lot of ethnic teams then," Gottlieb recalled. "I said, 'OK, you're the Italians.'"

After that, Iannarella started hanging around the office. "He was a printer," Gotty said to Bill Livingston in an article in *The Sporting News*. "So he could handle the posters advertising games. He got a lot of games that way."

Eventually, Iannarella worked himself into a full-time job with Gottlieb. He handled ticket sales and other duties with the SPHAS and Gotty's Philadelphia Stars and then became a one-man ticket department with the Warriors and later the 76ers during a career in pro basketball that spanned 48 years.

Another office regular was Harry Litwack, whose relationship with Gottlieb went back to the early 1920s. Litwack, who coached the SPHAS for three seasons and served briefly as an assistant coach with the Warriors, could often be found in the afternoons napping in the back office after his day's work as a schoolteacher was over.

"Eddie Gottlieb taught Harry not only about the game of basketball, but about the game of life," said Estelle Litwack in an article in the *Temple News*. "If there was one way to describe Eddie's relationship to Harry, Eddie was his guardian angel."

Gotty also was one of Litwack's early financial benefactors. In 1931, Hughie Black opened Pine Forest Camp, a summer camp for children near Lake Wallenpaupack in the Poconos. Black was joined one year later by Litwack and Mo Weinstein, a local football coach. The three owned and operated the business until 1946 when Black bought out his two partners. Two years later, Litwack opened Sun Mountain Camp near Stroudsburg with the help of a loan from Gottlieb. The amount, later paid back by Litwack, was said to be $50,000.

Of all the figures in Gottlieb's entourage, none was more conspicuous than Dave Zinkoff, the little man with the booming voice who would be The Mogul's best friend and confidant for more than 40 years.

The Zink, as everybody would call him, made his first connection with Gottlieb in 1935 while still a student at Temple. Gotty was looking for a public address announcer for SPHAS games at the Broadwood, and Zink, then the public address announcer at Temple football and basketball games, was recommended.

Summoned to the Market Street store, Zinkoff found Gottlieb in his second floor office. "He looked like a little Santa Claus," Zink said in a *Daily News* article written by Dick Weiss. "He had a wide girth, and he sat behind a desk and looked me up and down. He said, 'So you think you're an announcer, huh?' I said, 'Well, I've done a little bit of work, Mr. Gottlieb.' He said, 'Get over there about 20 feet away in the corner and shout at me for 10 minutes.' Then he had me get over by the wall, face it, and say something for about 30 seconds. He was checking the resonance of my voice. After about 15 minutes or so, I started thinking, 'What am I going through here? Is this the Inquisition?'"

But Gotty liked what he heard and hired Zinkoff. A few nights later, Zink's illustrious career began at a SPHAS game with Sisman sitting at his side as a spotter. Over the years, though, there were a few rough patches.

"One time when he was working for the SPHAS, Zink wanted a raise from $5 to $6 a game," remembered Frank Dolson. "He told Gotty, 'I see we're getting big crowds every night. They're coming because of the way I jazz up the game.' And Gotty said, 'No way I can give you a raise.' So Zink held out and wouldn't work. Gotty said, 'If he had said, I want a raise because I'm working hard and I think I deserve it, I would've given it to him. But because he said they're coming to hear me instead of to see the team, that didn't get very far.' But that was Gotty. He was stubborn. He would stand on principle." And he gave Zink his raise after the announcer staged a three-week holdout.

"For years," Brown said, "Zink would traipse in and out of the office every day, killing a couple of hours until it was time for his date, usually with a chorus girl from one of the shows at the Forrest or Shubert Theaters."

In the years on Market Street, Zinkoff would be a participant in another one of Gotty's passions. Nearly every afternoon, The Mogul, Litwack, Iannarella, and Zink would play gin rummy in the back of the office. "They'd do it for two or three hours every day," recalled Brown. Curses, laughter, and, at the end of the session, the noisy exchange of money resonated throughout the office.

For the better part of 50 years, the substantial voice of Zinkoff was heard at SPHAS, Warriors, and eventually 76ers games making colorful calls, such as "Dipper Dunk" and "Gola Goal" and "Wally by Golly" and "Two for Shue" and "Malone Alone" and "Two minutes left in the qua-tah," that became his trademarks. He also called out lucky numbers—some that earned for the winner items such as auto seat covers, wigs for women, gift certificates, dinners, cartons of cigarettes, cases of soft drinks, and game tickets—from the program called *The Wigwam* that he edited and for which he sold advertising, his main source of income. Zink also passed out rolls of salami procured from his father's delicatessen at 52nd Street and Girard Avenue.

All the while, Gotty and Zink were inseparable. Sometimes, Gotty shouted orders at Zink without much regard for diplomacy, and he often berated his friend. But the pair ate together, went to shows and movies together, and took two-week vacations to Florida together. Because Gotty didn't like to drive, Zink was usually the driver wherever they went, piloting first The Mogul's Buicks, then later his Cadillacs.

"They were like Mutt and Jeff," recalled Marv Bachrad, a longtime broadcaster and friend of the two in their later years. "Zink would say, 'I drive the car. Gotty pays the bills and I leave the tip.'"

Before each Christmas, the two traveled to Hershey where they bought numerous cases of chocolate bars, which they then brought home and distributed to friends and associates.

"Every year, you'd get a box of Hershey bars that were loaded with extra almonds," Williams said. "He'd come wandering in with his Hershey bars and Zink would be with him giving out salamis."

Brown himself became a fixture in the office. Having been a member of the staff of the student newspaper at Northeast High School, he moved from errand boy to publicist for the SPHAS, getting a raise to $15 a week. He wrote press releases and after Zinkoff went into the army in 1942 took over as editor of the *SPHAS Sparks*, the four-page game program.

"Each Friday I had to take money in envelopes to the different sportswriters at the newspapers," Brown said. "I never knew how much. They never opened the envelopes in front of me. These were people who took care of us and saw to it that our publicity got into the papers. Without money, they probably wouldn't have done that. Gottlieb understood well that one had to grease the old palms. I imagine he wasn't the only one who did that in those days."

While Gottlieb's sports undertakings reached far and wide, they didn't entirely involve booking, promoting, and running the SPHAS. Gotty had some other items on his resume that were perhaps not as well known.

In the 1920s, he ran amateur baseball teams called the Phillies and the Elks. Later, he skippered a baseball team that went by the name of SPHAS that played mostly black teams at 44th Street and Parkside Avenue.

"He had most of the best Jewish players in the city," said Sam (Leaden) Bernstein. "My older brother, Hymie, was a very good baseball player. He later had a tryout with the Philadelphia Phillies. Gottlieb came to the house, picked him up, and drove him to games. He'd say to our mother, 'Mrs. Bernstein, your son is in good hands.'"

Amazingly, Gottlieb also served two different stints as the head basketball coach at Philadelphia Textile School (later changed to Institute), now known as Philadelphia University. He coached the team from 1924 to 1926 and again in the 1930–31 campaign.

At the time, according to Bucky Harris, who spent 43 years as the college's basketball coach and athletic director, Textile was located in Center City at Broad and Pine Streets (where it stayed until 1949), its student body being primarily Jewish. The basketball team practiced in a gymnasium at the Strawbridge and Clothier department store on Market Street.

Textile, which first fielded a team in 1919, played in what was called the City College League. Other teams in the league included Penn freshmen, Drexel, Ursinus, Hahnemann College, Temple Dental School, Philadelphia College of Pharmacy, and Philadelphia College of Optometry. Textile also played industrial league teams.

Textile's 1924 yearbook made note of Gottlieb's hiring. "To make prospects for a favorable season seem more promising," it said, "the coaching services of Ed Gottlieb, a former Southern High star and at present a Philadelphia League player, were secured."

The record (probably incomplete) for Gotty's team that year is listed as 7–5. In a season divided into halves, the squad finished second to Temple Dental both times, although it was the only team to defeat the eventual league champions during the regular season.

The team's record for the 1925–26 season is unknown, but, according to the college yearbook, Gottlieb coached only half the season. No

"Record crowds flock to see Philadelphia Hebrews play."

PHILADELPHIA HEBREWS

REPRESENTING

סוימה פילאדעלפיא היברו אססאסיאיישאן

MANAGER
ED. GOTTLIEB
114 SOUTH ST.
PHILA., PA

PHONES
LOMBARD 5593-DAY
LOMBARD 0256-NIGHT

9/26/27.

Dear Bob: —

Following is probable line-up for Clifton Heights game: —

no.

2	Beloff	L. E.
1	Goldstein	L. T.
7	Golden	L. G.
8	Effenberg	C.
9	Medoff	R. G.
10	Brian	R. T.
11	Damsker	R. E.
5	Klein	Q. B.
4	L. Stein	R. H. B.
3	Shulman	L. H. B.
6	Braslow	F. B.

Subs — no.
Lewis 12
S. Stein 18
Josephson 14
Bertman 16
Preesen 15
Stamm 13
Herman 17
Conover 19

Ed. Gottlieb

Strictly all Jewish lineup of leading college and semi-professional players.

Gottlieb operated a semipro football team called the Philadelphia Hebrews. Here's the starting lineup that he sent before a game to the opposing Clifton Heights team. *(Courtesy of Rich Pagano)*

reason is given for his departure, although the team apparently fared better after he left, finishing second again to Temple Dental.

After his first stint at Textile, Gottlieb coached the basketball team at George Thomas Junior High where one of his players was future 76ers owner Irv Kosloff. Gotty returned in 1930 to Textile to coach for one more season. Again, there is no listing of his final record for that campaign.

Another sport in that era in which Gottlieb was involved was football. In the late 1920s, he was the coach of an independent team called the Philadelphia Hebrews, an all-Jewish squad manned by semipro and former college players. In a letter dated September 9, 1927, Gottlieb sent his probable starting lineup to the coach of a team in Clifton Heights, an upcoming opponent. The lineup had Klein (no first names) at quarterback, Braslow at fullback, Shulman at left halfback, L. Stein at right halfback, Beloff at left end, Goldstein at left tackle, Golden at left guard, Effenberg at center, Medoff at right guard, Brian at right tackle, and Damsker at right end.

In the 1930s and 1940s, Gottlieb
lived with his mother, Leah,
and sister, Belle, in a first-floor
apartment of this row home
at 6033 Catherine Street in
Southwest Philadelphia.
(Courtesy of Rich Westcott)

More than just a football
coach, Gottlieb also launched
and served as commissioner
of the Eastern Pennsylvania
Football Conference (EPFC),
a professional league that
operated in the Philadel-
phia area. The league began
in 1937 and lasted for four
years. Among the original entries were teams from Philadelphia (Seymour, Passyunk Square, Magnolia, Holmesburg, Olney, and the Philadelphia Angels) as well as ones from Chester (Lloyd AC and Sun Oil),
Clifton Heights, and Conshohocken.

By this time, Gottlieb was still working out of his office on Market
Street but had moved from the apartment at 114 South Street to a two-
bedroom apartment in West Philadelphia at 6033 Catherine Street. Gotty's mother, Leah, and his sister, Belle, still lived with him.

The job as commissioner of a football league may have been different, but for Gotty, it still had the same goal as his other jobs: keep
the operation organized and vibrant, promote it endlessly, and make as
much money as possible for both the teams and himself.

At least in the EPFC, most of those goals were easily attainable. The
league was enormously popular—games usually drew big crowds. In fact,
when Seymour and Passyunk, bitter rivals from South Philly, met, attendance often reached as high as 15,000 fans for games at 10th and Bigler
Streets.

"There is no stretching the point when it is said that the Eastern Pennsylvania Football Conference, started this fall by Ed Gottlieb as president,

As the commissioner of the Eastern Pennsylvania Football Conference, Gottlieb presided over a league that featured high-level competition and big crowds. *(Courtesy of Rich Pagano)*

has been a big success and really put independent football on the map," sportswriter Bill Dallas wrote in the Philadelphia *Evening Ledger.*

The Eastern Conference was not a league for the faint of heart. It was a rough and tumble circuit, and every team had its share of outstanding players. Among the big names were Swede Hanson, who had played with the Philadelphia Eagles; Jack Ferrante, a stellar receiver on the great Eagles teams of the late 1940s; and future coaching notables Lew Elverson, a member of Penn's famed Destiny Backfield (Swarthmore College), Phil Marion, a teammate of Vince Lombardi's at Fordham (Ridley Township High School), Charlie Tomasco (Clifton Heights, Bartram, and West Philadelphia Highs), Francis (Beans) Brennan (St. James High), Art Raimo (Villanova and PMC), and Jordan Oliver (Villanova and Yale). Vince Christy, whose son Dick was one of the great football players from Delaware County, former Penn captain Bob McNamara, former Villanova star Ray Stoviak, and Ridley Park High and longtime semipro standout C. D. Donato were also among the league's top players.

Games were always held on Sundays. Some of the top players often performed in several games that day. "They'd start in the morning and play two or three games, each in a different league," said Joe Ferrante, whose father Jack later coached at Monsignor Bonner. "Players were paid from $25 to $50 a game. Some of them made more than they did on their regular jobs."

Never one to let a good thing get past him, Gottlieb sometimes scheduled games at Municipal Stadium in South Philadelphia or at Baker Bowl, the Phillies' home park at Broad Street and Lehigh Avenue. In a memorable doubleheader in 1938 at Baker Bowl, a near-sellout crowd watched as Seymour and Conshohocken battled to a 0–0 deadlock in the first game, and Norristown upset Sun Oil, 7–6, in the nightcap.

Gottlieb held regular league meetings in his office. At one session the league officials tackled a critical problem that had surfaced involving players who violated their written contracts. With Gotty setting the tone, they levied a stiff penalty in which violators would be automatically suspended for six weeks.

The penalty bore Gottlieb's imprint. As always, it demonstrated what Paul Arizin said many years later: "Gotty dominated people," he said. "He was the boss. And you'd better do what he wanted."

O f all the business that Gottlieb did as a booking agent and promoter, none was more involved, of greater magnitude, or had a stronger impact than his activities with African American baseball teams. The Mogul's work in this area, especially with Negro League teams, was the biggest and most far-reaching of his many promotional enterprises during a period that reached from the mid-1920s until well into the 1940s.

The work gave Gottlieb national exposure as a promoter while positioning him in the inner circles of black professional baseball and setting the stage for him to become owner of the Philadelphia Stars. And, as a by-product of this, Gotty also carved inroads into white major league baseball, making a fortuitous connection that over the years would be applied in a variety of ways.

Gottlieb had made his first contact with black baseball in the early 1920s when the sporting goods company he owned with Harry Passon and Hughie Black sold supplies and equipment to the Hilldale Daisies. That gave Gotty entrée into black baseball, and soon, since there were no black promoters, he was booking and promoting the Daisies as well as other teams in games in Philadelphia.

Meanwhile, Gottlieb had become involved in booking white teams around the city. Eventually, he controlled most of the teams and most of the fields on which they played.

He also controlled the black squads and nonleague games played by the Hilldale Daisies of the Eastern Colored League. Gotty booked the games, promoted them, and took care of all the details. The Mogul's tight grip on sandlot baseball gave rise to the comment written by sportswriter Randy Dixon in the Philadelphia *Tribune.* "Gotty's word is law," Dixon penned, "and he can play you or slay you."

Gotty wasn't making big money. Typically, he got 5 percent of the gate from black teams. An entry in a Hilldale ledger showed that Gottlieb earned $34.55 from 12 games he booked during a one-month period in 1931. On June 2, 1931, Hilldale played Second Ward at a field at 26th Street and Snyder Avenue. The gate was $81.75 and The Mogul went home with $4.08.

Out-of-town black teams often came to Philadelphia seeking games. They, too, had to go through Gottlieb, who sometimes gave them enough games to span two weeks. Some of the games were against white teams. Other times they met black teams, including ones from South Philly, Chester, and Camden. And if a visiting team ran out of money, it could go to Gotty. "If you need $400 or $500, go down there and see him, and, bam, he'd give it to you," Buck Leonard told John Holway for his book *Blackball Stars.*

Gottlieb was sometimes criticized in the black community for what was perceived as his taking advantage of black teams. "But in all fairness," said New York writer Joe Bostic in the *People's Voice,* "Eddie Gottlieb has helped the individual members of the league over the many a monetary shoal and has helped the league in other ways. Not that he hasn't been well paid, mind you, but he still has helped."

That point was driven home early in the 1932 season when Hilldale owner John Drew decided that Gottlieb had such a tight hold on bookings that the Daisies could not even book their own games. Drew refused to do further business with Gottlieb. With the team losing and without Gotty promoting the games, Hilldale attendance began to fall, and one game attracted just 196 at Hilldale Field in Yeadon. That was enough for Drew. One week later, he folded the team.

As time went on, Gottlieb branched out. He aligned himself with Nat Strong, a former sporting goods salesman with ties to Tammany Hall who had become a powerful booking agent and promoter, controlling baseball games in New York City and the surrounding area. Both men were Jewish, a fact that was not lost on members of the black press, one of whom once portrayed the pair as "avaricious businessmen who preyed on black baseball teams." Strong had been connected with black baseball since the early 1900s when he was secretary of the National Association of Colored Baseball Clubs.

Along with Harlem Globetrotters and Indianapolis Clowns owner Abe Saperstein, who controlled independent baseball games in the Midwest, white promoters were regarded as "a necessary evil," even though they had a stranglehold on black baseball and teams that didn't deal with them simply could not get games. But it was readily acknowledged that in the absence of black promoters, black baseball couldn't do without the white entrepreneurs and the contributions they made to the economic conditions, especially during the years when black baseball was struggling.

As their alliance grew, Strong and Gottlieb—sometimes referred to as "the scourges" of black baseball—became increasingly powerful. Nobody from New York to Philadelphia and even through much of Pennsylvania and New Jersey played without their blessing. The two even split fees for games played between Philadelphia and New York. Gottlieb also developed an affiliation with William Leuschner, another East Coast white promoter. Although the three were often accused by black team leaders of collecting 40 percent of the gate, they usually booked Negro League teams for a fee of 10 percent, which at that rate seldom gave them a big payday. In fact, Gottlieb and Leuschner listed a combined income for booking games in 1939 of $2,267.21. Of that amount, $566.80 went to the league as part of an agreement to pay it 25 percent of the pair's earnings. Additional income had to cover office expenses.

With Strong's approval, Gottlieb even secured in 1939 the rights to book games at Yankee Stadium, acquiring a comfortable working relationship with Yankees' president and general manager Ed Barrow. It was reported that the original agreement to schedule games at the New York ballpark required no more than a five-minute conversation and a handshake to seal the deal.

Among the games Gotty brought to Yankee Stadium, the pinnacle of his booking career probably occurred in 1941 when he scheduled a four-team doubleheader involving Negro League clubs. Satchel Paige pitched for the Pittsburgh Crawfords against the Philadelphia Stars in one game, and the New York Black Yankees opposed the Chicago American Giants in the second clash.

"It rained the whole night before the game and really didn't stop until just before the first game started," Gottlieb remembered in Frank Deford's *Sports Illustrated* article. "But we had 25,000 there, and the concessions were just tremendous. Slim Jones was pitching for the Stars and Satchel for the Crawfords. It was a 1–1 tie, so we called it in the 10th inning with the idea in mind that we could repeat the whole damn game a few weeks later, which we did. And we got just about the same gate all over, even though it rained right up until the game started."

By then, Gottlieb was also booking games at Baker Bowl and Shibe Park. With Philadelphia then having the third-highest black population of any city in the country, he convinced Gerry Nugent, owner of the downtrodden Phillies, that games pitting black squads offered a way to enhance the team's barren bank account. He made the same pitch to Connie Mack, noting that the ballparks could be put to good use on Mondays when the home teams were typically idle. Both Nugent and Mack jumped at the idea.

In one memorable game in 1934, Gottlieb booked a game pitting the Stars against the House of David, whose players—one of whom was the legendary female athlete, Babe Didrickson—rode on donkeys. In 1943, four years after lights had been installed at Shibe Park, Gotty booked three games there between the Stars and the Kansas City Monarchs and Paige. In what was one of the largest crowds ever to see a black baseball game in Philadelphia, 24,165 attended the June 21 game. Altogether, 48,139 watched the three games.

Crowds at Shibe Park often reached 20,000 to 25,000. "About 40 percent of them were white," said former Stars catcher Bill Cash. "Whites wanted to see us play because it was a different brand of ball than the kind the major leagues played. They believed in the home run. We tried to score one run at a time."

Gottlieb also booked games at Ebbets Field in Brooklyn and at the Polo Grounds in New York. Most of the time, one of the teams was the Stars, a club that Gotty had owned since it started in 1933.

"Sometimes we'd play three games on Sundays," said Mahlon Duckett, a top Stars infielder in the 1940s. "We'd play a doubleheader in the afternoon at Yankee Stadium or the Polo Grounds, and there'd be 40,000 to 45,000 there. Then we'd go to Long Island for a night game. Then we'd play Monday nights at Shibe Park where we'd draw two to three times more than the Phillies or Athletics were drawing."

Gottlieb's role as owner and booking agent for the Stars gave him a tremendous amount of power in the Negro National League. Gotty, along with Strong and Saperstein, acted as virtually the sole booking agents for the league, despite attempts by other owners to schedule games on their own. Resentment built when the black owners found that their efforts were blocked, and as time went on, racial and anti-Semitic issues surfaced. Gotty became increasingly embroiled in league politics, a condition that ultimately caused deep divisions among the team owners.

Nonetheless, Gottlieb maintained his role as a booking agent. Well into the 1940s, he was still operating in that business, by then having become the dominant player in the field. And Gotty was nothing if not creative.

In 1941, he hired sprinting champion Jesse Owens to face the speedy Duckett in a 100-yard race before a game at the Stars' field at 44th and Parkside. Owens, five years removed from his celebrated Olympic victories in Berlin, was at the time a touring attraction with the Indianapolis Clowns, a traveling black baseball team that, like the Globetrotters in basketball, specialized in comedy.

The race was originally scheduled to pit Owens against local sprinter Tommy Norman. But when it was revealed that Norman would lose his amateur status if he ran against the now-professional Owens, Duckett was pressed into service. Gotty's plan called for Owens to run over hurdles and Duckett to run straight but in his baseball uniform.

Before the race, Owens told Duckett, "We'll run side by side." The race was a virtual tie with the trackman lunging across the finish line just ahead of the baseball star.

In 1947, Yankees' new president Lee MacPhail severed the club's relationship with Gottlieb, giving the rights to book games at Yankee Stadium to a black promoter named James Semler.

In mid-October that same year, Gottlieb scheduled a memorable exhibition game in Wilmington, Delaware, in which a team of white major league all-stars played an all-black team led by Jackie Robinson. The game came at the conclusion of Robinson's landmark season when he became the first African American to play major league baseball in the 20th century.

"The crowd was fantastic," recalled two-time American League batting champion Mickey Vernon, who played in the game. "One of the things I remember most about the event, though, was getting paid by Gottlieb after the game. He took each player, one at a time, into the men's room at the ballpark and paid us in dollar bills that he pulled out of his pocket. I'll never forget that."

That was the way Gotty handled his business. Secretively. Nothing written down. Done his way or no way. It was, he always thought, the way a born promoter should operate.

• • •

CHAPTER 6

Black Baseball Thrives

A frican American baseball in Philadelphia has a long and distinguished history. It is one that goes back nearly to the time when the game made its first appearance in the city.

Originally called base ball or town ball, a version of baseball was known to have been played by white club teams in Philadelphia in the 1820s, more than one decade before the erroneously attributed invention of the game by Abner Doubleday. In the ensuing years, as the game became increasingly popular, club teams proliferated. Scores of them played throughout the city.

The first game recorded in newspapers occurred in 1860 when a team called Equity beat Pennsylvania in anything but a pitcher's duel, 65–52. Five years later, Philadelphia had the world's first professional baseball player, a lefthanded second baseman from England (and first owner of the Philadelphia Phillies) named Al Reach. And in 1871, a team called the Philadelphia Athletics—no relation to later teams of the same name—joined and became the first champion of the National Association, the first professional league.

By then, baseball teams made up of African American players had been in existence in Philadelphia since the early days of the Civil War. In the late 1860s, teams such as the Excelsiors, the Pythians, the Orions, and the Keystone Athletics were the most noted of many black teams in the city. Although there were black teams throughout the Northeast then—some even playing in a loosely organized league called the League of Colored Baseball Clubs—Philadelphia was regarded as the mecca of black baseball.

Part of the reason for that resulted from the work of Octavius V. Catto, an ex-army officer and a schoolteacher at the Institute for Colored Youth (which became Cheyney University), located in the 900 block of Bainbridge Street in South Philadelphia. Catto was one of the organizers of the Pythians in 1867, as well as the team's principal promoter, its second baseman, and its manager. An intimidating, aggressive figure, known for his arrogance and disliked by many of his peers, he drove the Pythians to the top rung of black baseball.

Catto was never reluctant to schedule games against other leading black teams in the East. Usually, the Pythians beat them, as well as the white teams with which Catto occasionally arranged contests. The Pythians were the first black team to play a white team, beating the City Items, 27–17, in 1869. Later that same year, the Pythians lost to the white Olympians, 44–23. Home games were played before large crowds, mostly at 11th and Wharton Streets near Moyamensing Prison. Other "home" games were played at Recreation Park—later the first home of the Phillies—and in Camden. Banquets, dances, and picnics often accompanied games against leading visiting teams, making the occasion a social event as much as a contest between two baseball teams.

The pinnacle of Catto's success came in 1869 when the Pythians finished an undefeated season by beating the Uniques of Chicago in a game that was billed as the "World Colored Championship."

A civil rights leader and prominent Philadelphia political figure, Catto tried unsuccessfully in 1867 to get the National Association of Base Ball Players, an all-white organization that weakly oversaw baseball on a national level, to recognize and admit black players and teams. Later, Catto became embroiled in other civil rights issues, including an attempt to desegregate streetcars in Philadelphia. He was an ardent supporter of and worked tirelessly for the 15th Amendment, which allowed black males to vote. Even after the amendment was passed, white politicians in Philadelphia tried to prevent black men from voting in the 1871 mayoral race. The blockage resulted in riots, with Catto again involved in the battle. Ultimately, it cost him his life. Catto and other blacks voted. But after casting his vote, the 31-year-old activist was murdered by a white segregationist as he walked toward his home on South Street.

Catto's death—his funeral cortege was at the time the largest the city had held for a black man—fostered the end of the Pythians. The team folded soon after its leader's passing. Without the Pythians, the number of highly competitive games was greatly reduced, interest among fans waned, players moved on, and ultimately other black teams in the city, including the Excelsiors, met the same fate.

Black baseball continued to be played in the city on a club level, but it was a watered-down version of the elevated status that the Pythians had commanded. In 1887, however, a new team called the Philadelphia Pythians joined the newly formed National Colored Baseball League. All the while, baseball maintained its popularity in the African American community, and it remained that way throughout the rest of the century.

By 1900, numerous strong black teams were starting to appear in other parts of the country. Soon, black professional teams began to surface. One, the Cuban X Giants from New York, even played the American League's Philadelphia Athletics in a game at Columbia Park.

In 1902, Walter Schlichter, a white man nicknamed "Slick" who served as sports editor of the Philadelphia *Item*, and another white sportswriter named Harry Smith joined with Sol White to start a professional team called the Philadelphia Giants. White, whose full name was King Solomon White, was one of the premier early black players and later a history buff who chronicled early 20th-century black baseball in a book, *Sol White's Official Guide*. With Slick running the business operations and White serving as manager, the team quickly became a major force in black pro baseball, and later that season met—and lost to—the Cubans in a series billed as the Eastern championship.

In 1903, the Giants challenged the Cuban X Giants to a "World's Colored Championship" series, but lost, four games to one. The following year, the Philadelphia team again challenged the Cubans. This time, led by a marvelous hitter named Pete Hill and having lured a brilliant young Cubans pitcher named Andrew (Rube) Foster and several other top-rated players to the team, including standout second baseman Charlie Grant, the Giants won the unofficial world championship in a best-of-three series played in Atlantic City. Then, after joining the International League of Colored Baseball Clubs in America and Cuba in 1906, Philadelphia, paying players between $60 and $90 a month, again claimed the title with victory over the Cubans in a one-game playoff

Playing frequently at Columbia Park, the Athletics' home field, as well as at the National League Phillies' Philadelphia Park, and traveling throughout the Northeast to face just about anybody who would give them a game, the Giants claimed an overall record of 426–149 between 1903 and 1906. In the 1905 season alone, they were said to have a 134–21–3 mark. And in 1906, a year in which the Giants won the title in a four-team playoff series at Columbia Park—the deciding game played before a crowd of 10,000—they lost two games to the defending American League champion Athletics, 5–4 to Eddie Plank and 5–0 to Rube Waddell, both pitchers being future Hall of Famers. The following year they lost again to the Athletics, 3–0, with Rube Vickers getting the win with a four-hitter and pitcher Chief Bender playing second base.

Foster left Philadelphia in 1907, moving to Chicago where he pitched for and eventually became owner of the American Giants. Later, he was president of what was by then the Negro National League (NNL) and was eventually inducted into the Hall of Fame. The Philadelphia Giants, despite the addition of John Henry (Pop) Lloyd, who was one of the great players in early black baseball and another Hall of Famer, were never the same after Foster left. The Giants remained in the league through the 1912 season, then dropped out. They played as an independent team until 1917 before disappearing for good.

Black professional baseball, though, was still very much alive in the Philadelphia area in the form of the Hilldale Daisies (also sometimes called the Giants or the Darby Daisies). Formed by post office clerk Ed Bolden in 1910 as an amateur team made up of young men from Darby, Hilldale quickly became the area's top black team. And after moving into a new ballpark at Cedar Avenue and MacDade Boulevard in Yeadon, the team began attracting crowds of 4,000 to 5,000 fans, most of the time playing white teams.

The Daisies bloomed even brighter when the team turned professional in 1917. Under the strong-willed Bolden, Hilldale played an independent schedule, at one point in 1920 even facing two barnstorming major league all-star teams—one that included Babe Ruth—in a six-game series at the Phillies' Baker Bowl (formerly called Philadelphia Park).

"The race people of Philadelphia and vicinity are proud to proclaim Hilldale the biggest thing in the baseball world owned, fostered, and controlled by race men," Bolden told the Philadelphia *Tribune*.

In 1923, with Bolden taking the lead while at the same time feuding bitterly with Foster and his NNL, representatives of independent black teams met at the YMCA in downtown Philadelphia and formed the Eastern Colored League (ECL). Bolden was elected the league's first chairman.

Ultimately, with great stars such as Judy Johnson, Martin Dihigo, Biz Mackey, Louis Santop, Otto Briggs, Phil Cockrell, and Nip Winters dotting the roster over the years, Hilldale ranked at the top of the circuit, becoming one of the most successful teams in Negro League history while winning ECL titles in 1923, 1924, and 1925. The Daisies met the Kansas City Monarchs, champions of the NNL, in 1924 in the first official Colored World Series. They lost that series, five games to four, as 40-year-old pitcher Jose Mendez led the Monarchs to a 5–0 victory in the final game. The following year, the Daisies beat the same team for the national title, winning five of six games. With Cockrell gaining the win and Mackey hitting a decisive home run in a 5–1 triumph, nearly 8,000 watched the deciding game played at Hilldale Field in near-freezing temperatures.

A ll the while, Hilldale was playing not only league games but a strong exhibition schedule. It included local games held at Shibe Park, Baker Bowl, Hilldale Field, and various lesser ballparks around the city, and away games at places such as Atlantic City, Camden, and Paterson in New Jersey, and Chester, Reading, and Pottstown in Pennsylvania. The booking agent for these games was none other than Eddie Gottlieb.

Gottlieb had been wired to the Daisies since his early days in the sporting goods business when the company Harry Passon, Hughie Black, and he owned sold baseball equipment to the Hilldale club. By the mid-1920s, Gotty was booking games for baseball teams throughout the city, including those manned by African Americans. Helping to form that connection was Bolden, the only black member of the board of governors of the Philadelphia Baseball Association, an organization that comprised 60 of the top teams in the city, including Hilldale.

Bolden was a man of high moral standards, and he insisted that his men play cleanly. He stressed good behavior among the fans, too. Once, the Philadelphia *Tribune* reported that the Hilldale team issued warrants against five men for their rowdy behavior at a game. Four of them were fined. Soon afterward, Bolden hired uniformed security guards to make certain that the "pleasure and comfort" of the fans was ensured.

Following their 1925 championship, however, Bolden's Daisies had begun a downward slide. As players left for better pay elsewhere and other teams improved, Hilldale placed third in the league in 1926 and fifth in 1927. After that season, with Bolden ill and unable to devote time to baseball, the ECL folded. The following year, Hilldale played an independent schedule, then joined the new American Negro League in 1929. When

Long involved with Philadel-
phia's Negro League teams,
Ed Bolden was Gottlieb's partner
in the operation of the Stars.
*(From the Cash-Thompson Baseball
Collection. Provided through the
courtesy of the African American
Museum in Philadelphia.)*

that league folded, too, the
Daisies were bounced back
to the independent circuit
again, with Gottlieb scheduling local games. Like promoters in other cities, Gotty was
becoming increasingly neces-
sary for the survival of local black teams that, without their own booking
agents, had to rely more than ever on him for games.

The Daisies' latest setback was just about the last straw for Bolden.
Discouraged, with no money to keep the team alive, and on the verge
of losing his job at the post office because of his poor work record, Bolden bailed out. The operation of the team reverted to Lloyd Thompson,
a former player who had served in a variety of jobs, including business
manager of the team and most recently as secretary of the Hilldale
corporation.

Without funds himself, Thompson sought financial help from John
Drew, a wealthy black Darby politician who owned a lucrative transit line
in Delaware County (which he later sold to the Philadelphia Rapid Transit Company). Drew agreed to back the team, and in 1931, a reorganized
Hilldale company became the sponsor of the Daisies. The club joined the
newly formed East West League in 1932.

Judy Johnson, the fabled third baseman from Wilmington and one
of the first black players inducted into the Hall of Fame, was the Daisies'
highest-paid player. A dusty Hilldale ledger showed that he received $130
every two weeks. Of course, everything was cheaper in those days. Pitcher
Phil Cockrell paid $5.71 for a glove. Spikes could be purchased for $18.
The price of a ticket ranged from 35¢ to 75¢.

The East West League, however, died after a short illness. With teams not drawing because the Depression had left fans with no jobs and hence no money with which to buy tickets, the league collapsed before the end of the season.

Once more, Hilldale was reduced to independent status, forced to play games scheduled by Gottlieb. But there was an even more serious problem. Drew resented Gottlieb and his powerful grip on Hilldale's schedule. He wanted to book his own games and not have to pay Gottlieb a fee. That, however, was simply not going to happen. Gottlieb wasn't one to give away a job he had worked hard to get, regardless of the effect it would have on anything else. And in mid-July, with the team faltering badly at the gate and having drawn just 99 fans to a game two weeks earlier at Hilldale Field, Drew finally realized that he faced an unsolvable dilemma and folded the Daisies.

It was the end of a memorable era in Philadelphia black baseball during which eight future Hall of Fame players had worn the Hilldale uniform. But it was a victory for Gottlieb, the young entrepreneur who was rapidly becoming one of the most powerful people in Philadelphia sports. In the near future, he would also become one of the most powerful figures in Negro League baseball.

It was not hard to understand why black baseball was so popular in Philadelphia.

It was, after all, the main game in town for African Americans. Other than boxing and track—sports in which Joe Louis and Jesse Owens were among the few black national figures—the city's ever-increasing African American population really had no other sport in which to take an interest. Football was mostly for white guys. Basketball was for Jews. And ice hockey was in its infancy.

As for baseball, why should most African Americans follow the Phillies or the Athletics? Not only were these teams terribly inept and not worth watching most of the time, but black players weren't permitted to play major league baseball. No black had done that since the 1880s when Moses (Fleetwood) Walker, followed by a few others, made brief runs in what were considered the big leagues. Since then, black fans had resented the bigotry displayed by white baseball. Locally, according to Lloyd Thompson's son John, even the pennant-winning Athletics did not attract black fans because Connie Mack was viewed by them as a racist.

That left black baseball as the sport of the black population. And in Philadelphia that group, initially concentrated in South Philly, was growing rapidly. Increasing numbers of blacks were moving to Philadelphia and other northern cities in search of opportunities and security that did not exist in the racially divided South where lynchings were still prevalent and where most blacks were still denied advancement beyond the plantations.

In 1900, there were 63,000 blacks, roughly 6 percent of the population, in Philadelphia.

In the decade of the 1910s, Philadelphia's black population grew more than that of any other minority group in the city. By 1920, the number had grown to 134,000 people, which translated into 11 percent of Philadelphia's population, making it the city with the second-highest black population in the country.

Most of the city's early black residents lived in the area bordered by Lombard Street and Washington Avenue and by Broad Street and the Schuylkill River. But as Jewish people moved out of the lower end of South Philadelphia, blacks moved in. Over time, black neighborhoods also developed in West Philadelphia, North Philadelphia in the Broad Street and Girard Avenue area, and eventually in parts of Germantown.

Baseball fields in these areas were abundant. So were prominent black independent teams. Ones such as the Bachrach Giants (owned by Harry Passon), the South Philadelphia Giants, the North Philadelphia Giants, the West Philadelphia Giants, the East Philadelphia Giants, and the East End Giants of Germantown—all trying to emulate the Philadelphia Giants—developed large followings in their neighborhoods. Then, as the black population continued to branch out, new neighborhoods, shortly followed by new teams, were established beyond the city limits in Darby, Chester, Ardmore, Norristown, Ambler, Camden, and Wilmington. The baseball teams in those places were enormously popular. And they drew sizable crowds to their games.

Lawrence D. Hogan, in his excellent book *Shades of Glory: The Negro Leagues and the Story of African American Baseball,* cited the importance of black baseball to the social and economic life of the black community. Hogan wrote that neighborhoods that supported black teams "drew strength from a shared internal dynamic of community and identity generated within black America." Baseball, Hogan said, was one of the institutions that "offered [blacks] respite from American racism." He added,

"Within the boundaries drawn by segregation, a vibrant communal sporting world took shape in black America's urban archipelago."

Standing at the summit of this environment were, of course, the professional teams. First, it was the Philadelphia Giants. To the city's black baseball fans, the Giants were regarded with abundant admiration, a team of heroic figures who gave their followers a special reason to be proud of their race. Later, the same emotions were inspired by the Hilldale Daisies, especially in the towns of Darby and Yeadon where the team generated a wholesome blend of reverence and joy.

After Hilldale folded in 1932, these same feelings surfaced with a new black professional team. This team was called the Philadelphia Stars, and it was located in West Philadelphia where a large segment of the city's black population now resided. The team and the neighborhood would form a bountiful alliance that lasted nearly two decades.

The one person who more than any other made this alliance possible was Eddie Gottlieb. In the world of Philadelphia sports, no one was more qualified to make something happen than The Mogul, the master promoter, booking agent, and unchallenged go-to guy.

Gottlieb was already deeply involved in black baseball. From selling equipment to booking and promoting games to running white teams that had numerous black opponents, he had his hands in the game at all levels. "Everybody knew him," said Stanley Glenn, a fine catcher with the Stars. "If you wanted a game, you had to go through Eddie. If you didn't, you didn't play."

Gotty had the right connections, he knew all the angles, and, as John Drew had learned, he was somebody who could make or break you. Who better to get involved in a new sports venture than The Mogul?

Certainly, that's what Ed Bolden thought. After his departure from Hilldale, Bolden had stayed away from baseball for a while as he tried to get his job, his health, and his life under control. Once that was accomplished, Bolden decided it was time to get back in the game.

In 1931, Bolden attempted to form a new ownership group and wrest control of the nearly bankrupt Daisies. He enlisted the aid of former star player Pop Lloyd and none other than Gotty's old friend Harry Passon. By this time, Passon was a highly successful sporting goods dealer as well as the owner of Passon Field, a much-used baseball diamond at 48th and Spruce Streets in West Philadelphia. Although the deal fell through with Drew taking over the team instead, Bolden was hardly discouraged.

The NNL had ceased to operate in 1931, and with the ECL and the short-lived American Negro League and East West League already gone, there was a gaping hole in black professional baseball. There was no league for black teams. To make matters worse, the depression had brought the country to its knees, and, especially in the black community, there was rampant unemployment. That meant no attendance at games. Black professional teams were either going out of business or barely surviving.

Nevertheless, there were a few optimists in the ranks, notably Gus Greenlee, a Pittsburgh racketeer who made his money from running a large numbers operation out of his café and who had recently become owner of a prominent black team called the Crawford Giants. When Greenlee set up a meeting of black team owners in Gottlieb's Philadelphia office, still located at 507 Market Street, and proposed formation of a new NNL, Bolden was a willing participant. Soon after the meeting ended, Bolden began the process of putting a team together.

During the meeting, Greenlee had appointed Gottlieb as the booking agent for all NNL teams when they traveled east of Pittsburgh. Because he was also interested in getting Gotty directly involved in the league, Greenlee advised The Mogul that there was a tidy profit awaiting him if he launched a black baseball team in Philadelphia.

To make his point, Greenlee brought the Crawfords to Philadelphia to play Gottlieb's SPHAS baseball team at Baker Bowl. Josh Gibson and Satchel Paige were in the lineup for the visitors, and a huge crowd was in attendance as the Pittsburgh club broke away from a 3–2 lead with two runs in the ninth for an exciting 5–2 victory.

Shortly afterward, a union between Gottlieb and Bolden was formed. It was a natural fit—Gottlieb, the enterprising promoter who knew his way around Philadelphia sports better than anybody else in the city, and Bolden, the organizer who knew his way around black baseball better than anyone else in the city. Together, they assembled a team that was to be called the Philadelphia Stars.

Bolden was not a major investor. Gottlieb was the one who provided the main funding. But, preferring, as he always did, to keep his financial affairs unknown, Gotty made Bolden the titular president of the team and was seldom mentioned as being a part of the team's ownership. In due time, however, Gottlieb would become the team's primary owner, according to Bill Cash, a standout catcher with the Stars from 1943 to 1950.

Cash related the process, which was confirmed by John Thompson, by which Gottlieb assumed a controlling interest in the Stars. "Ed Bolden had a daughter named Hilda, who in the 1930s was going to medical school," Cash said. (According to the Philadelphia *Tribune*, she had been class valedictorian at Darby High School, she was a pre-med student at the University of Pennsylvania, and she earned her medical degree from Meharry Medical College.) "Bolden worked in the post office and wasn't paid much. So whenever he needed a tuition payment for college, he'd go to Gottlieb. And Gottlieb would give him money. Every time he did, he got some more stock in the team. Eventually, he got the majority interest in the team. He didn't want people to know he owned the team because he thought they wouldn't come out to the ballpark if they knew a white man owned it, and then he'd lose money. So he kept Bolden's name on the team. People thought Bolden owned it, but he was just on a salary like the rest of us." (Hilda Bolden Slie eventually became a prominent physician in Washington, D.C., and later a member of the staff of the United States Surgeon General.)

The partners, though, worked together beautifully with Bolden serving as the front man and Gottlieb running the business behind the scenes. The Stars, however, did not join the new NNL in 1933 when it was formed. Concluding that they could make more money operating as an independent team with Gotty booking games anywhere he could, the team played mostly white clubs. Most of the games were on the road where the gate receipts were often greater than they were at home.

Bolden had put together a formidable team, which included a number of former Hilldale players. Even the *Tribune*, which had strongly criticized Bolden during his later days with Hilldale, was complimentary, calling the Stars' roster "a choice coterie of diamond laborers whose past exploits and present records insure [Bolden] of fielding an aggregation that will doff the sombrero to no rival cast." The roster, the paper added, "will make the city forget its baseball headaches of recent seasons."

The roster included catcher Raleigh (Biz) Mackey, a 2006 Baseball Hall of Fame inductee, standout pitchers Phil Cockrell, Stuart (Slim) Jones, and Webster McDonald, also the team's manager, and hard-hitting first baseman Ernest (Jud) Wilson, another future Hall of Famer. In the early years, players got their pay by splitting the gate with Gottlieb and Bolden. Later, players were given salaries.

"It was a job, and it was money," Glenn told Rosland Briggs in the Philadelphia *Inquirer*. "This was our only chance because they weren't going to let us play in the major leagues."

In 1933, the Stars spent the month of April practicing at Passon Field, then opened their season with a doubleheader against the York Roses, a white minor league team in the Class A New York–Pennsylvania League. That twin bill was followed by a series of games against semipro and other professional teams, including ones from Frankford, Mayfair, and Camden, as well as Philadelphia Independent League teams such as the South Phillies and the All-Phillies. The Stars had games almost every day except Sunday, often playing doubleheaders and sometimes appearing at two different locations on the same day. All the games were, of course, booked by Gottlieb.

As the season progressed, the Stars upgraded their level of competition, facing some of the well-established NNL teams. In one particular outing, the Stars beat the mighty Pittsburgh Crawfords, convincing the *Tribune* to report that the team had "stepped in the front rank of eastern Negro baseball teams."

By July, the Stars had become so successful and were attracting such big crowds that Gottlieb and Bolden decided to move some of the games to the larger Hilldale Field, the Daisies' old home in Yeadon. The first game was played there against the New York Black Yankees. Some 5,000 fans, excited about the revival of black baseball, jammed the stands. Similar conditions prevailed for the rest of the season as the Stars met and often conquered some of their high-level opponents.

That winter, Greenlee renewed his attempt to persuade Gottlieb and Bolden to enter the Stars in the NNL. This time, the Crawfords' owner was successful. And when the 1934 season began, the Stars could be found perched in a reconfigured NNL with the Chicago American Giants, Pittsburgh Crawfords, Newark Dodgers, Baltimore Black Sox, and Nashville Elite Giants. Gotty's old friend Harry Passon had attempted to move his Bachrach Giants from Atlantic City to Philadelphia and join the NNL. But when Gottlieb and Bolden strenuously objected because they were not anxious to have another team compete with the Stars for the fans' attention—and thus their money—the Giants, like the Homestead Grays, were initially given status merely as associate members.

The 1934 season provided the Stars with their crowning achievement. Playing home games at Passon Field, newly renovated and considered much more accessible to the large contingent of West Philadelphia Stars fans than Hilldale Field, the club opened its season against Newark. Before the game, the Octavius V. Catto Elks Band led both teams in a march to the flagpole where it played the National Anthem. Then, before a crowd of 5,000, Dick Lundy hurled the Stars to victory.

The Stars finished second behind Chicago in the first half. At midseason, Gotty's team beat Passon's Giants in a best-of-five game series for the "city championship," winning three of four games. According to an account in the *Tribune*, Gottlieb was rumored to have collected a healthy sum from his friend as the result of a wager the two had on the series.

In the second half, the Stars roared into first place early. Then, despite losing four games to the Crawfords in a late-season, six-game weekend series at Baker Bowl, where the Stars often outdrew the downtrodden Phillies, they rode the strong arm of Slim Jones to the title. Ed Harris of the *Tribune* was moved to write that the Stars had helped disprove the view that "Negro baseball isn't worth a dime."

In a seven-game series with Chicago to determine the NNL championship, the Stars lost the first two games, then won three of the next four. In the sixth game of the series, Stars catcher Emile Brooks and first baseman Jud Wilson vehemently protested an umpire's call. During the argument, the umpire was knocked to the ground. But afraid that Wilson would carry out his threat to beat him up after the game if he was ejected, the umpire allowed the pair to stay in the game.

Giants manager David Malarcher was livid, and after the game filed a protest. NNL commissioner Rollo Davis, a Philadelphian and friend of both Gottlieb and Bolden, announced that he was suspending the two players for the seventh game. But when Gottlieb and Bolden went to his office to plead for their players' reinstatement, and Davis refused to change his mind, they threatened to pull the Stars from the series if the players were suspended. Davis backed down.

In the seventh game, a near riot erupted after a Giants player whacked an umpire with his bat after a called third strike. The game was called off with the teams tied, necessitating an eighth game. But with all the controversy and unpopular decisions turning off the fans, only 2,000 showed up at Passon Field to watch the Stars win their first—and only—league championship.

The Stars' victory also renewed claims by some NNL owners that Gottlieb, Bolden, and Greenlee controlled the league. It was a contention that surfaced repeatedly throughout Gottlieb's years in black baseball.

While his power was on the rise in black baseball, Gottlieb had become one of the most dominant sports figures in the city of Philadelphia. Other than Philadelphia Athletics owner and manager

Connie Mack, no one had a higher status in or a greater influence on local sports than Gotty.

That became particularly obvious in 1933 when Gottlieb teamed with Mack, Philadelphia Phillies owner Gerry Nugent, and Louis Schwartz, a member of the state House of Representatives from Philadelphia, to champion a cause in which they all had a special interest: making professional sports legal on Sundays in Philadelphia.

Since sports first started to become popular diversions to the everyday grind, games were not permitted in Philadelphia—or for that matter, the rest of Pennsylvania—on Sundays. Known as the blue laws, the ban was part of a series of regulations, including ones that governed gambling, the sale of alcoholic beverages, and a number of other activities. The rulings had become state law all the way back in 1794 and were largely the product of an era when Protestants viewed Sunday as a day of rest and religious contemplation that should not be interrupted by, as the statute described, "any worldly employment or business whatsoever."

Even in the early days of baseball, Philadelphia teams, especially the Pythians, tried to escape the blue laws by scheduling Sunday games in Camden. Over the years, there had been repeated attempts to get the ordinances repealed. Mack, realizing that without Sunday baseball his team was being deprived of a significant amount of income, even threatened to move the A's to Camden. In 1926, he went so far as to flaunt the ban by holding a Sunday game against the Chicago White Sox at Shibe Park. Mack's audacity was answered with a petition signed by 72 angry owners of property around Shibe Park who demanded that such a heathen practice be discontinued immediately. That was followed by a fine and reprimand from city government.

When a drive was finally launched to overturn the blue laws, Gottlieb was a key figure. "Think of what Sunday baseball will do for the unemployment situation in Philadelphia," Gotty told a reporter. "It will mean that at least 1,500 persons will be earning money, money they will spend."

The campaign worked. Legislators from the Senate and House in Harrisburg passed a bill that granted professional sports teams permission to play on Sundays in Pennsylvania if the local electorate approved. Although reluctant, Governor Gifford Pinchot signed the bill. Then on November 7, 1933, the final sanction was given locally when Philadelphians voted by a five-to-one margin to allow Sunday sports. For some reason—possibly because it wasn't considered important enough and games typically weren't played on Sundays, anyway—basketball (along

In an attempt to get Pennsylvania's "blue laws" overturned, Gottlieb teamed with (from left) the Athletics' Connie Mack, State House Representative Louis Schwartz, and Phillies president Gerry Nugent. *(Courtesy of Robert D. Warrington)*

with ice hockey, theater performances, and some other activities) was not included in the measure and would not be permitted on Sundays until Gottlieb raised the issue again two decades later. Finally, in 1957, Philadelphia mayor Richardson Dilworth approved a bill permitting Sunday basketball and other sports and activities.

The only stipulation in the first bill was that games could only be played on Sundays between 2:00 and 7:00 p.m. That made squeezing in doubleheaders almost impossible. But Mack repeatedly ignored the edict by scheduling the start of twin bills at 1:30 p.m. and paying the subsequent fine. Figuring he made more than enough money to cover the fine, Mack willingly dispatched an aide each Monday morning to City Hall with money to pay for the infraction.

For Gottlieb and the other baseball owners, overcoming the ban was a major victory. In Gotty's case, it gave him not only the chance to fatten the Stars' coffers, but to earn extra income himself from Stars games as well as from all the independent games he was now free to book on Sundays throughout the city.

• • •

CHAPTER 7

Owner of the Stars

By the mid-1930s, Eddie Gottlieb was well on his way to becoming one of the most powerful people in black baseball. Not only was he the principal owner of the Philadelphia Stars, he was also becoming a major figure in the league in which his team played. And he and his associates controlled the schedules of black teams throughout the East Coast.

Gottlieb's power did not always sit well with other black team owners. For one thing, he was white. For another, Gotty's control over the destinies of other black teams through his position as a booking agent was the cause of considerable resentment, even though some of his detractors readily admitted that he filled a role that black promoters were not able to because they had neither the contacts nor the influence.

Brooklyn Eagles owner Charles Tyler learned the strength of Gotty's power when he loudly objected at a league meeting to The Mogul's role as both an owner and a promoter. Soon afterward, Tyler found his team excluded from profitable dates. That led to a financial crisis that resulted in the Eagles being sold and moved to Newark.

As the effects of the depression spread, plunging the country into an ever-deepening economic hole, Gottlieb's power increased. Like all sports franchises, the teams of the Negro National League (NNL) suffered widening financial problems as attendance dwindled and money became more scarce. That made the teams' dependence on The Mogul

For many years, Gottlieb booked Negro League games, including this one at the Phillies' Baker Bowl. Games usually drew sizable crowds. *(From the Cash-Thompson Baseball Collection. Provided through the courtesy of the African American Museum in Philadelphia.)*

as their main source of games critical. But that didn't mean the other owners liked the situation.

There was no doubt that the NNL was in trouble. Along with their financial problems, teams were being hurt because players were jumping to teams in Latin America rather than playing for lower salaries in the NNL. And even the owners in their regular businesses were having problems. Greenlee, for instance, because of frequent police raids on his numbers operation, was experiencing a major decrease in his income.

The first tangible sign of a problem involving Gottlieb occurred in 1937 when Gus Greenlee, the owner of the Pittsburgh Crawfords, president of the NNL, and one of Gotty's early allies and supporters, tried to launch a revolt. Declaring that he was going to "shake off the sinister influence of the great booking agents of the East," Greenlee turned against Gotty and Nat Strong while saying he was going to reorganize the NNL.

Gottlieb didn't do himself any favors when he booked an exhibition game between a team of NNL All-Stars and blacklisted NNL players at Parkside Field. The blacklisted players were ones who had jumped from the NNL to the Dominican Republic to play for higher salaries in a league operated by the dictator Rafael L. Trujillo. They had been banned from the NNL, but after the season had put together a team and toured the United States. Gottlieb made a tidy profit, but also incurred the wrath of other NNL owners.

One of Greenlee's main adversaries had always been Cumberland (Cum) Posey, owner of the powerful Homestead Grays, son of upper level parents (his father was an engineer and a successful businessman and his mother was a schoolteacher) and a former Penn State basketball star. As the sponsors of Pittsburgh-based teams, the two were bitter rivals who, over time, made it a regular practice to pilfer each other's players.

Uncharacteristically, Posey did an abrupt about face. He had always opposed Gottlieb, railing against his 5 percent booking fee that he claimed turned into 10 percent whenever Gotty booked a black team against a white one. Once, writing in the Pittsburgh *Courier*, Posey said that Gotty and his associate in the booking business, William Leuschner, were attempting "to ensnare the various club owners by devious methods that have one objective, the destruction of the league." But now, he proposed to join forces with Gottlieb, forming a coalition that in addition to Gotty and himself would include a couple of numbers tycoons, Newark Eagles owner Abraham Manley, who had once run a gambling house in Camden before it was torched, and James (Soldier Boy) Semler, said to be a ruthless gangster who owned the New York Black Yankees. The purpose was to rally against Greenlee, thwarting his moves, eliminating his power, and forcing him out as president of the NNL.

Donn Rogosin, in his book *Invisible Men: Life in Baseball's Negro Leagues*, described Greenlee's meetings as "conclaves of the most powerful black gangsters in the nation." Among those he cited were Manley, Semler, New York Cubans owner Alex Pompez, and Tom Wilson of the Baltimore Elite Giants. But the tenor of the meetings was largely unchanged after Greenlee resigned and Wilson was named president. Constant arguments and disagreements about money and the way the league was run dominated every meeting.

Although there was no evidence that Gottlieb was involved in the shady dealings of the underworld or participated in the numbers racket as did many of his NNL colleagues, he was, in a way, a victim of guilt by association. Moreover, his power as a white Jewish booking agent who, rumors (according to Arthur Mann in *The Jackie Robinson Story*) often held, was making as much as 40 percent of the gate receipts—although the real amount was more likely 5 to 10 percent—continued to be an issue.

The anti-Gottlieb crusade led by Greenlee and Manley, who had left the pro-Gottlieb forces, reached its peak on February 4, 1940, when the NNL held its annual meeting—ironically in Gotty's office, now located at 1537 Chestnut Street. In a rancorous session that had no equal in NNL history, Effa Manley, the real brains behind the Newark Eagles, attacked Wilson for signing an agreement with Gottlieb to serve as booking agent for all games in Yankee Stadium at a fee of 10 percent. Yankee Stadium was the NNL's most lucrative site.

Manley, who posed as an African American although she was actually the child of white parents, was a native of the Germantown section of Philadelphia. She had married the black Abe Manley and developed a love of baseball. A woman ahead of her time, one who some described as "an early feminist," Manley in effect ran the Eagles and was a major figure in the NNL.

Although Manley demanded Wilson's resignation, her real targets were Gottlieb and Posey. And in a fiery speech, she was really making a direct assault on an issue that had for a number of years been festering among NNL owners.

"We are fighting for something bigger than money," Manley screamed. "We are fighting for race." When Posey defended Gottlieb, Manley called him a "handkerchief head," a derogatory term that at the time was comparable to calling someone an "Uncle Tom." Posey responded by telling Manley that she "should return to the kitchen where she belongs."

Subsequently, a vote was taken on whether to retain Wilson. The vote ended in a 3–3 tie, which meant that the status quo was retained. Wilson kept his job, and—the real issue of the vote—Gottlieb, who had threatened to pull out of the league—kept his contract to book games at Yankee Stadium.

In his regular column in the Pittsburgh *Courier* called Posey's Points, the beleaguered Homestead owner said that Manley gave a "disgusting exhibition." Posey claimed that Manley "took advantage of her sex in the deliberations." He called her a hypocrite for bringing in the race issue when she and her publicity man were white. Calling it an "irrational outburst," Posey wrote, "We have never heard so much senseless chatter and baying at the moon."

Posey even revealed that Gottlieb had actually used his influence to slice the fee NNL teams paid to rent Yankee Stadium from $3,500 to $1,000. That was a savings of about $10,000 per team per year, and even after Gotty's $1,100 booking fee, teams made some $16,000 in profit from

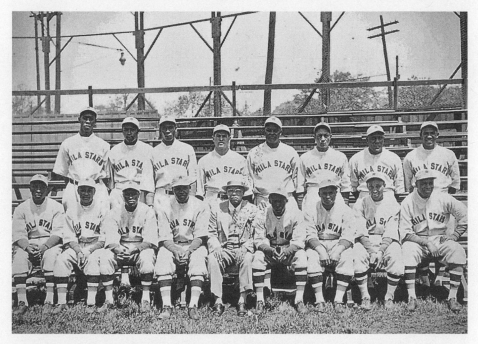

In their second year of existence in 1934, the Philadelphia Stars won the championship of the Negro National League. Among those pictured are (top row) Slim Jones (far left), Paul Carter (third from left), Biz Mackey (fifth from left), Jud Wilson (second from right) and (bottom row) Jake Stephens (second from left), Webster McDonald (fourth from left), Ed Bolden (wearing suit and tie), Mickey Casey (third from right), and Dick Seay (second from right). (*NoirTech Research, Inc.*)

all their games for that season. By contrast, Posey said, Semler had tried to book games at Randall's Island Stadium in the East River, and profits had amounted to about $12 per team.

Wilson was also angered by Manley's tirade. "It does not make sense to have a woman who positively does not know the first thing about baseball tell experienced men how to conduct their business," he said.

Eventually, Manley softened her stance. "Some white owners are the best of men," she admitted. "I even admire Gottlieb's business ability. He would be all right if the chairman [Wilson] could handle him. He needs to be whipped into line."

Manley, however, never fully lifted her opposition to Gottlieb. She continued to toss verbal assaults his way for the remainder of the NNL's existence. She wasn't alone. Gotty had his share of other antagonists, too. And they were not immune to making their views known.

While Gottlieb was deeply entrenched in the business of a league beset with financial problems and political skirmishes, he was also trying to run a team. That wasn't always so easy, either.

The Stars' championship in 1934 had turned out to be the crowning achievement in the team's history. Never again did the West Philly club come close to winning a title in a league that became dominated by Cum Posey's Homestead Grays.

For the remainder of the 1930s, the Stars had trouble attracting big crowds. Gottlieb had tried to remedy that problem in 1935 by moving the team's home games from Passon Field to a new location, which he leased at 44th Street and Parkside Avenue.

Sometimes called Penmar Park or Parkside Park, the ballpark had been built in the mid-1920s and owned by Pennsylvania Railroad, which used it mostly for company teams. The park was located along a trolley line, making it accessible for fans. While the grass was cut infrequently, the park, normally holding about 8,000, was otherwise suitable for professional teams. Its fences were 330 feet down the line in left field and 310 in right. And it had lights, which Gottlieb had installed with his own funds.

"The park was usually full," said Bill Cash. "Most of the fans were blacks who came from the surrounding area. Not many fans came from other parts of the city. There was only one problem. If you were wearing a white shirt when you came to the park, you left wearing a gray shirt."

That was because of the ballpark's one serious problem. It sat next to a roundhouse, and when locomotives were coming and going, they often spewed sparks and soot into the stands and smoke onto the field. People were sometimes burned, games often had to be delayed for 10 to 15 minutes, and the general conditions were both unhealthy and highly aggravating.

"Even fly balls could be lost," recalled Mahlon Duckett. "It never failed. Every time we played, the game would have to be stopped until the smoke cleared."

When they played at home, the Stars often wore their dark travel uniforms to hide the grime and dirt from the locomotives. The team usually played at Parkside on Wednesdays, Fridays, and Saturdays, but it appeared at other parks, too. Gottlieb scheduled games not only at Hilldale Field, but also in South Philadelphia, Chester, Camden, and at Wilmington Park, home of the Carpenter family's Inter-State League team, the Blue Rocks. The team often played on Monday nights at Shibe Park after lights were installed in 1939.

Gottlieb's buddy Abe Saperstein, a powerful booking agent in the Midwest, sometimes brought to Parkside his Indianapolis Clowns with Harlem Globetrotters star Goose Tatum playing first base. And once, Satchel Paige had one of his memorable games there. After pitching a perfect game for eight innings, Paige intentionally walked the first three batters in the ninth. He then ordered the seven fielders to sit down, after which he struck out the side on nine pitches.

The Mogul seldom let his team rest. "Some years, we played about 200 games," said Stanley Glenn, a Bartram High School graduate who caught with the Stars from 1944 to 1950, then played in the farm system of the Boston Braves. "We often played three times a day. We'd play a doubleheader at Parkside, then drive to Baltimore for a night game."

The Stars spent a lot of time on the road. But they seldom played below the Mason-Dixon line.

"Playing in the South was really terrible," said Duckett. "The KKK made it very tough on blacks. When we played there, our bus was often our hotel, too. We had to sleep and eat in it."

"Below Chester, they had a different name for us," said Cash, who went to Overbrook High School, played seven years with the Stars, then spent several years in the minor leagues, part of them as a member of the Chicago White Sox organization. "They called us 'niggers.'"

Travel was always difficult for the Stars. At first, they rode in a bus with reclining seats. Once, the bus turned over, injuring several players. Later, when the team had financial problems, it traveled in two station wagons. Most of the time, Gottlieb didn't send the team on long road trips so he could minimize expenses.

"One time, Gottlieb scheduled us for a 28-day road trip," Cash recalled. "We had a bus and three drivers. As we were going into Jackson, Tennessee, for a game, the bus blew an engine. They put in a replacement, but it was the wrong one. Then they put in another engine, and it was the wrong one, too. Finally, they put in a third engine, it was the right one, and we got back on the road at 4 p.m. We had a game at 6 p.m. in Jackson, but we had to cancel it.

"Our next game was in Tyler, Texas, and we drove straight through the night," Cash added. "We got there just in time for the game, but we had to dress under the stands. We were allowed just one short run around the field as a warm-up. Some guy in the stands yelled, 'Nigger, I'm going to shoot you.' After the game, they wouldn't turn on the hot water for showers. That night, we got to sleep for four hours in a motel. It was the only time during the whole trip we slept in a bed. The rest of the time we slept on the bus. From there, we had to go to Chicago and play a double-header at Comiskey Park. Right after the game, we drove to Philadelphia for a doubleheader the next night. It was brutal."

Spring training was no picnic, either. A few times the team trained in the South. "But that was only for a week or so," Duckett said. "Then we'd barnstorm until the season began." When funds were scarce and during World War II, the team held spring training at Parkside Field.

Although Gottlieb was never particularly close to the Stars players, his relationship with them was mutually agreeable. The players liked Gotty, and from all indications, he liked them.

"He was a likable guy," confirmed Duckett, an Overbrook High School graduate who later played briefly in the New York Giants farm system. "I never really had any contact with him on a personal level. I dealt with him at contract time, and that was about it, except when I'd go down to the office to pick up my paycheck.

"As long as we were winning, he was happy," Duckett added. "He'd call a meeting once in a while to talk about things like why we weren't winning. But the only other time I'd see him was when he'd come to games. He'd sit in the stands."

Glenn said that most of the players were friendly with Gottlieb. Many of them came from other areas of the country, wanting to play with the Stars because "Philadelphia was a nice place to live and they could find off-season jobs. But we saw very little of Gottlieb," he added. "He was a very busy man. Maybe you saw him once a week. He didn't come to games very much. He kept a low profile. But he was a good businessman. He knew what he was doing."

For whatever reason, there is not unanimous agreement about Gott-lieb's attendance at Stars games. Maybe it's because he did not make himself terribly conspicuous.

"You never saw him at the ballpark," said ex-pitcher Harold Gould. "He never came to games. The only time I saw him was when I signed my con-tract. But although he never showed up at games, we never questioned it. We were never even aware of what he was. Most players didn't know his role."

The one time players didn't find Gottlieb too agreeable was when they had to negotiate a contract.

"He was sort of cheap," said Duckett. "He didn't want to pay like some of the other teams did."

Cash, who claimed that Gotty "came to all the Stars' games," called him "a maneuverer," who "collected 10 percent of every game he booked, whether it was league games or exhibitions.

"He treated us all right," said Cash, "but he wanted us to come cheap. The most I ever made was $500 a month. He had plenty of money. But he just looked out for himself. He was hard to deal with over money. I'd have a good year and want a raise, and he'd say, 'Well, I have Glenn to catch.' He didn't believe in paying players what they were worth. But most players seemed satisfied with him, although I don't think he was fair with me. To make ends meet, I had to work a 12–8 night shift as a machinist at Westinghouse, then play that night. I had to play all winter and all summer. I got $2,500 a month playing in Cuba."

Gould, who played for the Stars from 1946 to 1948 and who is a native of Gouldsville, a South Jersey town named after his family, said his first contract called for a salary of $350 per month. "When I first got to the Stars, I was told that Mr. Gottlieb wanted to see me. I'd never heard of him. I went to Philadelphia, and he had a little office on Chestnut Street. He had a contract in his desk. He pulled it out, and said, 'Sign right here.' I never even got to talk about the amount. But, if you wanted to sign a contract, it had to come from him. Or, if you had a problem with money, you had to see him. He was the guy with the pocketbook."

For the Stars and Gottlieb, the 1940s were not devoid of turbulence. Numerous events made the decade a very difficult one for both the team and the owner. They eventually paved the way for the departure of both from the Negro League scene.

In 1937, black professional baseball had undergone major expansion with the formation of the Negro American League, a circuit originally consisting of teams from midwestern and southern cities such as Kansas City, Chicago, Detroit, Indianapolis, Cincinnati, Birmingham, St. Louis, and Memphis. The league would coexist with the NNL until 1949 when it was absorbed by the NNL.

Although both leagues floundered as the decade of the 1930s concluded, World War II returned economic stability to much of the population, including African Americans, who were starting to make appreciable gains in the employment market. That, plus the extraordinary talents of some players, particularly Paige and Josh Gibson, pumped new life into most teams in the Negro Leagues.

Philadelphia, however, was an exception. While other teams thrived, the Stars struggled as fans, disenchanted with Gottlieb, Bolden, and the team's long run of mediocrity, stayed away from the ballpark. Where once there were sellout crowds of men wearing coats and ties and women attired in dresses, gloves, hats, and high heels, the numbers dwindled to a few thousand and less as the team typically started well, but soon faded out of contention with lackluster performances becoming the norm.

"If the Stars had a more powerful team," Ed Harris wrote in the Philadelphia *Tribune* in the mid-1940s, "they would be playing to bigger crowds, including many whites who are disgusted with the antics of the A's and Phillies." He added that "if a man can sit at home and get almost all the thrills and joys of baseball competition [listening to the radio], he is not too apt to jump up and run to the game."

For Bolden—who had been elected, then a few years later quit, as league vice president—running the on-field operation was extremely difficult. The roster was constantly in a state of flux. Players came and went, and by the end of the 1930s, many of the better players had moved to higher-paying teams. Some fine players such as Stuart (Slim) Jones remained, but a salary squabble and a sore arm ultimately forced even his departure. In the winter of 1938, Jones, by then an alcoholic and unable to afford an overcoat, was found on a Philadelphia street frozen to death.

It didn't help that the team constantly changed its schedule. Nor did it help that none of the Philadelphia newspapers except the *Tribune* provided any coverage of the team. And certainly not in the Stars' favor was the fact that in Philadelphia only people from the area nearest the Parkside ballpark seemed interested in attending games.

"People just didn't travel a couple of neighborhoods away," explained basketball star and avid baseball fan Paul Arizin. "You stayed with your own group."

The sagging attendance—a condition that similarly afflicted the woefully inept Phillies and Athletics during the war—combined with continuing attacks from NNL team owners, especially Effa Manley, gave Gottlieb ample reason to display his hot temper. An example of his edginess was shown in an exchange he had with Bernie Brown, a front office employee of the SPHAS who sometimes worked at Shibe Park when the Stars were playing there.

"I was so happy at being involved that I would smile sometimes," Brown recalled. "Once, he was telling me something, and I was smiling. He said, 'What the hell are you laughing at?' I guess he thought I was laughing at him. He really tore into me. Oh, did he yell. I thought to myself, this is not a happy person."

All the while, Gottlieb was still under fire for his role as a white booking agent and one of the dominant figures in the world of black baseball. With the death of Cum Posey, The Mogul had tried to increase his own power, even taking over as league secretary. But the black press attacked him constantly. Especially outspoken was the *Courier*'s Wendell Smith, who sarcastically referred to Gottlieb as "Brother Eddie."

Even Gottlieb and Bolden were having problems between them. In 1941, Bolden insisted that a committee of men from the legal field in Philadelphia be named to investigate black baseball. Underscoring Bolden's request was his increasing disenchantment with Gottlieb's booking activities at Yankee Stadium. "No one should make a racket out of it by using the league's name," Bolden said.

Immediately, rumors began circulating that the Stars were headed for a change in management. It was even speculated that the club might withdraw from the NNL.

Neither conjecture became reality. But the Stars' future was anything but bright.

Although they seldom posted winning records, the Stars got a brief reprieve in the mid-1940s, particularly because Gottlieb was scheduling more games for the team at Shibe Park. It also helped that the team had been bolstered by some noteworthy players, including popular outfielder Gene Benson and future Hall of Famers Norman (Turkey) Stearnes and Oscar Charleston, who later became the team's manager.

Having persuaded Connie Mack a decade earlier that holding Negro League contests at Shibe Park was a lucrative endeavor, Gottlieb often scheduled not only single games but often doubleheaders at the venerable old ballpark. Usually, they were held on Monday nights when the Athletics or Phillies—whoever was at home—were off. The price of admission was $1.

"We often drew 15,000 to 20,000," said Cash. "Sometimes, we played white teams. I remember in one game against a white team, Bobby Shantz struck out 17 batters. Soon afterward, he was signed by the Athletics."

Shantz, playing for a team from the Tacony section of Philadelphia, said he was paid $35 for the game, but lost, 3–2.

Gottlieb even managed to get Negro League World Series games played at Shibe Park. In one memorable battle, Paige, arriving late after getting stopped for speeding in Lancaster, pitched five and one-third hit-less innings in relief to lead the Kansas City Monarchs to a 9–5 victory over the Homestead Grays in the deciding game. Thanks to Gottlieb's connections, the winning team was awarded the Mayor Bernard Samuel Trophy (Philadelphia's mayor at the time).

Gotty worked hard on the promotional aspects of Stars games, too, especially during the war. He summoned prominent local people to throw out opening day first pitches. In 1942, for instance, Captain George J. Cole, company commander of the Anti-Tank 372nd Infantry, made the opening day toss. The following year, Lieutenant Evelyn Green of the WACs delivered the ceremonial throw. Gottlieb also brought in distin-guished local citizens to participate in opening day activities by having them award gifts to players who got the first hit, the first home run, the first strikeout, and other noteworthy feats.

In a way, though, Gottlieb and Bolden may have missed one of the best promotional schemes when they overlooked a young Philadelphia youth who undoubtedly would have become one of the biggest gate attractions the Stars ever had. At the age of 13, Roy Campanella was a big, over-weight kid who hung around the team at its Parkside ball field. Although he lived at 1538 Kerbaugh Street in the Nicetown section of the city, the son of an Italian father and an African American mother, he was so smit-ten with baseball that he often traveled across town to watch the Stars in West Philly. Sometimes, the team took him on road trips. And even at a young age, he had enough talent that the great Hall of Fame catcher Biz Mackey began teaching him the finer points of his position.

When he became manager of the Baltimore Elite Giants, Mackey gave a contract to the now 16-year-old lad, who dropped out of Simon Gratz High School to play ball. In the ensuing years, instead of being a major figure with his hometown team, Campy became a star catcher with Balti-more. Often in the early and mid-1940s, he went to Shibe Park to ask for a tryout with the Phillies, a team for which he badly wanted to play. He was always told he needed minor league experience, which, of course, was not possible at the time. It was only after Jackie Robinson broke the color barrier that Campanella made it to the big leagues with—instead of the Phillies as it could've been—the Brooklyn Dodgers.

Even without Campanella, though, the Stars had regained some degree of popularity during World War II. But briefly challenging that status was the emergence of another black local professional team. With the formation of a new league called the Negro Major Baseball League, a new team with an old name appeared. It was called the Hilldale Daisies, it played at a refurbished Hilldale Field in Yeadon, and it was managed by Webster McDonald, the former skipper of the Stars. The team, however, never really caught the attention of local fans, and despite favorable coverage in the *Tribune*, it, as well as the league, soon folded.

Curiously, Gottlieb's affiliation with the Stars was rarely mentioned in the black press. Perhaps this was because of the animosity he generated among African Americans throughout his years with the Stars. When naming the leadership of the team, the press always cited Bolden, calling him either the owner, the operator, or the manager.

When Gottlieb was mentioned, it was often in derogatory terms. An astonishing example of this came in a scathing attack by Wendell Smith in a 1947 article in the *Courier* after The Mogul had formed the Philadelphia Warriors basketball team.

"Not too many years ago, a character by the name of Eddie Gottlieb was sauntering around the streets of Philadelphia, posing as a promoter," Smith wrote. "He had his office in his hip pocket and nothing in his head but some ideas about exploiting Negroes in sports. In those days, he was a very humble character and the sports mob classed him as a man free of prejudice. That's the way it usually is with guys who see a chance to move in and take over. They establish themselves as liberals first. That's the way it was with 'Brother Eddie.' He became the Negro's friend. He knew how tough it was to get along because other people had been booting his people around for thousands of years, too.

"So, 'Brother Eddie' got in good. He became a fixture in Negro baseball. He made piles and piles of dough as an owner of the Philadelphia Stars. Then somebody organized the Basketball Association of America, a league of the pro court world. 'Brother Eddie'—our friend—was named coach and general manager of the Philadelphia Warriors, an entry in this new league. That's where he showed his true colors, however. 'Brother Eddie' is running the team, now, but has forgotten his old friends. He refuses to give them a chance to play on his team. He contends that he can't find a Negro good enough. He hasn't tried to find one, of course, and we all know that.

"'Brother Eddie' has been disrobed as a liberal. Today he's a prejudiced, biased man. He's a traitor of sorts in the world of sports. He will have nothing to do with Negro basketball players in the winter months.

When baseball season starts, however, 'Brother Eddie' will be back with us. He'll be operating his Philadelphia Stars and raking in the dough of Negro baseball fans."

By the time the article was published, Gottlieb was embroiled in a deepening racial dispute that had been going on for many years. But it involved baseball, not basketball. And it would ultimately lead to the greatest upheaval the world of sports had even seen.

The racial barrier that prevented African Americans from playing major league baseball was an issue that had a long history, dating back to the early 1890s when Fleetwood Walker, George Stovey, Bud Fowler, Frank Grant, and their fellow black players had been cast out of professional baseball. The issue had simmered through the early decades of the 20th century, but by the 1940s, it had exploded into a major controversy that threatened the very foundation of professional baseball.

Largely because of the bigotry of the baseball hierarchy, championed for a number of years by commissioner Kenesaw Mountain Landis, even the very best black players—Gibson, Paige, Oscar Charleston, Judy Johnson, James (Cool Papa) Bell, Buck Leonard, Ray Dandridge, Mackey, and quite a few others—were not even remotely considered for the big leagues. Instead, they were left to spend the best years of their athletic careers toiling in mostly second-rate ballparks for low wages and with little recognition except in some areas of the black community.

Even Gottlieb could not escape being involved in the matter. In fact, as the 1940s progressed, his role in the dispute became increasingly pronounced. Much of the time, it was not a role that could be considered favorable to African Americans.

For one thing, Gottlieb had occasionally been accused of doing his part to keep baseball segregated because the sport without color barriers would hamper his booking activities with black teams and hence would diminish his income. That position was supported locally by Connie Mack, who in view of large Negro League crowds at Shibe Park, saw the potential for the same financial reductions if integration occurred.

On the other hand, in 1942, Gottlieb did join with the Levy brothers to try to buy the Phillies with the thought of adding Negro League players to the team.

And ultimately, he did play a part in moving black players into the major leagues.

Getting to that point, though, was no easy matter. There were many obstacles, not the least of which was overcoming the considerable rancor espoused by Dodgers general manager Branch Rickey.

By 1945, Gottlieb and Saperstein were the dominant figures in booking black baseball games. Gottlieb controlled the NNL and Saperstein commanded the Negro American League (NAL). And there was no room for debate, much less the intrusion of any outside interests.

To say the least, the situation rankled Rickey, who by then was starting to see the value, especially economically, of black players in the major leagues. When word—regardless of whether it was true or false—spread that the two booking agents were earning as much as 40 percent of the gate of the games they booked, Rickey exploded. He claimed that the Negro Leagues were "rackets" and that they needed to be cleaned up.

Some years later, in his book *Only the Ball Was White*, Robert Peterson asserted that Gottlieb and Saperstein did indeed "have a large stake" in the Negro Leagues. But the comment "that they were able to run the leagues as 'rackets' is insupportable."

One of the ways Rickey planned to "clean up" the two Negro Leagues was to start his own black league. In April 1945, he did just that, establishing the United States League (USL). Although it appeared on the surface that the formation of the league was an attempt by Rickey to undermine the other Negro Leagues, the new circuit, which included a team called the Brooklyn Black Dodgers, was really a thinly veiled attempt to allow Rickey to scout black talent for his real Dodgers. The USL was short-lived, but it thrust Rickey into the forefront of the movement to bring blacks into the big leagues.

That summer, Rickey signed the Kansas City Monarchs' Jackie Robinson to a minor league contract with the Montreal Royals, the Dodgers' top farm team. For the first time in the 20th century, an African American baseball player had crossed the line into white professional baseball.

Rickey, however, was far from done. Soon after signing Robinson, he issued contracts to Negro League players Campanella and pitchers Johnny Wright and Don Newcombe. Negro League owners were livid. "He took them from Negro baseball, and didn't even say thank you," Effa Manley fumed.

No one was more angered about Rickey's intrusion and corralling players from the Negro Leagues without compensation than Gottlieb. "Rickey is doing what he always does, getting ballplayers without spending a dime," he huffed.

Gottlieb was sufficiently perturbed that he tried to arrange a meeting with National League owners and Rickey. When that didn't work, he pushed for an agreement between the Negro Leagues and Major League Baseball that the latter would not sign black players without permission of the player's team and just compensation. All sales of players should be negotiated, the agreement stressed, and that relations between the leagues, teams, and players should be respected.

Before the agreement was negotiated, however, Rickey attempted to sign the Stars' stellar pitcher Roy Partlow. Gotty sent the Dodgers' general manager a message. "I'll save both of us a lot of time," he said. "I definitely have Roy Partlow signed to a legal paper. For your information, I [insist on] a standard National League contract without any variation."

Rickey was soon on a train to Philadelphia where he met with Gottlieb and finalized a transaction that satisfied The Mogul's terms.

Even then, Gotty had one more move up his sleeve. Rickey thought he was signing a player who was in his late 20s. Nobody told him that Partlow was actually 38. But after being assigned to Montreal of the International League, the hurler began showing his age. After three weeks in Montreal, he was sent down to Three Rivers in the Class C Canadian League. At the end of the season, he left organized baseball and returned to the Stars and played two more years.

By then, the agreement between the Negro Leagues and Major League Baseball had been consummated with the MLB commissioner Albert (Happy) Chandler, league presidents Ford Frick and Will Harridge, and minor league president William Bramham signing for white baseball.

While giving the Negro Leagues a temporary victory, in reality the agreement hastened its demise. Soon, the best players were leaving black baseball. Good, young talent was skipping over it altogether. And for the Stars and Gottlieb, the end was getting closer.

After the resurgence of the Negro Leagues during World War II, the popularity of black baseball remained high during the first two years after the war. In 1946, the NNL and Negro American League earned a combined total of $2 million in gate receipts, more than they'd ever made before. But the following season turned out to be the last big year for Negro League baseball.

The signing of Jackie Robinson, followed quickly by the entry into the big leagues of numerous other African American players, including the first black to play in the American League, Larry Doby, eventually weakened the rosters of Negro League teams. It also eroded the teams' fan bases as black spectators switched their allegiance to major league baseball.

In an astonishing doubleheader between the Phillies and the Dodgers in 1947, for instance, some 41,600 fans—about 8,000 more than the capacity of the stadium—crammed into Shibe Park, most of them to see Robinson in his first game in Philadelphia. Up to that point, it was the largest crowd ever to watch a baseball game in the City of Brotherly Love. Many of those in attendance were African American. Many of them were fans of the Stars. But as more players left the Negro Leagues, they would soon become fans of major league baseball.

Most of them, however, did not become new fans of the Athletics or the Phillies. The Athletics did not have a black player until pitcher Bob Trice made the team in 1954. And the Phillies were the last National League club to suit up a black player when shortstop John Kennedy opened the season in 1957 in red pinstripes. That was a full 10 years after Phillies general manager Herb Pennock had claimed, "We're interested in any player of any race, color, or creed who can help the club."

(The Phillies signed their first black player, Ted Washington from the Stars, in 1952. The first black player to wear a Phillies uniform occurred at spring training in 1956 when Glassboro High School graduate Chuck Randall briefly joined the team after hitting .351 the previous year with Bradford of the Class D Pony League.)

In 1947, Gottlieb was fighting to maintain his grip on the Negro Leagues. By then, he was immersed in his duties with the basketball Warriors and he was still running the SPHAS. But black baseball remained enough of a financial attraction that he was unwilling to relinquish his place in that sport.

Black baseball was still popular in 1947. The war had created jobs and put money in people's pockets, and now more fans were able to purchase tickets. The level of play was as good as it ever was. And with organized baseball now casting a spotlight on Negro League players—finally, an implicit admission that they had as much talent as white players—black baseball was generating considerable excitement. It was not unusual for a game to draw between 12,000 and 15,000 fans.

From a participant's standpoint, it was a great time to be a ballplayer. "We were like one big happy family," said Gould. "We had fun all the time. We were about the same as a Triple-A club. But looking back, we could've been much better if we'd had the luxuries that present clubs have."

Renewed attempts, however, were being made to strip Gottlieb of his power. Team owners in the NNL were refusing to let him book their games. A new league president, an Episcopal minister, Rev. John H. Johnson, who was completely free of Gotty's—or anybody else's—influence and had no financial interest in the league had been appointed. That was considered part of a move to clean house and to create an environment entirely different from the one Gottlieb and his colleagues had fostered.

In some ways it worked—the power structure changed hands. But in other ways, it was a miserable failure. Gottlieb continued to book games. And in 1948, with attendance dropping precipitously and many of the best players moving into organized baseball, the NNL folded. The following season, the Stars, along with the Baltimore Elite Giants and the New York Cubans, joined the NAL.

The Stars, though, were not without problems of their own. The team was still posting losing records. In 1948, Parkside Park, by then old, decrepit, and falling apart, was torn down, leaving the team without a home. Gottlieb had to schedule most of the team's home games on Monday nights at Shibe Park. Other games were played in Chester and Wilmington. The largest number of Stars games were played on the road, although that was not always objectionable to Gottlieb because he could make more money on away games than he could in Philadelphia.

The Stars opened their 1948 season playing the Black Yankees at Yankee Stadium. The game drew some 10,000 fans. Later, Gotty scheduled a four-team doubleheader at Shibe Park as part of the Stars' home opener.

But with minor league baseball teams in Wilmington, Reading, Allentown, Lancaster, and Trenton and with the two major league teams playing at Shibe Park, fans were shifting their allegiance away from the Stars, whom they seldom saw, anyway. Meanwhile, as an increasing number of African Americans joined previously all-white teams, black semipro teams in the area became virtually nonexistent, a condition that contributed further to the declining interest in black baseball.

Simultaneously, Gottlieb was selling off most of the Stars' best players to organized baseball in an attempt to cover the huge debts the team was incurring. Frank Austin, the 1944 NNL batting champion, was sold to the New York Yankees. Outfielder Harry (Suitcase) Simpson was shipped to the Cleveland Indians. Cash, Duckett, Glenn, and various others also were sent to teams in organized baseball.

"Gottlieb tried to sell as many players as possible," said Cash. "The players usually got a cut of the selling price." The selling price, however, was never too much. For instance, the Stars received a mere $1,000 for Simpson.

By 1949, with Charleston now serving as manager, the Stars were so financially strapped that they held spring training at the Sons of Italy field in South Philadelphia. And an invitation was extended to all young black players in the area to try out for the team.

It was hoped that a temporary reprieve would come in 1950 when Gottlieb signed Satchel Paige to a one-month contract. In his first game, Paige, whose short-lived stay with the Cleveland Indians was now over, pitched four innings and allowed three hits as the Stars beat the Brooklyn Bushwacks in an exhibition game. But the game was played on a little field called Dexter Park in the Woodhaven section of Northeast Philadelphia.

A few months later, the end of the Stars was virtually ensured when on December 27, Bolden died of a heart attack at Fitzgerald Mercy Hospital in Lansdowne. Bolden, who several years earlier had retired from his job of 44 years at the post office, was 68. He still lived in his original home at 300 Marks Avenue in Darby. Gottlieb was one of the pallbearers at his funeral.

According to Bolden's will, filed at the Delaware County Courthouse, his interest in the Stars was valued at $1,000 (the estimated value of Bolden's entire estate less debts was placed at $12,810.14). That winter, Gottlieb reached a settlement with Hilda Bolden Slie to purchase most of her father's few shares. Dr. Bolden, a resident of Washington, D.C., retained a few shares and kept a distant hand in the operation of the team. The real work of running the Stars fell to Charleston, now living in Chester.

But the Stars continued to fade. In part, Gottlieb blamed the team's decline—and that of all sports—on radio and television, claiming that they helped to make the public lazy and disinterested. "The sports fan who used to put on his overcoat, brave the cold weather, and drive 10 miles to an arena, now pulls on his bedroom slippers, gets out his pipe, and watches TV," he told an interviewer. "We have become a country of TV sitters."

That view was supported in 1951 when a mere 3,000 attended the Stars' home opener, a doubleheader against the Indianapolis Clowns at Shibe Park. Then during the 1952 season, gate receipts were sometimes as low as $50, the roster consisted mostly of young, local players, and the team finished with the worst record in the league. Except for a few games played at Shibe Park, the Stars had been reduced to strictly a traveling team. They journeyed throughout the Southeast and Midwest, often playing on successive days in different cities. It was a grueling schedule, and, according to the *Tribune*, the players often looked fatigued.

After the season ended, the Stars dropped out of the NAL. "It's been a matter of just breaking even or going in a hole every season for the past few years," Gottlieb told the *Tribune*. "Even though I think Negro baseball is going to become popular (again), it's too big a gamble."

While Stars fans—the few that were still left—complained loudly about the move, Hilda Bolden came up with another idea. She announced that she planned to meet with Gottlieb and attorney Carlyle Tucker to discuss the 1953 schedule and the future of black baseball. According to the *Tribune*, her plan was to emulate her father's role with Hilldale and restore the Stars to the lofty place the team had held nearly two decades earlier.

When the plan failed to materialize and figuring there was no easy solution, Gottlieb offered to sell the team. When he found no one willing to meet his $10,000 asking price, he withdrew the offer and resigned himself to continue operating the team.

But several months later, Gottlieb reversed his position. Claiming that he had explored every possibility and had reached the conclusion that the Stars would only lose more money if they continued, he announced that he had dissolved the team and given its players free agent status.

After 21 years, the Stars had ceased to exist. And so had black professional baseball in Philadelphia after a glorious run of more than one-half century.

• • •

CHAPTER 8

Trying to Buy the Phillies

In the long and mostly uneventful history of the Philadelphia Phillies, no period was bleaker than the one that began in 1918 and extended through 1948. It was a period in which the Phils sank to depths unmatched by any other sports team.

During the 31 seasons that comprised that miserable era, the Phillies managed to escape the second division just once—that with a fourth place finish in 1932. The club finished in last place 16 times, in seventh place eight times, and in sixth place on four occasions. With astonishing frequency, the Phillies lost 100 or more games 12 different times.

While the Phillies were losing on the field, they were losing just about everywhere else, too. They drew fewer than 200,000 fans for the entire season five times, including a low of 122,266 in 1918. In 23 of the 31 years, the team season attendance was less than 300,000. Once, the team had just 393 hardy souls show up for a game at Shibe Park.

The Phils were so financially strapped that briefly during that era they had to bring in three sheep to help trim the grass on the field. In the locker room, where players hung their clothes on nails, there was often no hot water for showers. Once, the team had to sell the office furniture to pay for its trip to spring training. And it always dumped its best players, including two, Bucky Walters and Dolph Camilli, who became National League Most Valuable Players, and scores of others such as Chuck Klein, Dick Bartell, Johnny Moore, Curt Davis, Pinky Whitney,

Phillies games at Shibe Park in the late 1930s and early 1940s were so poorly attended that the team suffered huge financial problems and eventually had to be taken over by the National League. *(Courtesy of Rich Westcott)*

Claude Passeau, and Kirby Higbe, all of whom had enjoyed banner seasons with the Phillies.

Over that period of overwhelming disaster, the Phils had 17 managers (counting interims). Players dotted the roster with nicknames such as Losing Pitcher Mulcahy, Weeping Willie Willoughby, Boom Boom Beck, and Shucks Pruett. And the team played most of the dismal era in a ballpark (Baker Bowl) that was often referred to as "a dump" or "the Toilet Bowl."

At no point during the years of hopelessness was the team's situation worse than during the five seasons that stretched from 1938 to 1942. In each of those years, the team lost more than 100 games, including a club record 111 in 1941. Naturally, the Phils finished last each year, once a staggering 62½ games out of first.

The excruciating futility hit rock bottom late in 1942 when club president and majority owner Gerry Nugent, who had run the Phillies since 1932, was forced to hand over control of the team to the National League. Nugent was said to owe the league a then-whooping sum of more than $150,000 and was two years behind in his rent for Shibe Park, where the team had moved midway through the 1938 season.

In an unprecedented act, the National League purchased most of the team's stock at, according to the Philadelphia *Inquirer*, "an agreed upon price" of $10 a share and assumption of the Phillies' estimated $300,000 debt. NL president Ford Frick, representing the team's highest creditor and backed by other NL owners, appointed a group from his office to operate the team while a new owner was sought.

This, then, was the situation when Eddie Gottlieb entered the picture.

As a catcher on the baseball team at South Philadelphia High School, Gottlieb had made no secret of the fact that baseball was his favorite sport. Although he realized he wasn't good enough, he occasionally fantasized that someday he might become a major league player.

That, of course, was not to be. Nonetheless, Gottlieb had become deeply involved in the sport over the years, running city teams and leagues, booking and promoting games, knowing virtually every manager and team in the area, and eventually becoming owner of the Philadelphia Stars. Gotty even traveled to Florida whenever possible to watch major league teams at spring training.

When Gottlieb was running the SPHAS, for a few years he also managed a Jewish semipro baseball team of the same name. The team played exhibition games, many against African American teams such as the Bronx Giants, which they often met at the ballpark at 44th Street and Parkside Avenue.

Gottlieb often caught. Both Harry and Chickie Passon were pitchers on the team. So was Hymie Bernstein, older brother of Sam (Leaden) Bernstein. According to Haskell Cohen, writing in the *Jewish Exponent,* sometimes, Gotty hired major and minor league players to masquerade as SPHAS so the team could play on the Sabbath.

In an era when Hank Greenberg, Harry Danning, Morrie Arnovich, Moe Berg, Andy Cohen, and only a few other Jews played major league baseball, most of the SPHAS' players were Jewish, although for a while the club had a catcher who was a Catholic priest. A junk-ball pitcher named Rube Chambers was also Irish. Once after Chamber slid into second base, an Irish friend playing shortstop for the other team said, "Hey Rube, what do all those funny-looking Jewish letters on your uniform mean?" "I better not tell you," Chambers answered. When his friend persisted, Chambers said, "OK, they mean, 'to hell with you Irish bastards.'"

In the 1930s, gambling was still evident in baseball, although the infamous Chicago Black Sox scandal had occurred in 1919, more than one decade earlier. Even after that, however, betting continued to surface in the big leagues. Locally, in 1920, Phillies first baseman Gene Paulette was banned from baseball for life for consorting with gamblers. Four years later, an attempt was made to bribe Heinie Sand, but the Phillies short-stop reported the incident.

Gottlieb himself liked to gamble. Baseball was his specialty, and according to Ed (Dutch) Doyle, a noted authority on Baker Bowl, Gotty often could be found at the ancient ballpark during the summer, sitting among a group of bettors who were always present at Phillies games. In fact, with attendance often numbering no more than 1,500 or 2,000, the gamblers—big-timers sitting in the lower grandstand behind first base and small-timers perched in seats down the third base line—represented a major portion of the crowd.

Doyle said that the third base gamblers would bet not just on the game's outcome, but on every pitch. "A quarter, it's a strike," someone would yell. All the takers would then raise their hands. Often, the group would even bet on whether a runner would score from second base or whether the batter was going to get a hit or make an out.

Gottlieb's first base group was more sophisticated. It included Center City nightclub owner Jack Lynch, who usually appeared with three cho-rus girls draped on his arms. Actor George Raft often joined the group, too, as did the usual cast of local mobsters accompanied by their own bevy of well-dressed beauties.

The big-timers, as Doyle and his friends called them, had as many as six different bets at once on the outcome of the game. The odds would change after a run scored or an inning was completed.

Although there is no evidence suggesting that Gotty ever exceeded the boundaries of recreational gambling, he was also often seen at Shibe Park where he sat in the upper deck in left field with his gambling pals and placed bets on various possibilities. "They would bet on whatever was going on," recalled Bernie Brown, who worked for Gottlieb in those days with the SPHAS. "Some of the gamblers were connected with the Latin Casino (a Center City nightclub).

"Gottlieb kept 3 × 5 cards in his office with all the pitching records and a rundown on who won and who they beat, and also the team per-formances against other teams in the league," Brown added. "He had ways of figuring out which pitchers he thought were going to win, and he would use these statistics to make bets. I don't know if he bet on other sports, but I know he was a pretty big gambler on baseball."

While much of Gottlieb's betting occurred at Philadelphia Athlet-ics games, the A's represented more than an afternoon of frivolity for

The Mogul. Along the way, he had become a close friend of Athletics owner-manager Connie Mack. With Mack's blessing, Gotty booked Negro League games at Shibe Park. And in 1935 when Mack and others were trying to convince Philadelphia politicians to eliminate the city's ban on Sunday baseball, Gottlieb joined the fray and helped to bring down the city's antiquated statute. As a token of his friendship, Mack always sent Gotty a season pass to A's games, one year enclosing a note that said: "Eddie, here is your season pass. We can never forget all you've done for baseball."

There was one thing, though, that Gottlieb hadn't done yet. That was to own a major league sports team. The opportunity seemingly presented itself in 1942. Having been taken over by the league, the Phillies' floundering franchise was in desperate need of new ownership.

Seizing the opportunity, Gottlieb quickly went to work. He summoned longtime friends Leon and Isaac Levy.

"Eddie was often at our house," recalled Leon's son, Bob Levy, a prominent Philadelphia sportsman, civic leader, and businessman. "He was a very good friend of my family's and became a very good friend of mine. I remember as a kid, I used to go to the Arena to watch Warriors games. When we were going in, Zink [Dave Zinkoff] would give me the lucky number, and I'd always win something. That really impressed my friends."

Both wealthy and prominent, the Levy brothers would make ideal partners, Gotty thought. Leon, a dentist (Isaac was an equally successful lawyer), was the founder in the 1930s of WCAU, which became the largest radio station in Philadelphia, and president of Atlantic City Race Course. He lived in a stately manor at the corner of Henry Avenue and Schoolhouse Lane on the outskirts of Germantown. The Levys were cousins of another Philadelphian, William Paley, who founded the Columbia Broadcasting System, and were major stockholders in CBS.

The proposed partnership wasn't commonly known at the time. There were no reports in the local media. Phillies personnel didn't know about it, either. "I never heard anything about it, nor as I recall did any of the other players," said Danny Litwhiler, a Phillies outfielder at the time.

"But it was absolutely true," confirmed Bob Levy. "Eddie and my dad and uncle were going to buy the Phillies."

While the Levys enthusiastically jumped for the idea, Gottlieb speculated that maybe, just maybe, he could add black players to the Phillies'

Dr. Leon Levy, with his son Bob (left) and his horse trainer Sid Jacobs (right),
attempted to purchase the Phillies with his brother Isaac and Gottlieb after
the team was put up for sale in 1942. *(Temple University Libraries, Urban Archives,
Philadelphia, Pennsylvania)*

roster (a move that would have been five years ahead of Jackie Robinson's entry into the big leagues and 15 years before the Phillies' first black
player). After all, as owner of the Stars and with a long connection to Negro
League baseball, he certainly was in a good position to try to do that.

T he Levy brothers had one condition. They wanted assurances from
Frick that their path to ownership would not be blocked because
they were Jewish. Even though major league baseball had few Jewish players up to that point—Hank Greenberg being the most prominent—the
question seemed moot inasmuch as Andrew Freedom had owned the
New York Giants from 1895 to 1902, Barney Dreyfuss was the proprietor
of the Pittsburgh Pirates from 1900 to 1932, and Sid Weil held the title to
the Cincinnati Reds from 1929 to 1933. All were Jewish.

Nevertheless, Gottlieb said he would get an answer to the Levys' question. He asked a friend, Bob Paul, a highly respected Philadelphia sports-

writer with the Philadelphia *Public Ledger,* for a favor. Many years later, Paul reconstructed the conversation, and in 1980, shortly after Gottlieb's death, Red Smith retold the story in a column in the New York *Times.*

"The Levys want to buy the club, but they've been told that because they're Jewish, they didn't have a chance," Gotty told Paul. "Since I can't ask Ford Frick this question, I'd like you to ask him."

"What are you going to get out of it?" Paul wondered.

"If the deal goes through, I'll become the general manager," replied Gottlieb. "And we would have enough money to have a winning ball club. But we don't want Nugent to know we want to buy the club. We have to go through somebody, and it was decided to try to go through you."

The next day, Paul contacted Frick. "Knowing the situation, you have no objections if the club is sold, do you?" Paul asked.

"No," said Frick. "I hope somebody buys it."

"I have an interested party, but there are certain questions that have to be asked," Paul said. "I don't think I can ask them over the telephone. Maybe I should come over (to New York) in a day or two when you're free, and ask you."

Frick replied that he was leaving town the next day to visit a number of major league teams, and wouldn't be back for a week to 10 days. "Will your people wait that long?" he asked.

Paul said he would find out. He called Gottlieb and told him the situation.

"I'll tell you what," Gotty said. "Call Frick and ask him what train he's getting on, and you get on the train in Philadelphia and ride to Harrisburg with him. Ask him all the questions, but the only big question is, will they accept a Jewish owner?"

Paul called Frick back. "Ford, what train are you taking?" he asked. "I'll get on at North Philadelphia and ride to Harrisburg with you."

"Ask me the main questions right now," Frick demanded.

Paul immediately complied. Would Frick and the National League hierarchy accept Jewish ownership, he wanted to know? Frick's answer was confusing, especially in view of reports that said Nugent had sold the team to the league.

"Of course, I wouldn't say to you they won't accept a Jewish man," he said. "I would never say a thing like that. But I've been thinking it over. I know there must be some important questions, and I know my answers will have an effect on whatever they say to Nugent. So I won't talk to you. If you get on the train, I won't talk to you. I cannot tell Nugent what to do with his ballclub. I'm not going to be put in a position to tell Nugent to talk to those men or listen to them or take their money. You have the answer to your question. Yes, a Jewish man can buy a ballclub."

Paul called Gottlieb. Gotty called the Levys. "They said that isn't enough of an answer," Paul remembered. "They said, 'We are not going to be put in the spot of having our religion being the main issue in buying a ballclub. That's not what we want. We want to buy a ballclub. We're not going to go to Mr. Nugent unless Frick tells us we'll be accepted if our finances are okay.'"

It was later speculated that it was really Frick, never a supporter of minorities, who did not want Jews owning baseball teams. Nor did he want black players in the major leagues. It was also said that Gottlieb's activity as a gambler might have been a factor that helped to squash the deal.

"Eddie would've made a great general manager," mused Bob Levy, who with his wife, Rachel, became stockholders in the Phillies when Bill Giles put together a group to buy the team many years later. "He knew sports inside and out and backwards and forwards. He was a very smart businessman. He was also a terrific guy. One of the classiest guys I ever knew. He was tough and maybe a little rough around the edges, but a great guy. I really loved him."

The Levy family—Bob owns and operates Atlantic City Race Course and several other race tracks and has been a major force in many Philadelphia athletic activities—wound up being involved in sports for well over one-half century. But the Phillies landed in the hands of a 30-man syndicate headed by wealthy New York lumber dealer William Cox. The group, which included future Philadelphia 76ers owner F. Eugene (Fitz) Dixon Jr., officially took over the team in March 1943 after paying in the neighborhood of $250,000 for the moribund franchise.

A popular story that made the rounds for many years maintained that Bill Veeck, son of the Cubs' owner, had at the same time also attempted to buy the Phillies. Veeck, who later became owner (at different times) of the Cleveland Indians, St. Louis Browns, and Chicago White Sox, revealed the idea in his book *Veeck as in Wreck*.

Ironically, Veeck's intention, or so he claimed, was to stock the club with outstanding Negro League players such as Satchel Paige, Roy Campanella, Buck Leonard, Monte Irvin, and Luke Easter. According to Veeck, the plan was vetoed by commissioner Kenesaw Mountain Landis once he learned of the possibility that black players might become major leaguers.

Eventually, Veeck's contention was found to lack credibility by John Rossi and other researchers from the Society for American Baseball Research (SABR). According to Rossi, a La Salle University history professor, he and his associates learned that the story was a myth, that it never happened, that Veeck may have secretly harbored such a plan, evidently even had a casual conversation with Nugent about the team's availability, but he never made any serious inquiries and most certainly never put the plan into motion.

In an article entitled "A Baseball Myth Exploded," the SABR report uncovered articles in Philadelphia newspapers that mentioned names such as Branch Rickey, Postmaster General James Farley, Philadelphia businessman and civic leader John B. Kelly, and several others as possible buyers. But no Philadelphia paper, including the city's black newspapers, ever mentioned Veeck as an interested buyer.

Ultimately, Cox, at 33, was made president of the Phillies. A meddler, impatient and inexperienced, and one who often put on a uniform, worked out with the team, and barged into the clubhouse to give orders, Cox didn't last long in that post. Having been hired and then fired at mid-season by Cox, future Hall of Fame manager Bucky Harris revealed that his boss bet on, among others, his own team. The accusation stuck, and in November 1943, Cox was banned for life from professional baseball following an investigation by commissioner Landis.

The team was then sold for a reported $400,000 to the Carpenter family, who owned the franchise until 1981. With Bob Carpenter presiding over the club until 1972 and his son, Ruly, running the team for another nine years, the Phillies not only became respectable again, but fielded a pennant winner in 1950 with the wildly popular Whiz Kids and a World Series championship team in 1980.

CHAPTER 9

A New League, a New Team

There had been a brand of professional basketball played since the 1920s when one of the teams was the SPHAS run by Eddie Gottlieb. But it wasn't the same as the big leagues that existed in other sports. Not even close.

Baseball had its American and National Leagues. Football had its National Football League. And ice hockey had its National Hockey League. By the mid-1940s, all had been around for many years, maintaining full-time schedules, playing in venues that could accommodate large crowds, and generally operating from a competitive standpoint at the highest levels of their sports.

The same could not be said for professional basketball. Over the years, there had been various pro basketball leagues, some good, some bad, all wearing the mantles of minor league operations. One of the most noteworthy was the National Basketball League (NBL), which had been formed and folded several times before starting again in 1937, with teams mostly from the Midwest.

From the 1920s to the 1940s, pro hoops were played mostly in dingy gymnasiums, before small crowds, usually on weekends, and money was as scarce as six-footers. Playing basketball was only a part-time job for those who wore uniforms. Booking agents such as Gottlieb and Abe Saperstein, who earned a percentage of the gate for arranging games, dominated the sport. And, except among the Jewish community, which provided many of the players and the largest audience, pro basketball was not a particularly popular attraction for most sports fans. It was a sport that was definitely not on a par with the other major team sports.

That did not mean, however, that pro basketball lacked the ability to climb to a higher level. Under the right circumstances, it surely had the potential to overcome its second-class status. In fact, by the mid-1940s, at another level, college basketball was already demonstrating that the sport had substantial appeal among the masses as players developed followings and crowds began flocking to games.

The rise in the popularity of the college game was hard to ignore. Among the more interested observers were members of an organization called the Arena Managers Association, a group that comprised men who owned and operated playing facilities in either the eastern or midwestern parts of the country. Along with their arenas, many of them also ran ice hockey teams.

The most prominent members were Ned Irish, who began his career as a sportswriter with the Philadelphia *Record* before moving to New York and running Madison Square Garden and the New York Rangers; Walter Brown, president of Boston Garden and the Boston Bruins; and Al Sutphin, operator of the Cleveland Arena and the American Hockey League (AHL) Cleveland Barons. Other members presided over arenas and ice hockey teams in cities that included Chicago, Detroit, Washington, Providence, St. Louis, Pittsburgh, and Toronto. Philadelphia was represented in the Association by Pete Tyrrell, who managed the Arena in West Philadelphia and the Philadelphia Rockets, a team in the AHL.

In addition to ice hockey, operators of the arenas tried to fill their schedules with wrestling and boxing matches, circuses, rodeos, dog and horse shows, political rallies, and ice-skating shows. But there were still numerous open dates. With college basketball beginning to blossom, it became readily apparent to the group of arena operators that pro basketball might be on the verge of becoming a popular attraction, too, and could provide a way to fill some of those dates.

Moreover, the arena managers were fully aware of the change in economic conditions brought about by the end of World War II. With an expanded economy, Americans now had more disposable income. They also had more free time, which translated into more time to seek entertainment. And with the people from the armed forces back in the country, there were hundreds of thousands of potential new fans.

The Arena Managers Association also thought that by putting teams in the big eastern cities, especially New York, there would be even more reason for success. And with their big arenas, an increasing number of well-known college players available to sign contracts, and the intention of putting forth teams and a league of considerably more substance than previous pro leagues, it wouldn't take long for their concept of pro basketball at a major league level to gain recognition.

With so many factors in their favor and with Max Kase, sports editor of the New York *Journal*, spearheading the concept, it was time, the arena managers decided, to form a new pro basketball league. A preliminary meeting was held in May 1946 at the Abbey Hotel in New York City. It was decided to call the league the Basketball Association of America (BAA).

The first organization meeting took place June 6, 1946, at the Commodore Hotel in New York. Representing Philadelphia were Tyrrell and Gottlieb, who had already been hired as a coach of the new team that was expected to operate in the city.

According to the minutes of that meeting, franchises were granted to Boston, Buffalo, Chicago, Cleveland, Detroit, Indianapolis, Philadelphia, Pittsburgh, Providence, St. Louis, and Washington. After action was initially deferred, New York and Toronto were also awarded franchises. (Buffalo and Indianapolis dropped out before the season began.) Among other items of business, it was decided that each team would play a 54-game schedule, the cost of joining the league was set at $1,000 per team, the minimum size of a court would be 60 feet by 100 feet, a roster would consist of 10 players, and the limit on total team salary would be $30,000. No "college boy" could be signed until after his class graduated, and teams could exercise a territorial draft within a radius of 50 miles of their city.

Maurice Podoloff, a lawyer and president of the AHL whose family ran the arena and owned the ice hockey team in New Haven and who coincidentally already had an office in New York City, was elected president. Not only was Podoloff well-known to the other owners, it was felt that his experience in dealing with matters involving a professional sports league made him especially suitable for the BAA position.

In a special follow-up meeting October 3, 1946, at the Roosevelt Hotel in New York, quarters were set at 12 minutes each, the salary cap was increased to $55,000, the roster was raised to 12 players (no fewer than nine could dress for a game), meal allowance for road trips was set at $4 per player per day, players on the team that finished first would get

$200 each, and a proposal to use other professional leagues as farm systems was rejected. In addition, because league founders thought that a fast-paced, offensive game would help to attract spectators, it was decided to prohibit zone defenses, permitting only man-to-man defenses.

According to the *Official NBA Basketball Encyclopedia,* the new league planned to emphasize four particular concepts, each of which differed from the way previous professional leagues were operated. They were as follows: (1) Because the owners of the teams also owned the arenas in which games would be played, each team was its own landlord, a condition that eliminated numerous problems, including scheduling. (2) The focus would be on college players instead of grizzled old pros, thereby giving the league a cleaner, fresher image. (3) Post-season playoffs, similar to the ones used in ice hockey, which staged series between two teams rather than elimination tournaments, would be used. (4) The league would present a unified front, which included promoting the league as a whole instead of individual franchises, a process that would help the smaller-city teams stay alive.

Ultimately, the first BAA game was held November 1, 1946, with the New York Knickerbockers meeting the Toronto Huskies. Ironically, the BAA's first game was held in Canada. Ossie Schectman, a star forward with the SPHAS just a few years earlier, scored the game's—and the BAA's—first field goal. He finished with 11 points to help the Knicks capture a 68–66 victory.

In Philadelphia, the Arena, where Warriors games would be played, was an unpretentious venue located at 45th and Market Streets. Built in 1920, it had a maximum seating capacity for basketball of 7,800. The original owner, local engineer and athletic official George F. Pawling, had installed $150,000 worth of ice-making equipment for what became an unsuccessful bid to boost interest in ice hockey. (Philadelphia's first pro ice hockey team, the Arrows, was not formed until 1927.)

Pawling stepped out in 1925, and over the next decade, the building, the principal asset of the Arena Corporation, had several owners and was used mostly as the site for boxing matches. That, however, proved to be a haphazard way to make a living, and in 1934, the facility was placed in receivership. A federal court judge appointed Pete Tyrrell as president and general manager of the bankrupt company. Tyrrell was still holding that job in 1938 when six local investors put up $10,000 each to buy the Arena Corporation.

The Arena at 45th and Market Streets was the original home of the Philadelphia Warriors. *(Temple University Libraries, Urban Archives, Philadelphia, Pennsylvania)*

Tyrrell was no stranger to the world of sports. After several jobs as a youth, he had become a sportswriter for a newspaper in Manayunk. He soon switched to publicizing and promoting boxing matches, at one point working for South Philadelphia bootlegger Max (Boo Boo) Huff, whose secretary was Tyrrell's mother, Elsie.

After taking over the Arena Corporation, Tyrrell had significantly enriched the programming at the venue. In 1936, he was one of the first arena managers to book the Shipstad and Johnson ice-skating show, which later became known as the Ice Follies. In 1940, Tyrrell formed an association with nine other arenas to finance another new ice show called the Ice Capades. Later, Tyrrell convinced a young ice skater named Sonja Henie to turn professional after the three-time Olympic champion had put on a dazzling show at the Arena. He also staged Philadelphia's first rodeo show, which featured Gene Autry. When Autry left the show several years later, Tyrrell replaced him with Roy Rogers.

Tyrrell would be involved with the Arena until 1965—after heading a group that purchased the corporation in 1959. During his tenure, he pioneered the televising of ice hockey, basketball, and boxing. He also staged swimming shows with Johnny Weismuller and Buster Crabbe. And he held performances by entertainers such as Elvis Presley, Bob Hope, and Nat (King) Cole and the Lippizaner Stallions and the Moscow Circus, as well as special events such as bicycle races, roller derbies, billiards contests, dance marathons, auto shows, and weddings.

With his broad experience in staging sporting events, it was not surprising when Tyrrell became one of the leaders in the drive to start a new pro basketball league. Like the others, he was convinced that the time was right for such a league. Offer something that would be an upgrade from the second-class circuits that had previously existed, he reasoned, and fans of all kinds would come out.

It was not surprising, either, when Tyrrell announced that he had hired Eddie Gottlieb as coach of the new Warriors team. After all, who better to become involved with such a venture than the man known as The Mogul?

Gottlieb, of course, was already firmly entrenched as one of Philadelphia's leading sports figures. He was owner of the SPHAS and the Philadelphia Stars and a promoter and booking agent with considerable power. And he was already a tenant of Tyrrell's at the Arena, where he rented the building for the wrestling matches he booked. To Gotty, it seemed like a prudent move up the ladder to the big leagues where he could make more money and still run his two other teams.

Tyrrell's son, Peter A. Tyrrell, Jr., clearly remembered when Gotty was hired. "Dad came home that night," he said, "and told us he'd hired Eddie Gottlieb as coach of the basketball team. I said, 'What are you doing, hiring a wrestling promoter to coach a basketball team?' Dad said, 'Look at it this way: I'm going to have a team. I need a coach. Eddie's got a team and he can coach. So I have two choices. I can hire Eddie as coach or I can buy his team and have him coach.' And that's how Eddie became coach of the Warriors. Dad hired him for $15,000. I think he was paying himself $10,000 or $12,000."

While Tyrrell as president ran the business side of the operation, Gotty was in charge of forming a team. Calling on his long years of experience in basketball, he wasted no time getting started.

One of his first moves was to hire former SPHAS standout Cy Kaselman as an assistant coach whose main responsibility was to work with players on their shooting. Gottlieb also signed a trio of young players, Jerry Fleishman, Art Hillhouse, and Petey Rosenberg from the SPHAS, who had won the American Basketball League (ABL) championship the previous year. Fleishman was still in the army when he signed, and before he was discharged, Gottlieb had him flown to weekend games from Columbia, South Carolina.

"Eddie only chose certain players from the SPHAS," remembered Red Klotz. "Those three were among the best in the ABL. They were great players and they could play with anybody in the BAA."

Former SPHAS player Cy Kaselman (left) was Gottlieb's first assistant coach with the Warriors, and ex-Penn star Howie Dallmar (right) was one of the team's top players. (*Temple University Libraries, Urban Archives, Philadelphia, Pennsylvania*)

Rosenberg was the only native Philadelphian of the three. (The number became four when Gottlieb acquired Ralph Kaplowitz from the Knicks during the season.) But he was soon joined by others. Although they weren't all Philadelphia natives, Angelo Musi and Jerry Rullo from Temple, Howie Dallmar from Penn, and George Senesky and Matt Guokas from St. Joseph's all became members of the team.

"I figured I should get as many local players as possible to help the box office," Gottlieb wrote in a guest column in 1971 in *Inside Basketball*. "But I didn't want to use all SPHAS players because we were stepping up from a representative club to major league status representing the entire city, and that required players from other geographic areas, too."

One of the nonlocals was an obscure player from Kentucky named Joe Fulks. Shortly, he would become the Warriors'—and the BAA's—first superstar.

When Joe Fulks signed with the Warriors, hardly anyone knew who he was. Even Gottlieb, the man who knew virtually everyone and everything in basketball, wasn't familiar with the 6-foot, 5-inch sharpshooter from a little-known college called Murray State in Kentucky.

Fulks spent most of his early years in the tiny backwoods town of Birmingham, Kentucky. An isolated village along the Tennessee River, it was noted for drunkenness, shootouts, and the otherwise lawless behavior of its residents. It was also a major supplier of bootleg whiskey to the Chicago speakeasies run by mobster Al Capone. Black limousines were often seen loading up with booze made by local moonshiners, who barely eked out a living from their illegal distilleries.

As a youngster, Fulks, whose father was a heavy drinker saddled with frequent fits of depression, was an outstanding basketball player, performing first in a high school attended by only 23 boys before his family moved to a bigger community some 14 miles and a ferry trip away. There, in a town called Kuttawa, Fulks attracted state-wide attention and eventually enrolled at Murray State, despite overtures from some of Kentucky's larger colleges.

After three years at Murray State, where he earned the nickname "Jumpin' Joe," Fulks joined the Marine Corps during World War II. Stationed much of the time in the Far East, he managed to play basketball. His play did not go unnoticed. Petey Rosenberg was one of those watching.

"Late in 1945, a SPHAS fan who was stationed in the Philippines sent me a newspaper clipping showing how several of our SPHAS players were making out in the Army," Gottlieb wrote in *Inside Basketball*. "The clipping showed Joe Fulks leading the league in scoring. I got in touch with Petey, who was playing in that league. He advised me that Fulks was very good, and would help the SPHAS win the title if I could sign him. I wrote to Fulks, but my letter never reached him.

"After the BAA was organized in 1946, I asked a friend, Russ Tuckey, who was with the Ice Follies appearing all summer in San Francisco, to go to the Fleet Marine Force office and find out where I could contact Fulks. Tuckey then phoned to advise me that Fulks had been discharged, was home in Kentucky, and could be reached through Murray State College. I phoned, told him who I was, and asked if he received my letter. He said he had not, and never heard of me. But he had heard of the BAA being organized, so I asked if he was interested in playing for the Warriors.

"He said, 'Yes,' if the price was right. I offered him $5,000. We had a salary limit of $55,000 for a 10-man team, so that was about the average. He said he would like to play, but wouldn't consider less than $8,000. It seemed very high at the time, but I was in no mood to lose him, and asked him to come to Philadelphia so we could discuss it. I wanted him to meet me as soon as possible, fearing that other clubs might hear of him and sign him before I could."

But Fulks couldn't make the trip right away. He promised, Gotty, though, that he wouldn't sign with another team before they met. A little while later, Fulks arrived in Philadelphia, unwilling to budge from his demands. Although Gottlieb had never seen Fulks play, and knew he was taking a huge risk, he told Tyrrell that if the player was as good as he was said to be and gets signed by another team, "we'll regret this for the rest of our lives."

Gottlieb said, "He told me about a meeting with Arthur Morse of the Chicago Stags, who tried to force him to sign a contract, which he refused to do. Joe, Pete Tyrrell, and myself then met, and we finally agreed to his demands."

The 25-year-old Fulks proved to be everything his supporters claimed he was. After scoring 25 points in his first game with the Warriors, he went on to reshape the way the game was played with his scoring exploits. He led the BAA in scoring in his first season, in scoring average his second season, and made the All-BAA first team in each of his first three campaigns. On the way to a spot in the Basketball Hall of Fame, Fulks became only the second player in league history to score 8,000 career points during the regular season. In 1949, while making 27 of 56 shots from the floor and nine of 13 from the foul line, he set a league record with 63 points in one game, a mark that was not surpassed until Elgin Baylor did it in 1959.

"He was better than anybody in the league," Musi said many years later. "He was simply unreal. He was probably the best shooter I ever saw."

Convinced that a prolific scorer such as Fulks attracted fans, Gottlieb, who at one point bought Fulks a new Buick Special, always told his other players to pass the ball three or four times, then get it to his star. "He had," Gotty said, "the finest assortment of shots and the widest variety of shots I've ever seen, bar none."

Fulks could shoot with either hand, a rarity in the early days of the BAA. He was also the first player to perfect a jump shot—something he had worked on since his early teenage years—and one of the first to dunk a ball.

"Hank Luisetti was supposed to have introduced the jump shot, "said broadcasting legend Bill Campbell, who did Warriors play-by-play starting in the club's first season. "But the first guy to do it successfully on a regular basis was Joe. He was magnificent. And a very nice guy, too."

Sharp-shooting Joe Fulks (10) was one of pro basketball's first superstars and the first scoring champion of the new BAA. *(Temple University Libraries, Urban Archives, Philadelphia, Pennsylvania)*

Other teams often used two or three defensive players to guard Fulks. "He had more moves than anybody I ever saw for a guy his size," Dave Zinkoff once said. *Time* magazine in an article in 1946 called him "The Babe Ruth of basketball." *The Sporting News* said he was "the greatest basketball player in the country."

"He didn't have a great shooting percentage, but he hit some of the damnedest shots you ever saw," said former *Inquirer* sportswriter Frank Dolson. "He'd get hot, and boy, was he exciting. He had all kinds of shots, and he could make any of them."

Despite such acclamation, "he never quite got the recognition he should have," said Rullo, who put in two stints with the Warriors and two with the SPHAS before playing in the Eastern League and launching a 40-year career as a college and high school basketball referee. "He helped to make the league what it is today. I remember there used to be a group of guys from South Philadelphia who sat on metal chairs behind the basket. Whenever Fulks made a sensational shot, they would jump out of their seats and bang their chairs on the floor. It made an awful racket. But that's how people reacted to Joe. They loved him."

"When I was in college, I would go to Warriors games and Joe was one of the main reasons," said Paul Arizin. "I loved to watch him play. People forget this, but he was also an excellent rebounder. But he was an absolutely great shooter. And I never saw him make an easy shot. Without Joe, I don't think the team would've lasted in Philly and the league might not have existed too long, either. He was the biggest star, the biggest attraction, and he carried the league."

A self-described hillbilly with a heavy southern accent, Fulks lived during the season with his wife in a row house at 1402 East Sharpnack Street in the East Mount Airy section of Philadelphia. Often, they rode the train to Center City to see a movie. Fulks was extremely popular with his teammates, a very likeable guy, most of them said.

"And he was a funny guy, too," remembered Arizin. "Joe was one of those typical southerners who was naturally funny. He didn't try to be funny, he didn't know he was funny, but some of the things he came out with were really humorous. He was a great person. Everybody on the team loved him."

After dominating the league for several seasons, though, Fulks resumed the drinking habits he had forsaken before he joined the Warriors. "He fell in with some wild guys, and they started taking him to clubs," Rullo said. "Soon, he was drinking too much. It cut his career short."

Fulks had several scrapes with the law for drunken driving. Once, a small-time gambler from North Philly tried to pay him to throw games. (Fulks declined, and the culprit was indicted on bribery charges.) And as his career quickly faded, Fulks was frequently sidelined with injuries.

After averaging more than 22 points a game in his first three years and in double figures in seven seasons, Fulks played his last game for the Warriors in 1954. Averaging just 2.5 points a game in 61 outings, Fulks was no more than a sad reminder of the player he once was.

Fulks returned to Kentucky where after holding numerous jobs, including a brief stint as a scout for the Warriors, he eventually got a job as recreation director at a prison. He returned to Philadelphia in 1971 for the 25th anniversary of the Warriors' first season. Gottlieb paid for his airplane ticket and bought him a suit.

The life of the man who was named one of the 10 best players during the first 25 years of the league came to a shocking end in Eddyville, Kentucky. In the early morning hours of March 21, 1976, broke and forlorn, he was shot and killed by the son of his girlfriend following a drunken argument between the two at a trailer park where the woman lived. Fulks was 54. The murder, for which the perpetrator served less than two years on a charge of "reckless homicide," rendered a tragic conclusion to a life that had once been so celebrated.

While Gottlieb was building the Warriors, he was also heavily engaged in building the BAA. Right from the league's inception, he had been involved in establishing and organizing the new circuit. He was, after all, the league's resident basketball expert. It was logical that he attend the meetings and share his wisdom. The others were arena managers and hockey team operators. What they knew about basketball could fit into an undersized sneaker.

Along with the normal problems of launching a new league, the BAA lacked the recognition enjoyed by the NBL, an organization that in its third incarnation had been around since 1937. The NBL had the top names in the game—ones such as George Mikan of the Chicago Gears, Al Cervi, Red Holzman, and Bob Davies of the Rochester Royals, Bobby McDermott of the Sheboygan Redskins, and Buddy Jeannette of the Fort Wayne Pistons.

The biggest names in the BAA belonged mostly to the coaches—Gottlieb, Honey Russell of the Boston Celtics, Joe Lapchick of the New York Knicks, and former New York Yankees third baseman and one-time Dartmouth basketball star Red Rolfe of the Toronto Huskies. Most of the players were either lesser lights plucked from the NBL or former college stars fresh from the campuses.

The job fell to Gottlieb to make some sense out of the chaos that usually surrounds a new venture. Unquestionably, The Mogul was the right man for the job.

"He was the driving force behind the formation of the league and he was in the middle of everything," said Ralph Bernstein, who was then a fledgling writer with the Associated Press. "He was the leader of the owners. He would say, 'I think we ought to do it this way,' and they'd say, 'All right, Gotty, if that's what you want.' In effect, he ran the league right from the start."

Over the years, the story was told repeatedly that whenever Podoloff was asked his opinion on a subject, he would say he had to ask Gottlieb first. "That was no joke," wrote Jack Kiser in the Philadelphia *Daily News*. "He had a way of stripping away all the fat and getting to the bone of the subject. Gottlieb was the most powerful man in the league's formative years. The league headquarters were wherever he hung his hat."

Put another way, it was sometimes said that if Gotty got hit by a car and died, the league would die with him. "He was the brains of the league," wrote Leonard Koppett in his book *24 Seconds to Shoot*. "Podoloff was the first commissioner, but to his dying day, he never understood basketball.

Gotty knew the game—how to sell tickets, how to get the arena cleaned, how to promote, how to sign up talent." He taught these and the ways many more jobs were handled to the band of basketball neophytes that ran teams in the new league.

Gotty also knew how to get along with people when he had to. He could be a good listener. He always tried his best to help people with their problems. And he could get things done. In that regard, "All Eddie had to do was to make a phone call," said longtime scout and executive Marty Blake.

"But Eddie could also be very argumentative," said early Syracuse Nats star and the first coach of the Philadelphia 76ers, Dolph Schayes. "Nobody ever won an argument with him. And he had the language of a longshoreman. He was very streetwise. And very persuasive."

"There was no con in Eddie," added former 76ers coach and general manager Jack Ramsay. "He was very straightforward. He was true to his word. And he knew the game from top to bottom."

It was characteristics like these that helped to make Gottlieb a power in the pro circuit.

"People understood how much he meant to the sport and how much he gave to it," said Dolson. "And I think everybody liked him. He got along with everybody. I know he drove hard bargains at times, but I never heard anybody say anything negative about him. Sure, he'd fight over a couple hundred dollars at times and piss people off, but that was Gotty. There might have been short-span enemies, but you'd have a really tough time finding someone who would say, 'I can't stand that son-of-a-bitch.' He was the biggest figure in pro basketball for a number of years, there's no question about that."

In the beginning, Gottlieb gave owners of the other teams crash courses in how to operate their clubs. Summoning the knowledge he had accrued during some 25 years of running sports teams, he helped them to get started. And then, when some of the teams and later the whole league skidded to the edge of disaster, he showed them how to survive.

"His advice was always excellent," Ben Kerner, owner of the Tri-Cities Black Hawks—later to become the Milwaukee Hawks, then the St. Louis Hawks—told Robert Burns writing in the St. Louis *Post-Dispatch.* "Over the years, we talked on the phone at least once a week. Eddie was a tremendous help to me, and he remained one of my most valued friends."

Perhaps Gottlieb's greatest contribution to the league came from his work on the rules committee and as the person who for 30 years put together the league schedule. In each case, he provided the league with a service that was simply unobtainable anywhere else.

The stories about Gottlieb's work putting together the schedule for the BAA and later the NBA are legendary. And nothing that The Mogul did during his 34-year connection with major league basketball gave him more notoriety. It was a job that probably no one else could have done, or—for that matter—would've wanted to do.

But Gotty did it willingly. And in an age before computers ran the world, he got more than a subtle pleasure out of being the person who year after year plotted the places and dates that every team in the league was to appear throughout the entire season. In fact, once when asked who was on the schedule committee, Sam Goldaper writing in the NBA's *Hoop* magazine said that Gotty bellowed, "I *am* the schedule committee."

He did the job without help, and with only a pencil, some pieces of paper, and train schedules from each of the cities that had pro teams. Gotty began putting together the league schedules in the first year of the BAA in 1946, and he was still doing the job—by hand—right up until 10 days before he died in 1979. "It keeps my brain going," an aging Gotty told a reporter who asked why he continued to subject himself to what was perceived as a torturous exercise. "When you stop using this," he said pointing to his head, "then you're in trouble."

Each summer after the season ended, Gottlieb began the exercise. He'd start by laying train (or later, airline) schedules from each city on a table. Then he'd make lists of holidays and call each team to get special dates on which they did or did not want to play and dates where the arenas were booked for other activities. In the beginning, he had to deal with only 11 teams, all from the East or Midwest. By the time he made up his last schedule, the league had grown to 22 teams scattered throughout the country and four divisions, and he was dealing mostly with airline schedules.

There were differing versions of how Gotty did the schedules. Some said he made notes on the backs of envelopes. Others said he carried scraps of paper in his pockets. Some said he kept a pack of 3 × 5 cards wrapped in a rubber band in his pocket. And then there were those who claimed he wrote his notes on napkins. Gotty was even believed to have kept a notepad at his bedside in case he had an idea in the middle of the night. All make good stories. But however he did it, the dates wound up on a big yellow pad that he always carried with him.

"He never talked about the process," said Stan Hochman, the astute sportswriter and columnist with the Philadelphia *Daily News*. "I guess his long experience as a booking agent helped. He sure had a special gift for the job."

It usually took most of the summer to complete the task. Gottlieb worked eight to 12 hours every day. He worked at home where longtime Temple University sports information director Al Shrier remembered that "Gotty's dining room table was always full of paper." He worked in his office. He worked when he went to Europe with the Harlem Globetrotters. He even took his work with him when he ate.

"Many nights we'd go to Horn and Hardart's for dinner, and he'd spread sheets of paper all over the table," said Harvey Pollock, who began working with the Warriors in 1946 and was still working with the 76ers in 2008. "The waitress would come with our food, and he'd say, 'Can you come back in a few minutes?'"

"I remember seeing him at the Olympics in Montreal," added Dolson. "He'd spend all day in his room working on the schedule, then at night he'd go out and watch an event. A 21-year-old would've had trouble following that routine. He was incredible."

It was always a juggling act. Sometimes, Gottlieb would have to call back and forth with teams to confirm certain dates. Typically, teams wanted to play at home on weekends. And they never wanted to travel long distances between away games.

Before the schedule was finalized, Gottlieb submitted several drafts. "I'd discuss it with the general managers during the summer, then send out the first draft," Gotty explained. "Then we'd discuss it some more. I tried to fulfill everybody's wishes. But I'd warn them, make sure it's okay now because I can't do anything about it once the games are played." Gotty always had the last word. And few argued with him. "They feared me like they feared the wrath of God," Gotty once joked.

Ramsay recalled a situation that emphasized the magnitude of Gotty's memory. "I remember going up to him one time when I was GM of the 76ers," he said. "I said, 'Eddie, you have us playing one night in Chicago and the next night in LA. How can we do that?' He looked at me, and said, 'American Airlines has a flight out of Chicago at 11 o'clock. With the time change, you'll be in LA in plenty of time. Your players will be well rested, and you'll be in great shape for the game.' He knew everybody's schedule and he remembered every game. He had a great mind."

In a publicity shot, Gottlieb posed for a picture that today would not be considered politically correct. *(Temple University Libraries, Urban Archives, Philadelphia, Pennsylvania)*

Gottlieb, of course, received a handsome fee for doing the job. When asked about it, one time, he exploded. "What the hell do you think I am, a charity worker? I'm not an amateur. I'm a pro."

When he was working in the NBA office in the late 1960s, Schayes went to Gottlieb with an idea. "I asked him, 'Why not see if some computer company could do the schedule?'" Schayes said. "I went to IBM and explained all that went into making up the schedule. After thinking about it, they said, 'Keep things the way they are. He does a better job than we could.'"

"When he was doing the schedule, you didn't interrupt him," Shrier said. "He didn't want anybody to break his trend of thought. He took great pride in his work."

In 1971 at a summer meeting in New York, NBA owners approved the sale of the San Diego Rockets and the subsequent relocation of the team to Houston. Immediately, Gottlieb rushed from the meeting to get airline schedules between Houston and other NBA cities. He was in the midst of the new NBA schedule, and time was of the essence.

Probably the hardest job Gottlieb's faced occurred in 1976 when the American Basketball Association (ABA) merged with the NBA. Without knowing whether or not the deal would be finalized, Gotty plotted a 738-game schedule for the NBA's 18 teams. He finished the job in June, but later that month he learned that four teams from the ABA were going to be added to the league. Gotty had to go back and redo the whole schedule.

"It was the toughest schedule I was ever confronted with because it all had to be done in six to seven weeks," Gottlieb, a notorious insomniac, told Goldaper in the article in *HOOP* magazine. "I worked on that schedule as long as 12 to 14 hours a day. I'd wake up in the middle of the night and think of a solution to a conflict, work on it for a while, then go back to bed."

Gotty had to deal with other problems, too. Syracuse could play at home on Saturday nights, but not on Sundays. St. Louis preferred playing on Sunday afternoons. Rochester could play any time except for three weeks in January when a bowling tournament was held at its arena. Games would get snowed out and have to be rescheduled. Or an ice show or college game would unexpectedly be scheduled at one of the arenas. "He used to call me every year in the NFL office and ask when the Super Bowl and the Pro Bowl were so he could schedule around those dates," said Jim Heffernan, a former *Evening Bulletin* sportswriter who later joined the public relations department of the pro football league.

"Sometimes, he'd have teams playing three or four nights in a row," Pollock said. "The teams always complained. "So he'd change the schedule for them. But he'd never do that for the Warriors. He always short-changed the Warriors. They never got a favorable schedule. I guess it was because he didn't want to be accused of playing favorites."

Gottlieb always paid attention to the desires of other teams and tried to accommodate them. "If you were unhappy with something," said Pat Williams, who, among a wide variety of posts, served as general manager for the 76ers, Atlanta Hawks, Chicago Bulls, and Orlando Magic, "he'd take out an eraser, erase a game, and put it somewhere else. Nobody ever liked their entire schedules. Everybody moaned and groaned about some problem. But he would sit you down, explain all the issues and problems, and try to work it out. He tried his best to make everybody happy."

Battles between Gottlieb and Red Auerbach often raged over the way that Gotty had scheduled Celtics games. Somehow, they'd always come to an agreement.

"You think this is fun?" Gottlieb once said to the New York *Daily News* columnist Mike Lupica about the job. "There is no fun attached to this whatsoever. At four o'clock in the morning I was working on this thing, and you ask me about fun? Ten hours I've been on this already today. Ten hours will make you crazy."

As the age of electronics arrived, turning the scheduling job over to a computer seemed like a logical approach. But, according to veteran broadcaster Marv Bachrad, who entered the radio business in the early 1960s, "the first time they tried to do the schedule on a computer, the computer blew out. It couldn't handle the huge amount of information."

Even when the job was put on computer, it had problems. It would, for example, schedule a team in New York one night and in California the next night. "The first few years, there were a lot of hitches," Pollock said. "You couldn't talk to the computer like you could to Eddie. And the computer wasn't told about distances between cities or travel times. After a while, they had to redo the whole operation."

Even that wasn't satisfactory. The league's reliance on a computer company to make the schedule lasted for about five years, said Matt Winick, who works for the NBA in New York. After that, the job returned to the league office where Winick has put together the schedule for more than 20 years.

• • •

CHAPTER 10

First Champions of the BAA

B y November 1946, the Basketball Association of America (BAA) was ready to launch its first season. League meetings had ended. Training camps were over. The teams were set. It was time to play ball.

Six teams were in the Eastern Division and five in the Western Division. Each team would play 60 games, a change from the earlier decision to play 48-game seasons. The first game of the Philadelphia Warriors was slated for November 7 at the Arena.

Unlike some of the others in the league who had assembled teams consisting mostly of players fresh out of college, Eddie Gottlieb took a different approach. Most of the players he chose had experience in the professional ranks. And most of the players on the roster had local ties.

Typical of both characteristics was Angelo Musi. A 5-foot, 9-inch guard from Philadelphia, Musi had played at Temple before joining the army in 1943. Stationed at a base in Aberdeen, Maryland, Musi spent his weekends playing with the Wilmington Blue Bombers, a team that was owned by Bob Carpenter and his father and that defeated the SPHAS in 1944 for the championship of the American Basketball League. After the war, Musi was signed by Gottlieb, became the team captain, and in the first season was the Warriors' second-highest scorer.

The Warriors trained their first season in Hershey, a place that in future years they often used to get ready for the upcoming season. They played eight exhibition games. Throughout the season, the Warriors held practice sessions on a court at Boathouse Row along the Schuylkill River or at the Palestra on the Penn campus. Although they played one game at Trenton High School, the Warriors staged most of their home games at the Arena in West Philadelphia. It was not always easy fitting in a game there.

"Before the Warriors came along, the Arena already had a heavy schedule," said Pete Tyrrell. "Monday night was boxing, Tuesday was ice skating, Wednesday was ice hockey, Thursday was ice skating, Friday was wrestling, Saturday was hockey, and Sunday was ice skating again. When the Warriors began, Tuesdays and Thursdays became basketball nights."

The Arena had other problems. "There was ice under the basketball court," remembered guard Jerry Rullo, another localite who played at Temple and for the SPHAS. "When it got hot in the building, the ice would start to melt, and you'd slosh around. When the ice was real cold, you'd slip all over the place. It got so bad one time that they were thinking about canceling the game, but Gotty wouldn't do it, so we played. Another thing, you were right on top of the crowd. Every once in a while, you'd go flying into the stands."

The court also had dead spots. If a ball was bounced off one, it wouldn't bounce back. Smoking in those days was also permitted at sporting events, and sometimes the air would be thick with smoke that covered the stands as well as the playing surface.

There were few parking spaces for fans. Although some players rode the subway to the stop at 46th and Market Streets, those who drove could always get spots because they came to the Arena early. The locker rooms, where players hung their clothes on hooks and only three or four could take showers at one time, were not only tiny but dingy and antiquated. And there were stains on the ceilings, and the water pipes leaked. "You put your clothes where you could and hoped you got them back," Musi said.

As they always did during what some called the "dark ages of pro basketball," players had to wash their own uniforms, socks, and jocks in the hotel sinks when they were on the road. With no security vaults in the locker rooms, players put their valuables in a bag. The bag, often containing as much as $10,000 in cash and jewelry, was then kept under the players' bench during the game.

But those who were on the team were glad to be there. "It was a lot better than playing for the SPHAS," said Jerry Fleishman, who had experience with both teams. "The conditions were better, and the players were better. It was just a better league in every respect."

The style of play was vastly different from that of today's game. "We didn't use as many fundamentals," said Musi. "The most important thing was to pass the ball. Eddie told us, 'Don't dribble around, pass the ball.' That was the way you got things done. And nobody could touch the rim."

For the most part, hook shots and two-hand set shots from as far away as 35 feet from the basket were standard offensive weapons. At 7 feet, one inch, one-time SPHAS player Elmo Morganthaler of the Providence Steamrollers was the only seven-footer in the league. And fistfights, even in practice, were common.

Players on the same team usually had a different relationship with each other, too. "Everybody got along," Rullo said. "We always went out to dinner together when we were on the road. We didn't make much money, but we loved playing ball, and it was a lot of fun."

Rullo said he was paid $4,000 for the 1946 season. Players got $4 meal money a day. "Gotty would give you meal money before the game because he knew if we lost, he'd be too pissed off to give it to you," Rullo said. "When you won, that was the best time to catch him."

The Warriors won more than they lost during the 1946–47 season. The biggest win of all came in the last game.

The Warriors began their first BAA season with an 81–75 victory over the Providence Steamrollers at the Arena. The team then played five more home games before going on the road.

With a starting lineup that included Musi and George Senesky at guards, Joe Fulks and Howie Dallmar at forwards, and Art Hillhouse at center, the Warriors could put a formidable club on the floor. Reserves Fleishman, Rullo, Matt Guokas, Petey Rosenberg, Fred Sheffield from Utah, and Philadelphian John Murphy completed the original roster. When Sheffield, a medical school student, decided he could no longer mix basketball and academia, he left the team. Gottlieb filled his spot by making a trade with the Knicks for Ralph Kaplowitz.

The quality of the BAA at the time was an uneven mixture ranging from very good to not so good. The new league had top players such as Max Zaslofsky and Chuck Halbert of the Chicago Stags, Ernie Calverley of Providence, Bob Feerick and Horace (Bones) McKinney of the Washington Capitols, Stan Miasek of the Detroit Falcons, and Ed Sadowski, who played for both the Toronto Huskies and Cleveland Rebels.

Members of the first Warriors team participated in a pre-season drill. They included (from left) Joe Fulks, George Senesky, Angelo Musi, Jerry Fleishman, and Johnny Murphy. *(Courtesy of Rich Westcott)*

The best teams were Washington, Philadelphia, Chicago, and the St. Louis Bombers. The worst was certainly the Pittsburgh Ironmen, who would turn out to be winners of only 15 of 60 games.

While Gottlieb ran the Warriors, he was also the owner of both the Philadelphia Stars and the SPHAS. Although he left the coaching of those two teams to others, he continued to oversee their business operations, and that, combined with his new responsibilities with the BAA, kept him busy most of his waking hours.

"Eddie was a businessman," said Harvey Pollack. "Whatever he was involved in, whether is was a semipro baseball team or the Warriors, he put all his energy into it. And he was not a guy who went for frills. He was only interested in the players, winning, and making a living. He'd fight you for every dollar. If he saw the dancing girls, the cheerleaders, the 300-pound black guys dance team of today, he'd turn over in his grave."

The Warriors' two-room office was still located on the second floor over a movie theater at 1537 Chestnut Street. Mike Iannarella was still in charge of ticket sales, and Dave Zinkoff edited a program called *The Wigwam*, sold advertisements for it, was the public address announcer, and sometimes did secretarial work for Gottlieb. Publicity was handled on a part-time basis by two sportswriters, Herb Good of the *Record* and Pollack, who worked for the *Evening Bulletin*. There were always a handful of guys just hanging around, waiting to run errands for The Mogul.

"Everything about Gotty was centered behind his desk or in his pocket," said broadcaster Bill Campbell. "I don't know how he kept track of all those notes he kept in his pocket. It was amazing. But Eddie was one of the most intuitively bright guys I've ever been around.

"He was very articulate," Campbell added. "But he was also very opinionated, very stubborn, and very hard to argue with. He had a rough exterior. But he was more bark than bite. He had a real soft spot, but didn't want to show it."

Gotty still lived at 6033 Catherine Street with his mother and sister. Ken Berman, owner of a jewelry store on Sansom Street, worked part time for the Warriors and 76ers for 51 years starting in 1954. Most of those years, he served as the operator of the 24-second clock. Berman grew up across the street from Gotty on Catherine Street. "We never saw Gottlieb around the neighborhood," he said. "He was always too busy. I knew he hung out at Lew Tendler's restaurant at Broad and Sansom with a lot of the other sports people. But he never had any contact with those of us who lived in the same block as he did."

Unlike legions of coaches who ignore their players once they're off the court, Gottlieb dealt with his athletes on an everyday basis. He seemed to relish that part of the job.

"He always had contact with his players," Fleishman said. "Often, I'd be his whipping boy. One time, I was sitting on the bench, and he yelled out on the floor at me. Rullo said, 'Gotty, Jerry's here on the bench.' He was so involved in the game that he hadn't realized that. But he was a helluva guy. He was always willing to help you out if you had a problem. Compared to the other guys who ran teams in the league, he was the best."

Gottlieb always warned his players not to ignore their fans. "He always told us, 'Anytime somebody asks you for an autograph, you sign it,'" Rullo recalled. "Same for banquets. He said, 'If somebody wants you to come to a banquet, you go.' He was always trying to make fans for the team."

"He was tough. A hard taskmaster," said Musi. "You did things the way he wanted them to be done. Although he was a very nice guy, to a certain degree he was a little bit of a loner. And he wasn't cheap, but he watched every penny. I remember in one city we stayed in a hotel two miles from the arena because he got a better price there."

Bernie Brown, who worked for Gottlieb in the 1940s in the front office, had a less flattering description of him. "He was a little self-centered," Brown said. "I wouldn't say he was selfish, but I don't know how much sympathy he had for people who worked for him. He was a little like a dictator. To some extent, he was hard to get along with. He wasn't an easy person to like."

By the end of the regular season, Joe Fulks had averaged 23.2 points per game to win the scoring title with 1,389 points, 463 more than second place Feerick. The only other Warrior to rank among the league leaders was Dallmar, who placed fourth in assists.

Red Auerbach, who had never coached above the high school level before joining the BAA, led Washington to the regular-season title in the Eastern Division, finishing with a 49–11 record, including a 29–1 mark at home. Gottlieb's Warriors, who by the end of January were only 18–16, came in second with a 35–25 log. Chicago (39–22) and St. Louis (38–23) were the top teams in the West.

In the quarterfinals of the playoffs, the Warriors beat St. Louis, two games to one, in a best-of-three series, while the New York Knickerbockers downed Cleveland by the same count. That led to one of the oddest semifinal schedules in sports history. It was decided by the league's board of governors that as regular-season winners, Chicago and Washington would meet in a best-of-seven series. Meanwhile, the two quarterfinal winners, Philadelphia and New York, would square off in a best-of-three set. The winner of each series would meet in the final.

Chicago won its series, four games to two. The Warriors took the Knicks, 82–70 and 72–53, setting the stage for a best-of-seven final against the Stags.

The Warriors won the first game, 84–71, as Fulks scored 37 points. Gotty's team also won the next two games by scores of 85–74 and 75–72. With Fulks in foul trouble, the Stags won the fourth game, 74–73.

The fifth game was played on April 22 at the Arena before a sellout crowd of 8,221. Another 5,000 were turned away at the gate. After leading 22–7 in the first quarter, the Warriors held only a 40–38 edge at halftime.

At the end of the third quarter, Chicago had moved ahead, 68–63. Then, behind a red-hot Fulks, the Warriors came back to tie at 78-all with 1:20 left in the game. Playmaker Dallmar, who missed much of the second half because of calluses on his left foot, dropped in a 15-foot set shot. Kaplowitz followed with a foul shot, which added another extraordinary dimension to the game. Actually, it had been Rosenberg who was fouled, but when he walked to one side and the deadly shooting Kaplowitz stepped to the foul line, referees Pat Kennedy and Eddie Boyle never detected the switch. With the wrong man shooting, the Warriors closed out an 83–80 victory for the championship.

Fulks finished with 34 points, followed by Musi with 13 and Senesky with 11. Tony Jaros scored 21 for the Stags, while Zaslofsky was held to five and Halbert to eight.

"They are a great team," Stags coach Harold Olsen told reporters. "There is not a team in the league that I would rather have lost to."

The winning team received $14,000. The Warriors had also won $10,000 from their previous two series, which, when the total was divided, came to $2,150 per man. Chicago was awarded a losers' share of $10,000.

Gottlieb was as happy as he'd ever been. "I have never coached a finer group of boys," he advised the assembled writers. "They were easy to handle, and I never had to fine a single one. We never had a bit of dissension. The fellows never thought of anything but winning games. Another thing, I've never been connected with a team that was as popular all around the league as this one. They are a credit to the game of basketball."

Later, Gotty revealed to Ed Delaney of the *Evening Bulletin* a little secret. "You often hear of a fighter leaving his best punch in the gym," he said. "Well, it's the same way in our league. But do you know, we scrimmaged less than any team in our circuit? We held one scrimmage during the entire playoffs. Daily workouts weren't necessary with these kids. They always were in perfect physical condition. That's why I say a better group of athletes can't be found."

After the final game, the Warriors celebrated with a raucous victory party at Sam Framo's seafood house at 23rd Street and Allegheny Avenue. "Gotty used to throw a lot of parties for the players," remembered Fleishman. "But that party was one nobody will ever forget."

The victory gave Philadelphia its first major league sports championship since 1930 when the Philadelphia Athletics defeated the St. Louis Cardinals in six games to win the World Series. And it launched local

Surrounding team president Pete Tyrrell, the Warriors celebrated their 1946–47 championship. The happy group included (from row from left) Cy Kaselman, Jerry Fleishman, Jerry Rullo, Angelo Musi, Tyrrell, Petey Rosenberg, and George Senesky (Gottlieb is behind the hand) and (back row) Howie Dallmar, the team doctor, Art Hillhouse, Matt Guokas, Ralph Kaplowitz, and Joe Fulks. *(Philadelphia Jewish Sports Hall of Fame, Adolph and Rose Levis Museum)*

teams on a run in which the Eagles won NFL titles in 1947 and 1948 and the Phillies captured the National League pennant in 1950.

Over the entire season, the Warriors had drawn a paid crowd of 128,950, the highest in the BAA. Net receipts for the team were $191,117, second best behind New York, but far ahead of third place Providence's $117,740. Although the size of the crowd depended on the opponent—teams such as the Knicks, Stags, and Capitols drew much bigger audiences than other clubs—the Warriors averaged more than 4,000 fans per game, the top figure in the league, and well in excess of the league average of 3,000. It looked like pro basketball in Philadelphia had made a strong impression on the city's sports fans.

The BAA had a vastly different look when the 1947–48 season opened. The most conspicuous change was in the number of teams. Cleveland, Detroit, Pittsburgh, and Toronto had gone out of business, which left the league with seven teams and the possibility of an unbalanced schedule. To remedy that problem, the league summoned the Baltimore Bullets from the ABL, the same circuit in which the SPHAS still played. At the time, no one could have forecast what that addition would mean to the league.

When they entered the BAA, the Bullets were hardly considered a first-class operation. They played in a funky, little arena in one of the low-income sections of Baltimore. The place held just 4,000. And, because its main function was to serve as a roller-skating rink, basketball was not only secondary, but the team played on the same floor, ruts and all, that was used for roller-skating. "It was a real dump," said Bullets owner Jake Early, whose team had no other place to play. "I'll tell you how bad it was," said player-coach Buddy Jeannette. "When they quit using it as an arena, they made a garage out of it."

Another major change for the new season was the schedule. To help the teams cut travel expenses, the regular-season schedule was reduced from 60 games to 48 for each team. That made Gottlieb's summer job as the league schedule-maker considerably easier.

While there were major changes in the league, the Warriors experienced an important change, too. The Arena Corporation, which had been created in 1938 and under the stewardship of Pete Tyrrell had played a key role in the formation of the BAA and the Warriors, was sold to Triangle Publications, Inc. The sale included the Arena, the Warriors, and the Rockets, an ice hockey team that played in the American Hockey League.

"Every time the company got ahead, made a little money," Pete Tyrrell, Jr., said, "the other owners wanted to give themselves a little bonus or buy a new Cadillac. My dad sold his share because he wanted to get away from the other five shareholders."

Triangle Publications was owned and operated by Walter Annenberg and was the parent company of the Philadelphia *Inquirer*, the *Daily News*, the *Daily Racing Form*, and several magazines and radio/television stations, including WFIL. Annenberg had assumed command of the company after his father, Moses (Moe), who had purchased the *Inquirer* in 1936 for $15 million, was jailed for income tax evasion and subsequently died in 1942.

Tyrrell remained as president and general manager of the Arena, while Gottlieb maintained his various duties with the Warriors. Other than the apparent conflict of interest of a team being covered by newspapers that owned it, and Annenberg's construction of a new television studio next to the Arena, there was no perceptible change in the Warriors' operation.

Gottlieb's job with the Warriors, however, had intensified. Now, as reigning champions of the BAA, other teams were gunning for them. Among those who were true professionals in mind and body, facing the champs always made an opposing player elevate his game. Gotty had to make sure the Warriors improved.

One of his first jobs was to bolster his roster. His biggest move was to draft All-American Francis (Chink) Crossin, one of Penn's all-time greats whose father Frank had played major league baseball in parts of three seasons (1912–14) with the St. Louis Browns. Just two years earlier, Crossin had teamed with Dallmar to give Penn one of its finest teams.

Guokas, Rosenberg, and Rullo were gone from the championship team. Bob O'Brien from Kansas, Jack Rocker from California at Berkeley, and Stan Brown, an 18-year-old who had played with the SPHAS after leaving Central High School, were added to the roster at the beginning of the season. Hank Beenders from Long Island University and former Stags star Chuck Halbert from West Texas State joined the squad during the season.

The starting lineup was the same as that of the previous season: Musi and Senesky at guards, Dallmar and Fulks at forwards, and Hillhouse at center. Fleishman and Kaplowitz, along with Crossin, formed a valuable group of reserves.

"We had a great team," Fulks said in an article in the *Evening Bulletin*. "Senesky took care of the defensive work, Dallmar liked to pass off, and Musi did the outside shooting. I did it from in close. Gotty liked to have his players pass the ball three or four times before there was any shooting, so I tried to make sure the other guys moved the ball before it came to me. Then nobody would holler if I took a shot."

With Fulks leading the league in scoring average with 22.1 points per game, although after missing five games because of an injury, he scored 949 points to finish behind Zaslofsky's 1,007, the Warriors won the Eastern Division regular-season crown with a 27–21 record. Providence finished last in the division with a 6–42 mark.

Some years later, Gottlieb recalled for Frank Deford in the *Sports Illustrated* article his strategy when the Warriors faced the Steamrollers. "Providence was Ernie Calverley and all those firehouse guys from Rhode Island State," he said. "Run, run, run. But one reason they were so bad was that mostly everybody held the ball on them and wouldn't let them run. Everybody but me. I wanted them to run. I knew from a coach's standpoint that was bad, but it was what the public wanted. What the hell's the use of playing Providence if it's not Providence playing?"

In the playoffs, the Warriors drew a bye in the first round, then beat the Western winner, St. Louis, four games to three, in the oddly format-ted semifinals. The Warriors lost three games by a total of 14 points, won one game by one point, and two others by scores of 84–56 and 84–61 before romping to victory in the deciding game, 85–46.

Baltimore, which featured Jeannette, Chick Reiser, and Clarence (Kleggie) Hermsen, shocked pro basketball followers by finishing tied for first in the Western Division (the Bullets lost in a playoff game to break the tie with St. Louis). Under the weird BAA playoff schedule, the Bullets beat Chicago in two games in the semifinals.

The championship series began at the Arena with the Warriors win-ning the first game, 71–60. In Game Two, Baltimore held the Warriors to seven points in the third quarter to gain a come-from-behind 66–63 vic-tory. Then, with the series moving to Baltimore, the Bullets triumphed, 72–70 and 78–75. Back at the Arena, the Warriors won, 91–82. In the sixth game in Baltimore, the Bullets captured the title with an 88–73 triumph.

As a team that had won the championship one year and had gone to the final the next, the Warriors were attracting a considerable amount of attention around Philadelphia. The newspapers were cover-ing the team with big stories. A radio station was broadcasting games. And people were jamming the Arena whenever the team played there. In their second year, the Warriors again averaged more than 4,000 per game, a figure matched only by the Knicks.

Gottlieb, though, wasn't content. "It's a shame the Arena only seats 8,000 [actually 7,700]," he said in a publication called *Basketball Illus-trated.* "We could sell seats to 20,000 for some games. In fact, I would book 400 exhibition games for the Warriors if I could. That's how much we are in demand."

Crowds were one of Gottlieb's specialties. It was often said that the size of the crowd determined Gotty's mood. He liked to tell people that he was a promoter-coach. "I always thought I was a pretty good coach," he confided to Deford. "I could get a team up. But my primary thing was box office." And virtually everything Gotty did was with an eye for attracting fans, even if, as many claimed, he did fudge attendance figures on occasion.

No one was a better witness to Gotty's promotional mindset than Campbell, who first broadcast Warriors games in 1946 and continued in that role into the mid-1950s. "We'd walk into an arena on the road, and you'd say, 'Eddie, what's the attendance?' He'd look around and come up with a figure within 100 people every time. I don't know how he did it. But numbers were a big part of his life. Attendance was very important to him."

While attendance was booming in Philadelphia, that was not the case everywhere else in the BAA. Some cities were drawing crowds suitable only for high school games. Moreover, the BAA had entered into a full-scale war with the rival National Basketball League (NBL), whose president, Ike Duffy, regularly predicted the imminent demise of the BAA.

The two leagues had met as early as May 21, 1947, to explore the possibility of merging. The NBL, which had most of the best players, got together again on June 2 with the BAA's board of directors, which included Gottlieb. But an agreement could not be reached, and eventually negotiations broke off, and the hostility resumed.

The battle got more intense before the start of the 1948–49 season when four of the best teams in the NBL—the Fort Wayne Pistons, Indianapolis Jets, Minneapolis Lakers, and Rochester Royals—joined the BAA, expanding that league to 12 teams. With the new clubs came some of the top players in the NBL, including a 6-foot, 10-inch center for the Lakers named George Mikan. The bespectacled giant would not only revolutionize the way the game was played with his inside scoring and rugged rebounding, but would give pro basketball the first-class status it had coveted while leading the Lakers to five championships in six years.

With Mikan topping the BAA in scoring with a record 1,698 points (28.3 average) and averaging 30.3 points per game in the playoffs, the Lakers captured the league championship, defeating the Washington Caps, guided by former high school coach Red Auerbach, four games to two in the playoff final. As for the Warriors, they placed fourth in the Eastern Division with a 28–32 record, then, with the playoff format finally changed, lost to Washington twice in a division semifinal. During the season, Fulks placed second in scoring with 1,560 points (26.0 average), while newly acquired center Ed Sadowski, playing with his sixth pro team, ranked sixth in scoring with 920 tallies.

Meanwhile, the fight between the BAA and the NBL was still raging. Duffy continued his attacks, saying among other things that the Warriors and seven other BAA teams were on the verge of disbanding.

"Take it from me," an angry Gottlieb fired back, "as long as there's a BAA, there will be a Philadelphia team in it. Duffy should worry more about his NBL and quit sticking his nose into the BAA. He should particularly pay attention to his own Anderson (Indiana) team, which drew less than 1,000 spectators recently."

Duffy, a wealthy meat packer, replied that at a recent game in Philadelphia, the paid attendance was fewer than 200. "The game he refers to," stormed Gotty in an article in the *Inquirer*, "was last Thursday night when the PTC [Philadelphia Transit Company] strike was underway and a snowstorm hit the city. Our paid attendance that night, despite the strike and the weather, was 1,199." Duffy, he continued, should have seen the previous game when the Warriors drew a record 8,475 to a meeting with Minneapolis.

The feud between the two leagues was not destined to last forever. With a number of its entries coming from smaller cities and its arenas generally being inferior to those of the BAA, the NBL had become the weaker circuit. Eventually, it had a choice: either give in or perish. When BAA commissioner Maurice Podoloff, with the backing of Gottlieb and the rest of the board, invited the NBL's remaining teams to join his league, the offer was accepted.

Following the merger, the new league was named the National Basketball Association (NBA). Six teams, Anderson, Denver, Sheboygan, Syracuse, Tri-Cities, and Waterloo—some obviously not from cities of big-league caliber—moved from the NBL to the new league, while Providence and Indianapolis of the BAA disbanded. A new team, the Indianapolis Olympians, which featured 1948 Olympic gold medalists Alex Groza and Ralph Beard, replaced the city's Jets, bringing the final number of teams in the NBA to 17.

For the 1949–50 season, the league was divided into three divisions, with five of the old NBL teams and Indianapolis forming the Western Division. Syracuse was placed in the Eastern Division. That winter, Dolph Schayes and Al Cervi, two players who would later be heard from again in Philadelphia, led Syracuse to an amazing 51–13 record during the regular season. The Warriors, with Fulks nowhere to be found among the league's top 10 scorers, finished fourth with a 26–42 record.

In the playoffs, the Nats topped the Warriors two games to none in the division semifinal. Ultimately, Syracuse reached the last round where it lost four games to two to Minneapolis, led by league scoring champ Mikan, future La Salle College coach Jim Pollard, and Vern Mikkelsen. The Lakers' final win by a 120–95 score—only the second time in 32 of that year's playoff games in which a team had scored more than 100 points—ended what had been a landmark first season for the new NBA.

The draft of college players in 1950 was one that would chart future Warriors' seasons for more than a decade. It would also once again confirm two long-held theories of Gottlieb's. Attendance at Warriors games, Gotty firmly believed, was greatly enhanced by a roster filled with local players. And fans would also come to games in greater numbers if the team had one major scorer, a player to whom others on the team would willingly defer.

The first theory was verified by previous Warriors teams, all of which were staffed by numerous local players. The second opinion was supported by the scoring exploits of Joe Fulks. Gottlieb credited both theories as being significant reasons the Warriors drew well at the gate.

In their last two seasons, however, the Warriors had been highly mediocre, finishing fourth in the Eastern Division each time and getting knocked out in the first rounds of the playoffs. While Fulks, except for an off year in 1949–50, was still one of the league's dominant players, the number of local players on the roster was rapidly dwindling. So was the Warriors' attendance.

The 1950 draft, though, provided what looked like an instant fix. Paul Arizin grew up in South Philadelphia, attended La Salle High School, and then became a sensation at Villanova. Although Gottlieb could have chosen La Salle College star center Larry Foust, another South Philly guy, he snatched Arizin as a territorial pick in the first round of the draft. In support of his theory about local players, Gottlieb also picked George Senesky's brother, Paul, from St. Joseph's, Ike Borsavage from Temple, and Brooks Ricca and Leo Wolfe, both from Villanova.

It was Arizin, though, who was the big catch. The hustling forward had an intriguing background. He never played basketball in high school; in fact, he was cut from the team in his senior year. He then went on a basketball binge, playing in an assortment of local amateur leagues, sometimes as many as six at a time. Arizin enrolled at Villanova as a chemistry major in 1946, but didn't try out for the team until his sophomore year. When he did, however, his talent was quickly evident.

The 6-foot, 4-inch youngster, who had by then perfected the relatively new technique called a jump shot, made such a strong impression on Wildcats coach Al Severance that he offered him a scholarship. During the season, Arizin not only became a starter, he led the team in scoring.

Arizin continued to blossom the following season, once scoring 85 points in one game and leading Villanova to a 23–4 record. By now, Arizin had become a familiar name around the country. In his senior year, as he sparked the Wildcats to a 25–4 record while becoming the first Villanova player ever to score 1,000 points in a career, he added to his laurels by leading the nation in scoring with the second-highest total (735 points) and the second-highest average (25.3) in college basketball history. After the season, "Pitchin' Paul," as he had become known, was named first team All-American and College Player of the Year.

Arizin was everything Gottlieb—and the Warriors—needed. Gotty quickly signed the future NBA great to a contract.

"When I went up to negotiate with Eddie," Arizin recalled, "the office was over a movie theater. We began talking, and he said to me, 'How much money do you want?' I didn't know what to say—you didn't have agents in those days—or know what anybody else was making, so I said, '$10,000.' I pulled the figure out of the air. He looked at me and laughed. He said, 'If I give you $10,000 you're going to bankrupt the team.' Personally, I didn't care if I played or not. I didn't have any burning desire to play pro ball. I wanted to get out in the business world and start making a living. But then we negotiated some more. Finally, he agreed to the $10,000. After I signed, he said, 'I have a bonus for you.' He took me downstairs and got me a free ticket to the movie. He knew the manager. The ticket probably cost all of 75 cents."

In terms of players' salaries of the era, Arizin's was high. But it turned into one of the best bargains Gottlieb ever made. Arizin went on to score 1,121 points in his rookie season to rank sixth in the league. Ultimately, he led the NBA in scoring twice (1952 and 1957), finished second twice, and third once. He was named to the All-Star team in each of his 10 years in the NBA (Arizin spent two years in the Marine Corps). When he retired after the 1961–62 season, he was the third-highest scorer in NBA history with 16,266 points. Arizin was named to the Basketball Hall of Fame in 1978, and in 1996 was selected as one of the 50 greatest players in NBA history.

At a time when help was desperately needed, Arizin was one of the players who gave a much-needed boost to the Warriors as well to the entire NBA. A fan favorite, Arizin joined with players such as Mikan, Schayes, and Bob Cousy to give the NBA certifiable big league status.

Bringing Arizin to the Warriors was undoubtedly one of Gottlieb's shining hours. But it was not the only major story during what turned into an extraordinarily eventful year for both Gotty and the Warriors.

Cousy, a flashy guard from Holy Cross, was in the same draft as Arizin. He was picked by the Tri-Cities Black Hawks, a former NBL team from Indiana, but failed to come to terms with owner Ben Kerner and was traded to the Chicago Stags. Before the 1950–51 season began, however, the Stags disbanded. While most of the Stags players were distributed to other NBA teams, Zaslofsky, Andy Phillip, and Cousy—Chicago's most valuable commodities—were given special treatment. Because an attractive fee could be earned by the NBA by selling each player, league officials decided that one would go to the Knicks, one to the Celtics, and one to the Warriors, three teams that could afford the price and that would benefit the most by having the players.

But when the three teams couldn't agree on who would get whom, Podoloff decided to break the stalemate by dropping the three names into a hat while putting a $15,000 price tag on Zaslofsky, $10,000 on Phillip, and $8,500 on Cousy. Picking second, Gottlieb drew Phillip, a spunky playmaker who had been one-half of an excellent backcourt duo at the University of Illinois with future baseball great Lou Boudreau.

Thus, the Warriors barely missed out on having Cousy perform his Hall of Fame magic in Philadelphia instead of Boston. But Phillip was no slouch himself. Joining with Senesky to give the Warriors an excellent backcourt, he led the league in assists for the next two seasons.

Meanwhile, Gottlieb continued making moves off the court. He arranged for some Warriors games to be televised, the first time that had been done in the NBA. He took away seats from the press section and sold them to the public. He even had the Warriors fly to some away games, the first time an NBA team had traveled in the air.

Gottlieb also began scheduling a few home games at Convention Hall, a much larger venue near 34th and Spruce Streets on the edge of the Penn campus. Convention Hall, which held 12,000—more than 4,000 higher than the Arena—was regarded by Gottlieb as a more appealing place to play. It offered more desirable playing dates, too. That point was readily apparent during one month in 1950 when the Warriors could play only four home games at the Arena because the Ice Follies took up six dates, 10 more were used for ice-skating, two for wrestling, and one for boxing (Sunday basketball games were still prohibited).

Although players weren't subjected to the obstacles created at the Arena such as ice on the floor, Convention Hall was no Taj Mahal. It had its own set of flaws.

"It had the worst dressing room in the world," Arizin declared. "There were no hooks for your clothes. You had to drape your clothes on a wooden chair. Each dressing room was on the side of a stage, and each one had only a single shower. We had to use it, and so did the referees. And if you were playing a game and you had a plane or train to catch afterward, it was a mess getting out. Really, the Arena was better. At least, it had hooks for your clothes."

Few teams in the NBA in those days played all their home games in the same facility or even the same city. Team owners moved games around to different locations in an attempt to attract big crowds that didn't usually see pro basketball. It was all part of the effort to remain solvent, otherwise interpreted to mean staying alive.

Once in a while, when both the Arena and Convention Hall were occupied, the Warriors played at the Palestra. As the years went by, they also played home games in Allentown, Bethlehem, Hershey, and Camden, and at Lincoln High School in Northeast Philadelphia and Sayre Junior High in West Philly. They even played home games in places like Toledo, Cleveland, Tulsa, Fargo, North Dakota, and Saratoga Springs, New York. "A promoter would sell the games. If nobody came, he would take a bath," observed Arizin.

Gottlieb, who, according to Jim Heffernan, once considered having a court built and relocating the Warriors to 30th Street Station but never received the support necessary for such a venture, was one of the first men in the NBA to schedule doubleheaders. That gave fans an outstanding bargain. A fan could see four different NBA teams for the price of one ticket. Gotty also brought in his SPHAS to play in the first game of doubleheaders. He arranged for the Harlem Globetrotters to participate in twin bills, too. In the years in which the Warriors were performing poorly and attracting small crowds, the Globies often were the main attraction. "Some years, they needed us to keep them alive," remembered Red Klotz. "We'd go in and pack the place. Then the NBA game would start and everybody would go home."

Over the years, preliminary games were standard fare at Warriors games. Gottlieb staged meetings between high school teams. He scheduled games between independent teams such as the B'rith Sholom League All-Stars versus the Norristown Blocks. Games involving girls' teams such as ones that pitted the Ford and Kendig Girls against the Woodbury Starlets were often held. And basketball teams made up of players from the Phillies and later the Eagles also played in the early games.

By 1950, college basketball, including that played in Philadelphia, had become extremely popular. Although the Big Five had not yet been formed, the colleges that later comprised that group drew sellout crowds to doubleheaders at the Palestra. If he was worried, Gottlieb didn't let it show. "We aren't trying to compete against colleges," he said. "We think there are enough fans to support both pros and colleges here in Philadelphia."

During the season, Gottlieb sometimes attracted as much attention as his players. Once, in the midst of a game at the Arena, fans were razzing The Mogul. "Whoever said you could coach?" yelled one of them. "You're a bum." Gottlieb started into the stands after the heckler, then stopped and returned to the bench. Later, when asked why he had stopped, Gotty explained that it was "for business reasons. I realized," he said, "that the guy was sitting in a $2.60 seat. He'll come back again to give me the bird, and he'll pay $2.60 every time he does."

Nevertheless, Gottlieb was not reluctant to bolt into the stands to engage in a battle with an unsympathetic fan. Another time at the Arena, he charged after a spectator who had screeched at Gotty to "drop dead." "His makeup comprises equal parts coach, promoter, and showman," Edgar Williams wrote in the *Sporting News*.

The Warriors were playing in Moline (one-third of the Tri-Cities), and according to an account in the *Inquirer* by Fred Byrod, "a wildly partisan crowd turned out vociferously demanding that the 'big leaguers' be put in their place." One fan threw a punch that hit Gottlieb, who immediately charged into the stands. Cooler heads prevailed, but after the game, Gotty filed a protest, claiming that "the actions of the fans had not been conducive to good officiating."

In Syracuse, the Nats had a large, bald-headed fan who was a few clowns short of a circus. He was called "The Strangler." Frequently, as visiting players walked up a ramp to the locker room, he tried to reach down and choke them. Once, he made the mistake of trying to grab Gottlieb. "I'll put $50 in an envelope in Philly, and we'll get rid of you," Gotty advised the chump.

Generally, Gottlieb got along well with referees, who in the early days of the NBA made $50 a game and were sometimes accused of being intim-

Gottlieb always went through an array of emotions while coaching a game. Harry Litwack sits next to Gotty (above). *(Temple University Libraries, Urban Archives, Philadelphia, Pennsylvania)*

idated by fans and not taking control of the game. "Gotty never gave the refs a bad time," claimed Norm Drucker, the only referee still living who officiated in games that The Mogul coached. "He was more interested in attendance and publicity. He seldom protested a ref's decision, and I don't recall his ever being thrown out of a game."

That view could be contradicted. Once, Gottlieb had a young ref thrown out of his job after he did protest loudly about his calls. The next day, Gotty called the league office to complain. The man never worked another NBA game.

Williams wrote in the *Inquirer* that "few enraged bulls can bellow louder then Eddie when an official calls a questionable foul." Gottlieb responded that he was "not a referee-baiter. I just stand up for my rights," he said. "You have to yell to make yourself heard above the crowd."

According to Dolph Schayes, though, screaming at the refs wasn't a regular Gottlieb habit. "When he was coaching," the former Syracuse star said, "the referees were his best friends. He respected them and didn't like to antagonize them. He liked the good ones. He didn't think refereeing was a difficult job. Sometimes, when he didn't agree with a call, he'd say, 'I could pick a knowledgeable fan out of the stands who could do a better job than you.'"

A long with Gottlieb's antics, the Warriors enjoyed a banner season in 1950–51. They won the Eastern Division title by one game over the Celtics after drawing sizable crowds to their games all season, especially when they played Boston, New York, or Minneapolis. Phillip and Senesky went one-three in the league in assists, and Fulks was fourth and the rookie Arizin sixth in scoring.

"You never saw in my day players who could shoot with such amazing accuracy and consistency as today's boys," Gottlieb said. "Take my own scorers, Joe Fulks and Paul Arizin. Both of these boys make shots we never dreamed of taking. We never had shooters to compete with these boys."

The only weak spot in the Warriors' lineup was at center. Ron Livingston, a 6-foot, 10-inch Wyoming native who had been acquired from Baltimore the year before, manned the post, but averaged only 4.5 points and 4.7 rebounds per game.

"He could run like a deer, but he was not a very good basketball player," said Arizin. "Worse than that, he didn't like basketball. He quit after the season. I heard that he wanted to be a forest ranger. He went back to Wyoming, and I never heard from him again."

In the opening round of the division playoffs, the Warriors met fourth place Syracuse, which, despite finishing the season two games under .500, was a tough team led by Schayes and two feisty guards, Cervi and Paul Seymour. "If you didn't play hard, they would eat you up," Arizin recalled.

Playing the first game at the Arena, the teams fought to an 89–89 tie in regulation. In overtime, after Fulks missed a shot, the Nats held the ball for four minutes and 50 seconds. With less than 10 seconds to play in the five-minute extra period, Fred Scolari threw up a one-hander that went in and gave Syracuse a 91–89 victory. "A lot of people blamed Eddie for not telling us to foul," Arizin said. "But in those days, you didn't foul intentionally because you felt you were good enough defensively to stop them."

The Nats won handily, 90–78, in the second game played at Syracuse, knocking the Warriors out of the playoffs. Later, Syracuse lost to the Knicks in the division final, and that was followed by a New York loss to Rochester in a seven-game league final.

In 1951–52 Arizin won his first scoring title with 1,674 points (25.4 average), while Mikan finished second and Cousy third. But the Warriors wound up in fourth place. With the roles reversed, first place Syracuse slammed the door on the Warriors, winning the first round of the playoffs, two games to one. Again, the Nats lost to the Knicks in the division final. This time, Minneapolis beat the Knicks in seven games for the NBA title.

The Warriors were once again relegated to the level of an also-ran. It was not a position that Gottlieb found easy to tolerate. But before he could turn his attention during the off-season to improving the team, he had to attend to more important business.

CHAPTER 11

New Owner of the Warriors

In their first five seasons in pro basketball, the Warriors achieved a high level of success. The team won a league championship and finished first two other times during the regular season. Two of the league's scoring leaders were Warriors. And the team was regarded as a bona fide member of Philadelphia's major league sports fraternity.

The Warriors were an interesting team with a colorful coach and a roster dotted with outstanding players, many of them native Philadelphians. Over their first five years, the team posted a 156–146 record during the regular season. The Warriors certainly ranked among the elite of the NBA.

But as the 1951–52 season began, the team was in trouble. Attendance, which originally had been among the highest in the league, decreased dramatically, dropping from a high a few years earlier of 4,500 per game to an average of 2,500. The Warriors' vagabond sneakers were forced to roam far from home in an attempt to attract crowds. The team was barely staying afloat financially. It was definitely on a downward spiral.

It was not an appealing picture, and Walter Annenberg and his henchmen at Triangle Publications were fully aware of the possible disaster looming ahead. It was, they concluded, time to get out of the sports business.

Annenberg developed a plan. He would ask Pete Tyrrell, the president and general manager of the Arena Corp., to sell the Arena, disband the Rockets ice hockey team, and either fold, sell, or move the Warriors to another city. The most likely possibility for the Warriors was simply to cease operations. Because the team had fallen on hard times and was no longer a major attraction, who would care if it was gone?

There was at least one person, though, who didn't embrace Annenberg's plan. Eddie Gottlieb had poured his heart, soul, mind, and body into the Warriors franchise, and there was no way he was going to let it die without a fight. Gotty told friends he was going to try to save the franchise, no matter what it took, keeping it in Philadelphia instead of moving it to some other city.

Gottlieb's first move was to have a talk with Annenberg. By then, the publisher of the *Inquirer* and *Daily News* had already folded the Rockets. Now, it appeared that he was about to pull the plug on the Warriors. Gotty set up a meeting between the two.

When they sat down together, Gottlieb wasted no time getting to the point. Harvey Pollock recalled the way Gotty told him the conversation went. "He said to Annenberg, 'Don't get rid of the team. I'd like to buy it,'" Pollock remembered. "Annenberg said, 'What do you want this team for? It's a losing proposition. Nobody comes to games. You'll do nothing but lose money.' Then Annenberg said he'd sell the team for $25,000."

Gottlieb, of course, didn't have $25,000. At the time, he wasn't a wealthy man. He had rented a place for years on Catherine Street, then in 1949 had relocated to a duplex at 2201 North Salford Street, near Upland Street in Wynnefield. There, in a three-bedroom, two-bathroom second floor apartment that he also rented—Gotty never owned real estate—he supported an aging mother and a sister who required treatment for mental illness and spent time as a patient at Friends Hospital at Roosevelt Boulevard and Adams Avenue in Northeast Philadelphia. His domestic expenses absorbed much of his income.

But The Mogul had several good friends who were willing to help him finance the purchase. One was Jules Trumper, whose family owned Perlstein Glass Company in Philadelphia. Another was Lou Glazer, owner of a large clothing factory in the city that, among other products, made swimwear for Jantzen. Each would invest $5,000, thereby each owning 20 percent of the team. Gottlieb would put up the rest, although all of it turned out not to be his money.

Both Trumper and Glazer were longtime pals of Gotty's. Alan Trumper described his father's relationship: "He and Eddie were friends growing

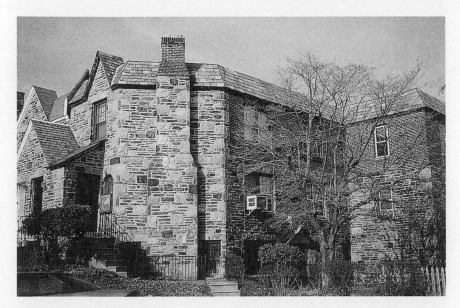

For many years, Gottlieb lived on the second floor of a large duplex at the corner of Salford and Upland Streets in Wynnefield. The house extends around to the right. *(Courtesy of Rich Westcott)*

up in South Philly," he said. "Later, my brother, Jerome, was an usher at SPHAS games. Eddie became part of our family. He and my father had dinner three or four times a week. They'd go everywhere together—to see Penn at the Palestra, Temple at Convention Hall, later to Harry Litwack's camp, and to the Hall of Fame each year. Eddie was always at our house. And we were always at Warriors games, my father, my mother, Jerome, me, and later my wife, sitting right behind the bench. My father went to every game and many away games from the time Eddie bought the team until he sold it."

The sale was announced on April 25, 1952. No stockholders were named, nor was the purchase price announced. New owners were merely described in area newspapers as "a local group headed by Eddie Gottlieb." The Mogul was reported to have made "a substantial offer," which prompted the owners to sell the team. Some said he had to be crazy to buy a basketball team at that time.

The *Jewish Exponent*, though, wrote in glowing terms about the new president, general manager, and coach of the new company called Philadelphia Warriors, Inc. "He has long been regarded as one of the country's more progressive and intelligent sports promoters, and is considered without peer when it comes to knowledge of basketball," said an article in the newspaper. "Despite more than 30 years' active association with the game, Gottlieb has never lost his zest for victory."

Other accounts of the sale hailed Gottlieb as the savior of the franchise. "It's safe to assume that if a purchaser wasn't forthcoming, the former owners would have given it (the team) up as a lost cause. He rescued it when it was on the way out," wrote Bob Vetrone in the *Evening Bulletin*.

Three weeks after the sale, Gottlieb revealed the name of one of the Warriors' new stockholders. It was Abe Saperstein, Gotty's friend and fellow promoter, the owner of the Harlem Globetrotters, a stockholder in the St. Louis Browns baseball team, and a man with whom The Mogul had been doing business for some 25 years. While claiming that he had "the majority interest in the team," Gotty called Saperstein "a principal stockholder." But, Gotty told Sandy Grady a few years later in the *Evening Bulletin*, "Abe has no more to do with running the Warriors than I have with the Trotters. And I have no interest in them."

Many years later, Alan Trumper revealed that when his father received his stock, he divided it into thirds, keeping one-third for himself, and giving one-third each to Jerome and Alan. "My father knew when he got the stock that it was just a favor," he said. "He knew there would be no dividends. And stockholders didn't have any input. That was not part of the deal. Eddie ran the show 100 percent."

The sale effectively ended speculation about the Warriors' future. Meanwhile, Annenberg's company retained ownership of the Arena, eventually holding it until 1958 when it was sold to a group headed by Tyrrell. With Tyrrell as president and general manager, that group owned the building until it was sold at auction in 1965 to James Toppi Enterprises. Later, it was sold again, this time to an alleged drug dealer. Soon afterward, the Arena was destroyed by a fire that was said to have been set by an arsonist.

Gottlieb couldn't have picked a worse time to take full control of the Warriors. For one thing, the team was coming off a highly mediocre season in which it had been knocked out of the NBA playoffs in the first round. College basketball in Philadelphia was becoming increasingly popular. Fans had stopped coming to see the Warriors play. The team that Gottlieb would send out to battle in 1952–53 was putrid.

Making matters even worse, Paul Arizin, having led the league in scoring the previous year and become an enormously popular player, had been called into the Marines and would miss two full seasons. The team was seemingly left with no superstar, something Gotty always thought was a necessary part of the lineup based on his belief that one great player would attract fans.

What remained for the Warriors was a roster peppered with names that nobody ever heard of. Names like Mark Workman, Danny Finn, Ralph Polson, George Radovich, and Fred Kadelka. Names that made brief appearances in Warriors uniforms and then were hardly ever heard from again.

The Warriors' roster was in such dire straights that Gottlieb sometimes had to summon players from the Eastern League, a weekend minor league consisting mostly of teams in the Mid-Atlantic states. One such player was future Penn coach Jack McCloskey.

At one point, it was rumored that Gottlieb was considering moving the franchise to Chicago where Saperstein wanted to place a team to replace the defunct Stags. The Stags had been dropped from the NBA after the 1949–50 season for defaulting on a debt to the league. Saperstein had attempted to assume ownership of the team, but when his terms weren't met, he refused to conclude the deal. He still wanted to have a team in Chicago, but his effort to persuade Gottlieb to move the Warriors there ultimately failed.

That was not all that failed. During the season, the Warriors finished in last place in the Eastern Division, winning only 12 of 69 games. The situation got so bad at one point that Gottlieb tried to buy young center Lew Hitch from Minneapolis, although Hitch had never averaged as much as four points per game in the NBA. Uncertain about the health of center George Mikan, the Lakers declined. But Gottlieb persisted. He offered to trade his whole team except Arizin for Mikan. "I'm not kidding," he said. Lakers general manager Max Winter wired back. "Throw in Convention Hall," he said, "and you've got a deal."

All was not lost, however. As a territorial first round pick in the 1952 draft, Gottlieb selected Bill Mlkvy, a deadly shooter from Temple. Called "The Owl Without a Vowel," Mlkvy was an All-American who had led the nation in scoring in his junior year. A native of Palmerton in upstate Pennsylvania, Mlkvy was not only a talented player, he had a huge local following that made Gottlieb dizzy with anticipation.

Gotty could hardly wait to sign his new player. "I was in class, and the dean came in and gave me a message that Gottlieb had called," Mlkvy recalled. "He wanted to see me in his office. So, when I got out of class, I called my girlfriend, Barbara [who became his wife], and said, 'I'm going to sign a contract, and I'd like to take you out for dinner afterward.' We got on the subway, and rode downtown. We still had our books with us. We went to the office, which was on the second floor at 1537 Chestnut Street. Barbara said she didn't want to go up; she was too embarrassed. I went up myself, up these winding, dirty steps. Boxes were all over the place. And there was Gotty in this very cluttered office.

"He gave me some papers to sign. I said, 'Mr. Gottlieb, what am I signing?' He said, 'Don't worry, kid. Just sign them. You're going to be rich.' After I signed them, he said, 'You just signed for $1,200.' That was my contract for the whole season. The newspapers took some pictures, then he said, 'Let's go get something to eat.' I thought, this is going to be the best part of the deal. I'm on a hot dog diet, but I'd always heard that he liked to eat dinner at big restaurants downtown like Lew Tendler's. I figured this was a chance to show off for my girlfriend. We walked down Market Street. We came to a White Tower and went inside. Gottlieb put a dollar down on the counter. We each had a hamburger. I think they were 10 cents apiece. We had Cokes to drink. The whole bill came to 95 cents. Gotty got a nickel change. He picked it up, and put it in his pocket. No tip. And that was my signing bonus. My entrée into the NBA."

When he signed, Mlkvy was a first-year student in dental school at Temple. Not wanting to take a temporary leave of absence to play basketball, he stayed in school and played only home games. "I'd go to school from 8 in the morning until 5 in the afternoon, then play a game that night," Mlkvy said. "It was either, do it that way, or play ball and get drafted into military service."

As a result of his schedule, Mlkvy played in only 31 games during the season. At the end of the year, Gottlieb called for a meeting with the dean of Temple's dental school to try to clarify the situation. Gottlieb, Mike Iannarella, Jules Trumper, and Mlkvy all went to the meeting. "Eddie comes in wearing this big, floppy hat and big overcoat," Mlkvy recalled. "The first thing he says is, 'How are you, Dean? Do you need any tickets?'" At the meeting, it was decided that Mlkvy would give up basketball and return full-time to dental school. Ultimately, he became a successful local dentist.

While Mlkvy had joined the Warriors, another young player, almost completely devoid of fanfare, had also become a member of the team. Neil Johnston had played just one year of varsity basketball at Ohio State, averaging a mere nine points per game for a highly mediocre Buckeye team. While his college performance had not been particularly note-

As Gottlieb watches, two NBA scoring champions, Paul Arizin (left) and Neil Johnston, take shots at the basket during a practice sessions. *(Courtesy of Rich Westcott)*

worthy, basketball, in fact, wasn't even Johnston's primary sport. He was a baseball player who had quit college to become a pitcher in the Phillies farm system where he had played for three years until an arm injury cut short his career.

When that happened, Johnston managed to get a tryout with the Warriors. He realized he had no future as a professional baseball player. "I'd like to try pro basketball," he said. "I couldn't be any worse." Gotty took one look at the 6-foot, 8-inch player with only brief college basketball experience and quickly offered him a contract. Then Johnston made the team, although in his first season, he was strictly a reserve, playing mostly behind Ed Mikan, younger brother of George, who was on a six-team, six-year nondescript sojourn through the NBA.

In his second season, 1952–53, with his majestic hook shoot and precision one-handed jumpers hitting with uncanny accuracy, Johnston came out of nowhere to lead the NBA in scoring while averaging 22.3 points per game. Johnston would lead the league in scoring in each of the next two years, too, en route to earning a place in the Basketball Hall of Fame.

Johnston joined with the veteran Senesky to give the Warriors two bright spots on the team. A third shining ray would have been Andy Phillip, but Gottlieb sold him to the Fort Wayne Pistons at mid-season for $15,000, a move for which he was strongly criticized. "There's no doubt that Phillip is one of the league's best players," Gotty answered his critics. "But is he one of the best for our purposes? Phillip is 30 years old. His best days are past him. I'm looking for the future." While Gotty revealed that he had tried to acquire young stars Larry Foust and Jim Pollard in trades, Phillip, an outstanding playmaker, went on to perform five and one-half more years in the NBA and eventually gain a spot in the Hall of Fame.

One of Gottlieb's strengths was his ability to evaluate players. Over the years, he proved that by his choices of players who became useful if not excellent pros. "He didn't make many mistakes," said Bob Paul, a noted sports publicist for many years at Penn (and a son of the *Record* sports editor of the same name). "He was an excellent judge of talent."

Gottlieb was always in search of good ballplayers. Because no team had scouts in those days, Gotty performed the duty himself. He regularly attended local college games. He even showed up frequently at independent league games. One of his favorite gyms was one at Fifth Street and Allegheny Avenue. "Everybody knew him there," said Alan Levitt, Gotty's longtime accountant. "When he came in to watch a game, everybody wanted the ball. Nobody except the guy with the ball was ever going to shoot."

Gotty's exceptional talent for grading players was once again evident during the 1953 draft when he chose as his top pick and territorial choice Ernie Beck from Penn. He also drafted Jack George from La Salle. Although he didn't play after originally being drafted in 1952, Walter Davis from Texas A&M was also a rookie on the team.

All three had interesting backgrounds. Davis was a 6-foot, 8-inch high jumper who had won the Olympic gold medal in 1952 and held the world record in the event. Married and an off-season sheriff, he had overcome polio as a child and gone on to a career in which his leaping ability had helped him become one of the top college centers in the nation. With the Warriors, Gottlieb used him on opening and second half tapoffs. Davis could jump as high as any player in the league and was one of the first in the NBA to dunk the ball with some frequency.

George, a native of Washington, D.C., had gone to La Salle, played guard and in just two seasons had set the school's scoring record (which was quickly broken by Foust). After his sophomore year, however, George was drafted into the army. He played service ball for two years, then signed with the Warriors rather than return to college. Also an outstanding baseball catcher, George was sought by a number of major league teams. But Gottlieb, exercising his strong powers of persuasion, convinced George that his path to success in sports would be through basketball. "You see some players just once or twice and know they're ready," Gottlieb was quoted as saying by *Bulletin* writer, Bob Vetrone. "That's the way it was with George."

Gottlieb's top pick in the 1953 draft was Beck, a high-scoring guard who had gone to West Catholic High School. An All-American, Beck had led the Ivy League in scoring in three straight seasons while becoming Penn's all-time leader in scoring and rebounding, two records he still holds. In his senior year, while playing mostly center, the skilled, 6-foot, 4-inch ball handler had led the Quakers to their first Ivy League title in nearly 10 years. It was Gottlieb's dream to have three Philadelphia All-Americans—Beck, Arizin, and Tom Gola—on the same team. Although Beck had to spend two years in the navy after his rookie season with the Warriors, Gotty's wish eventually came true.

"I remember when I signed my first contract," Beck said. "It was for $9,500. Then I went into the service, and when I came out two years later, he said, 'I can't pay you any more than $8,500.' So I got docked for being in the service. A few years later, he said to me, 'I hear you got married.' I said, 'Yes, I did.' He wrote a check for $250. He said, 'Here, this is your wedding present.'"

There was one other player that Gottlieb fervently desired. His name was Marques Haynes, a ball-handling wizard who had played for the Harlem Globetrotters for seven years. In the absence of a point guard on the Warriors, now that Phillip was gone, Gotty thought that Haynes was the perfect solution. Saperstein sold him to the Warriors for a reported $30,000. But Haynes refused to report to the Warriors. He then rejected a new contract offer from Saperstein and went home to Tulsa, Oklahoma, amidst a storm of controversy in which black newspapers bitterly criticized him for his actions. Soon afterward, the man who might have been the greatest dribbler ever to bounce a basketball formed his own all-star team, which toured the world for the next 40 years as the Harlem Magicians.

The Warriors had Davis, George, and Beck, though, and with their signing, Gottlieb was looking toward the future. But he had to look past the 1953–54 season in a scaled-down league that had been reduced to nine teams. Although much improved over the previous year, the Warriors still managed no more than a 29–43 record, finishing above only the forlorn Baltimore Bullets in the division.

After purchasing the Warriors in 1952, The Mogul tried to peer into the future.
(Temple University Libraries, Urban Archives, Philadelphia, Pennsylvania)

When he wasn't making the club's decisions, something he and only he did, Gottlieb busied himself with extemporaneous affairs. He continued without success to lobby his friends in City Hall to allow Sunday basketball games. "Basketball has the potential to attract at least 20,000 fans to Sunday college and pro doubleheaders at Convention Hall and the Palestra," he said. "I can't see what crime there is in basketball on Sunday. If football and baseball are allowed, why not basketball?"

While arranging for five Warriors games to be televised on Annenberg's WFIL-TV—a certain revenue producer—Gottlieb was also growing increasingly unhappy with what he viewed as extravagant players' salaries. He claimed that NBA salaries consumed 75 to 80 percent of a team's costs, while in other pro sports, they amounted to just 25 to 30 percent. To offset the high pay in basketball, he proposed smaller rosters and more time on the court for players. "What's so strenuous about 30 or 35 minutes of basketball to make a good buck if you don't have anything else to do in a 24-hour period?" he asked.

Gottlieb was as unsuccessful in getting that proposal accepted as he was in convincing the city fathers that basketball should be played on Sundays in Philadelphia. (That finally happened in 1957 with the backing of Mayor Richardson Dilworth.) He was also once again unsuccessful at yanking the Warriors up from the dregs of the Eastern Division. Although the team's record improved to 33–39 and Johnston and Arizin —now back from the Marines—finished one-two in the league in scoring (Johnston also led the league in rebounds), the Warriors finished fourth out of five in the division and failed to make the playoffs for the third straight year. The team drew so poorly that it played games in places like Collingswood, New Jersey; New Haven, Connecticut; White Plains, New York; and Grand Rapids, Michigan.

Of even more significance, though, was Gottlieb's physical condition. Late in the season, he had become ill. Ultimately, he appointed his assistant, George Senesky, as interim coach and was admitted to the hospital where he underwent gallbladder surgery. As he recuperated, eating a diet heavily loaded with parsley and watercress, Gottlieb lost 50 pounds. He also made the difficult decision not to return as coach, announcing that he was leaving the job at a Chamber of Commerce luncheon. Thus, after piloting basketball teams for more than 30 years, Gotty's career on the sidelines of basketball courts throughout the country had come to an abrupt end.

In nearly nine years as coach of the Warriors, Gottlieb finished with a 263–318 (.452) record. His teams appeared in six post-season playoffs, winning 15 and losing 17. Under Gotty, the Warriors went to the league final twice, winning the championship once.

What kind of a coach was Gottlieb during his nearly nine years of guiding the Warriors?

Opinions vary. There is no dispute, however, over the intensity the man brought to the bench.

He'd yell and curse. He'd frown and cast dirty looks. He'd throw his coat. His blood pressure would rise. His face would turn red. "He coached like a busted fire hydrant," wrote Sandy Grady in the *Evening Bulletin*. It all gave the appearance that Gotty was putting himself through some brutal form of torture. Or was it just an act, some wondered? "If it's an act, then I ought to be in Hollywood," The Mogul said.

Charley Eckman, originally a referee before becoming coach of the Fort Wayne Pistons, had a special description of Gotty's antics on the sidelines. "When Eddie was coaching," Eckman said, "he didn't just sit on the bench. He owned it. He'd take off his coat and throw it on the floor if he didn't like an official's call. In some games, he was throwing so many clothes around, you had a feeling he would be down to his drawers by the time it was over."

After blowing up, Gottlieb would usually calm down quickly. A fit never lasted more than a few minutes. Unless, of course, the Warriors lost.

"He absolutely hated to lose," said Jerry Rullo. "When we did, he'd get very upset. He was a very hard loser. Once, we lost a couple of games on the road, and we're coming home on a train. We had a two-hour layover. He made us all go into the men's room for a meeting. He paid the janitor a couple of bucks to tell people the room was out of order. When we all got inside, he started going around the room. The first guy he started to pick on was Matt Guokas. Eddie's saying, 'Here's what you need to do,' and 'Here's what you're not doing.' Matt hated to lose, too, and he's getting madder and madder. Pretty soon, they get into a big argument. We thought they were going to come to blows, right there in the men's room."

Arizin said that Gottlieb "was not a good man to be near if we'd lost. If a loss came on the road, and afterward we were going to the airport or back to the hotel, the players would scramble to stay away from him. There would be six or seven players in one cab and maybe one or two in the other cab with Gotty. And if you did wind up riding in the cab with him, you had better either keep your mouth shut or not be in any sort of a happy mood. If you were talking about anything else but the game, he'd really let you have it."

The great Warriors forward remembered the time that Gottlieb became particularly angry at the play of freshman center Ron Livingston. "We'd lost a close game in Rochester, and a lot of the players were sitting around the hotel lobby," Arizin said. "There were a lot of people in the lobby, and they didn't know who we were. Suddenly, Eddie comes in, and he starts yelling at the top of his lungs at Ronnie. 'If I was as big as you,' he screamed, 'I'd be the best player in the world.' And then he went over and kicked Ronnie in the shins. People were looking at him like, what is this guy, crazy? But that's the way Eddie operated. And you had to be ready for it."

On the other hand, Gottlieb presented an entirely different picture when the team won. "If we won, he would be very, very happy," said Beck. "He'd smile and congratulate everybody. He simply loved to win and hated to lose."

After every game, Gottlieb grabbed the stat sheets and poured over them. He critiqued each player's performance. If he didn't like what he saw or if the team had lost, the locker room would reverberate with the sounds of Gotty's tirade.

There was a game against the Knicks, for instance, when Joe Graboski led a fast break down the court with less than one minute to play and the Warriors up by one point. Grabbo went up for a dunk shot, missed it, and the ball bounced off the rim. Carl Braun snatched the rebound, raced the length of the court, and bagged a layup as the buzzer sounded. The Knicks won by one.

"Eddie chewed us out up and down," remembered George Dempsey. "It was unbelievable. He used words I didn't know what they were. They sounded like cusswords. He went on for about half an hour. I've never seen anybody so mad."

Players had to report to the locker room 45 minutes before a game. Gottlieb did not make an appearance in the room until about 15 minutes prior to game time. Before that, he spent his time at the ticket office, checking on ticket sales, money, and looking after other administrative affairs. After he arrived, Gotty gave the team a pep talk, went over the opposing lineup, and sent his men out to the court.

"Eddie always painted a dismal picture," Arizin said. "He'd say those stars on the other team could shoot from outside, they could drive. Those guys are great. If you listened to him talk about them, you'd get the idea that we can't beat this team. But I think that was his way of getting us to play at full speed."

Once they got to the floor before a game, Gottlieb always had the club perform snappy, enthusiastic warm-up drills. A lot of movement and a lot of chatter were trademarks of the team's pre-game activities. Meanwhile, Gottlieb busied himself being sociable. He was, according to Williams in an article in the *Inquirer,* "the picture of composure, chatting with the officials, greeting newspapermen, shaking hands with the fans. But when the referee tosses up the ball for the opening tap, 'I begin to bleed,' said Gotty."

In a game in Toronto one time, the Warriors had a 22-point lead with less than one minute to play. But one of the Warriors threw a bad pass. Gottlieb immediately called a time out. "What the hell was the idea of that?" he roared. "Cool off," one of the players said. "We're a mile ahead, aren't we?" "You should get so careless," Gotty screamed. "Do that again, and you'll all walk home."

Gottlieb, who wouldn't change his clothes when the Warriors were winning, was often known to plead with his players when they were performing poorly. "My boys, my boys," he'd say. "What are you doing to me?" Most of the time, if a player did something Gotty didn't like, he'd do more than plead. He'd scream and yell at the unfortunate rascal, which, of course, is not considered in the coaching manuals as a recommended way to instill confidence in your players.

Nevertheless, The Mogul was quite adept at getting the maximum effort from his players. "He knew how to handle players," observed Ralph Bernstein. "He had some real characters, but he always knew how to handle them."

If somebody gave him trouble, though, Gottlieb usually knew how to deal with the problem. "If you missed a couple of shots or otherwise were messing things up, your tail was on the bench," said Bill Campbell. "He didn't stand for any crap. He was a disciplinarian, and he ran a real tight ship."

"Gottlieb had a different relationship with each player," Mlkvy said. "He treated Fulks differently. He tried to coddle him. He would scream at Senesky. 'You're the captain of the team. I want more out of you.' Some guys he'd yell at. Others, he'd just let them alone. 'Play the game you want to play,' he'd say."

Gottlieb's technical ability as a coach produced differing views. Some said he had little to do with the shape of a game. Others credited him for his keen knowledge of the game.

"He was not much of a coach," claimed Jack Ramsay, who compiled a splendid record as a coach himself at St. Joseph's College, and with the 76ers, Buffalo Braves, and Portland Trailblazers, who beat the 76ers for the 1976–77 NBA title. "He was not an X and O guy by any means. His strength was getting good players to play together and win."

Dolph Schayes said that Gottlieb "coached by the seat of his pants. He didn't have a lot of strategy," he said. "He coached based on the star theory. He thought a big scorer would bring in people. That was important to him. He also thought it was very important to get local players on the team so they would draw. These theories were not true. It was better to have a winning team."

Gottlieb sometimes arranged exhibition games during the season when the Warriors had a couple of days off. One time, the team was playing in Allentown. "Somebody had put together an amateur team and guaranteed Eddie a few dollars," recalled Beck. "At halftime, we're only winning by a couple of points. In the locker room, he screamed at the top of his lungs at us. 'You're professionals, and you better not lose to these guys,' he yelled. He didn't always know why we were losing. I don't think he knew much about the science of the game. He couldn't really analyze why you did or didn't do something. He couldn't say that the defense did this or did that. In general, he would just let you know that you weren't playing well."

The way Norm Drucker saw it, Gottlieb had both pluses and minuses. "He was a hands-on coach," the referee said. "I think you would consider him a good coach. But he didn't put fire into his teams like Red Auerbach did. Philadelphia always had good players, even after Gotty stopped coaching, but the difference in his teams and Red's showed up in the fact that Boston won nine titles."

Gottlieb's skills as an organizer provided strong support to his skills as a coach. "His practices, his drills were very well organized," Mlkvy said. "We always had scrimmages, five on five. He'd set up plays. But he never really coached. He'd say, 'I'm not going to spend time with you and tell you how to shoot. You already know how to shoot.' To be honest, he was really more of a promoter, an organizer, an administrator than he was a coach. He was an expert promoter. That was his gift. I remember if we didn't have too many in the stands he'd get very upset."

"He was really a combination coach and promoter," recalled Frank Dolson. "His primary interest was getting a good crowd at the game. He was very conscious of how many people the club was drawing. Of course, he realized that a winning team had a lot to do with that. So he always wanted to put a good club on the floor."

Both before and during the season, Gottlieb brought the Warriors to Temple three or four times a year for a scrimmage with his friend

Harry Litwack's team. Sometimes Gotty also took his team to La Salle for practice sessions. One year, Gotty scheduled a game in Hazelton so Mlkvy's Palmerton fans and followers of Senesky from his nearby hometown of Mahanoy City could see their local favorites in action. This, The Mogul believed, was another way that the Warriors could spread goodwill among basketball followers, thereby building attendance at their games.

Although his willingness not to engage in the finer points of the game was well known, Gottlieb's knowledge of basketball was seldom dismissed. "He knew the game, and he knew it well," said Bernstein. "Gotty was one of the smartest people in the NBA. He knew how to plan the offense. Of course, defense in the league at that time was just a rumor. It was all shooting."

When you had shooters such as Fulks, Arizin, and Johnston and one coaches the way Gottlieb did, the technicalities of the game become less important. There were few set plays. Just let the boys go out and pepper the basket. And then let them know how they're doing.

"Eddie's sitting on the bench, and you'd take a shot," said Arizin. "Maybe he didn't think it was a good shot, so he'd be yelling, 'No. No. No.' But if the player took the shot and it went in, he'd give a big cheer. He'd jump off the bench and yell, 'Yea.' So, his opinion of whether it was a good shot or a bad shot changed. If it went in, it was a good shot. If it didn't, it was a bad shot."

Gottlieb also had his views on dribbling. He didn't like it. "We had many practices with a ball that had the air taken out of it so you couldn't dribble," Arizin said. "He emphasized passing. He wanted the guards to bring the ball up court passing it back and forth. When we had Phillip and Senesky, they controlled the whole game. He didn't want me to dribble unless I was going to the basket. He told us that every time we put the ball on the court, there's a chance that a good defensive man will steal it. So don't do it, he'd insist."

Dempsey was a rookie in 1954, having been summoned to the Warriors after playing with the SPHAS. In his first game, held at Madison Square Garden against the Knicks, Dempsey didn't play during the first half. "I figured, I could sit on the bench and look at Gottlieb and maybe learn something," Dempsey remembered. "We were losing pretty badly at the half, and when we went into the locker room, he laid into me because I was looking at him. The way he operated, if he could blame something on somebody, he would. If we lost, he'd blame it on somebody. So, when we went back out, Graboski was sitting next to me on the bench. He

On one of the summer tours he made with the Harlem Globetrotters, Gottlieb viewed the sights in London with Red Klotz. *(Temple University Libraries, Urban Archives, Philadelphia, Pennsylvania)*

said, 'Don't look at him. Put your head down and look at the floor.' From then on in the rest of the games I played for Eddie, I never looked at him.

"The funny thing about that game," Dempsey added, "was he put me in in the second half. He told me I'd be guarding Dick McGuire. 'Do whatever you want to do,' he said. "I held McGuire down, scored 15 points, and we won. Then we came home and the next night we're playing Syracuse. Now he's all buddy-buddy. He said, 'When I put you in, you do whatever you want to do.' I was a shooter in high school and college, and I scored 15 points again while holding Paul Seymour to five. I figured that was pretty good. Afterward, Gotty said to me, 'I want you to feed Paul and Neil.' It was all kind of confusing."

Many times, Gottlieb's duties as a coach strayed into off-court issues. One of those involved Howie Dallmar, who for one season tried to split his time between playing with the Warriors and serving as head basketball coach at Penn. Occasionally, Dallmar had to miss a Warriors game because of a coaching obligation. That infuriated Gotty. He told the former Stanford and Penn player that he had to make up his mind: either play or coach, but don't do both.

"The Warriors were playing in Boston one night, and Howie couldn't travel with the team because he had an afternoon game at the Palestra," recalled Campbell, who was then broadcasting the club's games. "I was going up on a plane later because I had an afternoon game, too. Eddie called me and said, 'Make sure Howie gets on the plane with you.' He didn't care about me being there. He wanted Howie there. So I called Howie and told him I'd meet him at a certain time, and we'd go to the airport together.

"When we got to the airport, we had about a half hour to kill," Campbell continued. "We went to a lunch counter, and we're sitting there, and Howie looks out the window. 'Look at that plane against the setting sun,' he said. 'Isn't that a beautiful sight? Somebody ought to paint that.' Then he said, 'Holy shit, that's our plane.' We got a later plane and arrived at Boston Garden just before the game. Eddie didn't say a word to Howie. But he jumped all over me. 'I told you to make sure he got on the goddamned plane,' he roared. Oh, did he lay me out."

Travel in the early days of the NBA was always a hit or miss proposition. Often, a trip to an away game was blotted with foul-ups. Mishaps and mistakes were ever-present parts of a team's itinerary.

Trips were not without humor, too. Once, Senesky was driving the lead car from Philadelphia to a game in Toronto. "How do I get there?" he asked Gottlieb. "It's easy. Just go north to Wilkes-Barre and turn left," came the reply.

Originally, the Warriors traveled mostly by cars, usually two or three at a time. First they were Fords. Then they were Buicks. As time went on, the team increasingly used trains and airplanes. Although Gottlieb dreaded airplanes—often moaning and complaining on flights that he was sick—the Warriors were the first team to fly.

"Even in the early years, we did some traveling by plane," recalled Ralph Kaplowitz. "Senesky always sat next to me because he was afraid to fly. I had been a pilot in World War II, so if he heard a strange noise, he had me to tell him what it was." During one plane flight, oil from an engine kept splashing on the windows. "That's all right," Kaplowitz told a frightened Senesky. "We still have three more to go."

Then there was the time Kaplowitz and his teammates were flying on a plane that was supposedly trying to set a record for the fastest time from Philadelphia to St. Louis. "About five minutes into the flight, we saw smoke," he recalled. "We told a hostess, and she called the captain, and all of the sudden the plane banked sharply. 'We are turning around because we forgot the dinners,' a voice said. As we approached for a landing, we could see emergency equipment all lined up. They fixed the problem, and soon we were back in the air."

Traveling by airplane was often somewhat strained. "Once we got lost in fog," recalled Beck. "We were supposed to land in St. Louis, but landed instead in Kansas City."

Senesky seemed to be in the center of many Warriors travel stories. Take the time the team was sitting in a plane at the Newark Airport awaiting a flight to Rochester. After the flight had experienced a two-hour delay, Senesky looked at his watch. "If we don't do something, we're going to be in trouble," he told Gottlieb. With that, Gotty ordered the pilot to taxi the plane back to the terminal. He then sent the players, most of whom had been asleep, off the plane, went to the nearest phone, and hired three taxi cabs to drive the team to Rochester. Mindful that by not appearing, the Warriors faced a league fine of $5,000, Gottlieb elected to pay about $800 for cab fare. The Warriors arrived at the arena 15 minutes before game time. Royals owner Les Harrison, thinking of the big crowd on hand, delayed the game for another 15 minutes. With no warm-ups, the Warriors took the floor and proceeded to suffer one of their most one-sided losses of the season.

Another time, the team was again flying to Rochester. Senesky was hurt and didn't make the trip. Temple alumnus Nelson Bobb was scheduled to take his place in the lineup, but on arrival discovered he'd forgotten his uniform. "Call George at the deli where he eats," someone suggested. Bobb complied, but when he asked for Senesky, the counterman who answered the phone, said in broken English, "We have sturgeon, sardines, sable, and salmon, but no Senesky." When Bobb persisted, the man told him, "We even have lox, but no Senesky." Then he abruptly hung up. Gottlieb fined Bobb for not having a uniform.

Bill Campbell remembered a quite different traveling experience. "Eddie hated to fly," he said. "And he got sick almost every trip. We're coming back from somewhere, and he's sitting in a seat on the aisle. Matt Guokas is sitting on the opposite side in an aisle seat. All of the sudden, Eddie got very sick. He's not only sick, but he's mad as hell because the team had just played badly. He's about to throw up, and Matt hands him one of those containers they carry on airplanes. Eddie throws up, and as sick as he was, he turns to Guokas. 'Matt,' he said, 'that was the best pass you made all night.'"

For the most part in the early days, automobile was the preferred mode of transportation. "We'd travel all over the Midwest in cars during the exhibition season," said Arizin. "Some days, we'd make trips of several hundred miles in a day. Everybody would be saying, 'Let's stop and eat, Eddie, we're hungry.' But he'd say, 'No, we have to get there.' He wasn't a big eater, so it didn't bother him. A lot of times, we'd get to where we were going without eating at all. Once in a while, though, we'd stop and have an ice cream cone."

Beck remembered the time the team was driving to upstate New York for a couple of exhibition games. For some reason, Gottlieb was down to one car. Beck had just bought a new car, and Gotty asked him if he'd drive it to the game. Beck agreed. "But somewhere between Saratoga and Elmira, we had an accident," he said. "A guy sideswiped me. Arizin, Graboski, and Tom Gola were with me. The car was a mess. The insurance company paid for part of the repair work, and Eddie picked up the rest. To me, that was Eddie. He didn't have to do it, but he did."

On short trips, Gottlieb often hired a bus. "Twelve or 13 players plus a couple of writers and broadcasters would get on," recalled Campbell. "Gotty would figure right off the top of his head what the charge was and what the change should be. He'd give the bus driver $40 and say, 'Give me $1.75 back.' He knew exactly what the charge and the change were."

On long-distance trips, when the team had a few days between games, Gottlieb usually packed the players on a train. Trips, such as ones to St. Louis, were overnight jaunts with players using sleeper cars. That saved Gottlieb money because he didn't have to pay a hotel bill.

For Gottlieb in those days, money was scarce. And a dollar saved was a dollar earned.

It would not be long, though, before The Mogul's financial condition took a decidedly upward turn.

CHAPTER 12

Integration Arrives

Although the Warriors did poorly as a team, the 1954 season was filled with milestones. Eddie Gottlieb handed the coaching reigns to George Senesky. Neil Johnston and Paul Arizin finished one-two in the league in scoring. And Gotty had begun putting together a team that one season later would carry the NBA championship back to Philadelphia.

The 1954 season was also noteworthy for another reason, one that had more long-term significance than any of the others. It was the season in which the first African American player became a full-fledged member of the Warriors.

His name was John (Jackie) Moore, a former Overbrook High School and La Salle College player. Moore made his debut with the Warriors during the season, then joined the roster for the entire campaign the following year.

Despite Gottlieb's long affiliation with African American athletes, Moore's presence on the Warriors did not place him among the NBA's earliest black players. The first black athlete to play in an NBA game was Earl Lloyd, who made his debut on October 31, 1950, with the Syracuse Nationals. Chuck Cooper was the first black player drafted (on April 25, 1950), but he made his NBA debut with the Boston Celtics one night after Lloyd. The following week, Nat (Sweetwater) Clifton made his first appearance with the New York Knicks.

Before the three players signed, Gottlieb had already made his feelings known at an NBA meeting in 1949 where Knicks owner Ned Irish first sought to bring Clifton into the league. Irish had brought the matter of accepting black players to a vote, but lost. Six months later, he raised the issue again, and, threatening to pull his team from the league if the other owners wouldn't let him sign Clifton, he won backing by a 6–5 margin.

Gottlieb was not happy. "In the first place," he said to Irish, "your players will be 75 percent black in five years, and you're not going to draw people. You're going to be a disservice to the game." Having said that, Gottlieb stomped out of the meeting, calling Irish "a dumb SOB." Gotty added: "You've ruined professional basketball."

During his career, Gottlieb, who once made the statement that "black players can't play basketball," was never one to avoid controversy. Often outspoken, always opinionated, and as Ken Berman said, "would argue until doomsday if he had to prove his point," Gotty was frequently a willing participant in contestable issues. The greater the debate, the better he liked it. The dispute over integrating the NBA was no exception, and The Mogul was heavily involved.

The controversy was still swirling when a few weeks after the NBA meeting Gottlieb told team owners, "We [the Warriors] will never sign anybody because he is a Jew, a Negro, Irishman, or a Chinaman. We sign players purely on the basis of ability." To this he added, "We will continue to run a white club as long as possible."

Long before that proclamation, African American basketball had a long and distinguished history, dating all the way back to 1902 when Harry (Bucky) Lewis became the first black professional player while competing for a team in Lowell, Massachusetts, in the otherwise all-white New England Basketball League. The first all-black league was formed in 1912 as the Colored Intercollegiate Athletic Association.

By the late 1920s, black basketball was becoming increasingly popular in the African American community. Both the New York Renaissance in the East and the Harlem Globetrotters in the Midwest were attracting big crowds. There were even black women's teams, one of the best being the Philadelphia Tribunes, a group that played from the 1920s until 1940 and was sponsored by the local newspaper of the same name.

In 1931, George Gregory of Columbia University became the first black All-American basketball player. Six black players on a team of 10 performed with the Chicago Studebakers when they won the National

Basketball League championship in 1942. In 1948, Don Barksdale, an All-American from UCLA, was the first black member of the United States Olympic basketball team, and in 1953 he was the first black player to appear in an NBA All-Star Game.

At the end of the decade of the 1940s, as a major segment of the African American population relocated from the South to the North, blacks had begun to replace Jews and other minority groups on the basketball courts in the inner cities. Although it was not reflected by the presence of African Americans on most high school, college, or even pro teams, basketball was rapidly becoming the second most popular sport of blacks, ranking behind baseball.

Nevertheless, by the late 1940s black basketball was mainly viewed in the context of the Globetrotters. The Globies, stressing magical ball-handling, sleight-of-hand tricks, their own rules of play, and rollicking comedy, were the only truly visible representative of black basketball, and they were extremely popular among fans wherever they played. And they were regarded as a major source of income by NBA teams, which frequently scheduled them to play one game of a doubleheader, often giving them top billing and almost always being the recipients of a sold-out house.

As always, Gottlieb put the size of the crowd above all other matters. And he, as well as other team leaders, was unwilling to disrupt the benefits that the Globetrotters brought to his bank account by signing players from their roster. Sometimes Globies games drew three times the crowd that the Warriors attracted. There was certainly no desire to tamper with the whims of Globies owner Abe Saperstein; no one, least of all Gotty, wanted to be on the wrong side of such a good cash cow. Because it was also believed that Saperstein really controlled the destinies of black players, they were routinely ignored by the NBA. Some felt, there was even an unwritten agreement among team owners to ban blacks from the NBA, although Celtics coach Red Auerbach, who had invited four black players to training camp in Cooper's first year in 1950 (one was future Phillies' infielder Chuck Harmon), led a chorus of denials.

With Gottlieb, the hands-off approach had additional angles. Eddie and Abe had been friends since their days together as booking agents for black baseball teams. When he bought the Warriors, Gotty had taken in Saperstein as one of the team's stockholders. The Mogul, as well as Dave Zinkoff, also traveled with the Globetrotters on their annual summer trips to Europe, arranging the team's schedule and handling promotion. It was a special time of year for Gottlieb, one he always relished.

Abe Saperstein (left) was a long-time friend and associate of Gottlieb's before they parted ways. Here Gotty is about to begin one of his many summer overseas trips with the Harlem Globetrotters, along with Red Klotz (second from left), Dave Zinkoff (right), and (back row from left) Cy Kaselman, Rookie Brown, and Frank Washington. *(Courtesy of Jim Rosen)*

"When we took those trips, you always saw a different side of Eddie," noted Ernie Beck, one of a number of Warriors, including George Senesky, Paul Arizin, Bill Mlkvy, George Dempsey, and others, each of whom made the trip as a member of the opposing team. "He just enjoyed himself. During the season, he was always very tense. But on Globetrotters trips, he was much more friendly, much more relaxed."

In the summer of 1952, Gotty had accompanied Saperstein on his most ambitious junket, a 168-day world tour during which the Globies played 141 games against a team of college all-stars before 1.5 million people on five continents. There was no way Gotty was going to cut himself out of such perks or to rob Saperstein of any of his essential assets by signing black players for the Warriors. Beside, when Cooper and Clifton, both former Globetrotters, had entered the NBA a few years earlier, Saperstein blew a gasket. Gottlieb didn't want to see that happen again. "I have no intentions of arguing with Abe over his players," Gottlieb told Malcolm Poindexter in the Philadelphia *Tribune*.

When it was pointed out that a roster that included African American players might put black people in the stands at NBA games, Gottlieb rejected the idea. "Look at how many colored people come out to see the Harlem Globetrotters play," he said. "If we had to depend on them to support our club, we would have been out of business a long time ago."

Slowly, though, Gottlieb's position softened. Perhaps, he thought, it was okay to invite black players into the NBA because they just might bring black spectators to games. But he issued one caveat. "He thought the NBA should negotiate with Saperstein for every black player it wanted to sign," said Dolph Schayes. "Presumably, Saperstein would get a cut from each sale."

That was about as far as Gottlieb went. He didn't try to sign black players for his own team. Nor did he encourage others to sign them. It could not be said at the time that Gotty was in the forefront of the Civil Rights movement.

But his lack of action on behalf of black players was not viewed by most of his acquaintances as being a case of moral turpitude. "It certainly wasn't fueled by racism," said Frank Dolson. "I know he was not a racist by any stretch of the imagination. I think more than anything, he thought people wouldn't come out to see black players in the NBA. His motivation was strictly money."

Paul Arizin verified Gottlieb's open-minded regard for blacks. "I don't think Eddie had any prejudice at all," he said. "Black players weren't going to college in the numbers they are today, and I don't know if there were that many to choose from. As a player, I never thought about whether a player was black or white. I played against John Chaney, Zack Clayton, guys like that, in the schoolyards. They were accepted. The only rule you gauged a black guy by was whether or not he was a good player. That was no different than the way you gauged a white guy."

Nevertheless, Gottlieb and the Warriors were roundly chastised by African Americans and in some areas of the press for not signing black players, although in 1952 he actually had scouted an African American player in a black church league. Gotty claimed later that it was merely as a favor to a black preacher he knew. But hadn't he tried to sign Marquis Haynes in 1953? "He was very sensitive to the fact that he didn't have any black players," said Alan Levitt. "He was looking very hard for ones he could sign."

It was generally agreed that Gottlieb was really more interested in the accuracy of a player's jump shot than the color of his skin. "It didn't matter to him whether you were black, red, or green," Jack Ramsay claimed. "If you could play, that's all he was interested in."

Even those who had played with the Philadelphia Stars claimed that they saw no traces of prejudicial behavior on Gotty's part. Stanley Glenn summarized that view when he said: "Color had nothing to do with the way he saw the players. If you were a good player, he put you on the team. It was as simple as that."

Moore was such a player. He had an exceptional jump shot, he could leap high into the air, he worked hard, and he hustled all the time. That's all that mattered. When Gottlieb needed a player late in the 1954–55 season, Moore was his man.

"I was playing in the Eastern League at the time," recalled Jerry Rullo. "Gottlieb was always looking for players. He'd ask me all the time, 'Have you seen anybody?' One time I told him about Jackie. He was a very good player, and I thought he'd fit in with the Warriors."

Moore was a home-grown athlete who had helped Overbrook High win three straight city titles, leading the team in scoring in his senior year. He had gone to college at La Salle where he was a solid contributor on the Explorers' 1952 NIT championship team. The 6-foot, 5-inch forward had a tryout with the Syracuse Nats in 1954, but was cut after the first few games of the season. He then tried to hook on with the Milwaukee Blackhawks, but again lasted only a couple of games. He wound up in the Eastern League and was still playing there when Gottlieb signed him to a Warriors contract late in the season.

The West Philly native appeared in 23 games with the Warriors in 1955, averaging 4.8 points per game. "He was a good player," Rullo said. "He was a very steady player. He got things done."

Although he was the Warriors' first African American player, Moore said that his joining the team wasn't regarded as a big deal. "Nothing was really made of it," he claimed. "There was no fanfare. It was just something that happened. Why did Gottlieb wait so long to sign black players? I don't know the reason. But I was happy to join the team because I already knew most of the guys. La Salle had scrimmaged the Warriors several times."

Ironically, when Moore became the Warriors' first African American player—the Warriors were the sixth NBA team to sign a black—he preceded the first black player to appear in a Phillies regular-season game (John Kennedy) by three years. And that was despite the fact that Jackie Robinson had joined the Brooklyn Dodgers three years before black players entered the NBA. (The Athletics had a black pitcher named Bob Trice in 1954.)

Jackie Moore came out of
La Salle College to become in
1955 the first African American
player on the Warriors. *(Courtesy
of LaSalle University)*

Like black baseball play-
ers, black basketball players also suffered the pains of
bigotry.

"Sometimes, we had exhi-
bition games in Virginia, and
had to eat in separate restaurants," Moore recalled. "We
played in Dayton, and they wouldn't serve us. In St. Louis, we stayed in a
different and smaller hotel."

Beck recalled those days with a bad taste in his mouth. "I remember
one time in the train station in St. Louis, Jackie, Paul, and I went into the
bar to have a beer while we were waiting. The bartender said to Jackie,
'Get out of here.' That was terrible."

Moore said that Gottlieb treated him no differently than he did white
players. "He was fair. If he saw something good, he'd let you know. If he
saw something he didn't like, he'd let you know about that, too. It didn't
matter who you were. His relationship with black players was nothing special. With everybody, he maintained the usual owner-player relationship.
He tried to work with everybody as much as he could."

When the 1955–56 season began, Moore had beaten out some
tough competition to become a full-fledged member of the team. He
was no longer a late-season pickup. He was an integral part of a team
that was headed for the NBA championship. And he made a substantial
contribution.

Coming off the bench as a key reserve, Moore was a valuable rebounder
and a timely scorer. "He was always rated a very good driver, as the opposition was prone to find out in crucial moments," wrote Bob McGowan of
the *Daily News*. "Now, rival teams can't lay off him on the outside anymore
because he can pop those shots in with accuracy or drive up the middle.
Most experts will agree that Moore is a handy fellow to have around."

While Moore broke the ice for black players on the Warriors, others soon followed. Woody Sauldsberry, a fine outside shooter who had played with the Globetrotters, joined the team in 1957. One year later, another former Trotter, Andy Johnson, became a Warrior. By then, Gottlieb was also drafting black players as first-round territorial picks, too. In keeping with his plan to choose local players in an attempt to attract fans to the Warriors, he selected a pair of flashy lefthanded Temple guards who had led the Owls to the Final Four in the NCAA tournament in 1956, Hal Lear in 1956 and Guy Rodgers in 1958. Then he exercised the territorial rule for high school players that he had initiated several years earlier by choosing Wilt Chamberlain in 1959.

Even as late as the early 1960s, there was thought to be an unwritten rule among owners that no team could have more than three African American players on its roster at one time. Moreover, in the early years that black players entered the NBA, they were for the most part not supposed to be high scorers. They were expected to rebound, set picks, and play good defense.

Auerbach broke the code when he became the first coach to start an all-African American lineup when he did it with the Celtics in 1960. That convinced other teams to relax the so-called agreement, and by the mid-1960s, most teams were amply staffed with black players. By then, Gottlieb had erased any lingering thoughts about his unwillingness to play black players, even becoming a man who was regarded as a leader in the effort to put blacks on his team.

That view was echoed in an article in the *Evening Bulletin* by Frank Brady. "He is one of the few men I have known who can say in an hour of conversation 'colored,' 'Negro,' and 'black'—and use each adjective with dignity and without phoney condescension," Brady wrote. "Gottlieb grew with his years. He helped open doors for the black athlete."

In recent, years, Sonny Hill praised Gottlieb's role in the black community. "He was always good to me, and I know how good he was to other black players," Hill said. "Ultimately, the Warriors had more black players than anybody else. He was a role model for all of us in the Philadelphia area. To have someone of his magnitude take an interest in us was something that all of us cherished. He was ahead of his time. And I'm not sure they've caught up with him yet."

For many years, Hill ran the Baker League, a league in which pros and college players performed together in what was one of the most highly regarded summer circuits in the country. When he died, Gottlieb left money in his will to the league. "That was an indication of the kind of relationship the two of us had," Hill said. "We [the Baker League] were strictly a hand-to-mouth operation, but the money gave us stability. When you say Eddie Gottlieb to me, you are talking about a great man."

In 1960, Gottlieb drafted guard Al Attles out of North Carolina AT&T in the fifth round. Attles went on to a 40-year career with the Warriors, first as a player for 11 years with Philadelphia and San Francisco, then as a coach for more than 13 years, during which time he became the first black coach to guide a team (the Golden State Warriors) to an NBA championship, and finally as a top executive with the team.

A relatively unknown black player such as Attles, a native of Newark, New Jersey, might have been short-changed by some owners. But that was not quite the case with Gottlieb. "When I went into his office to talk about a contract, he was shuffling some papers and looking really busy," Attles recalled. "He said, 'How much do you want?' I said, '$7,500.' Without looking up, he said, 'That's too much.' Now, I'm thinking, I'll go back to Newark and get a job teaching school. But he took a piece of paper, wrote something down, and slid it across the desk to me. It said $5,000. He saw the look on my face, and said, 'I'll give you $500 more.' At the end of the season, he gave me a bonus, and we made some money from the playoffs, so I wound up with $7,500.

"Eddie Gottlieb was one of the pillars of the league," Attles added. "He had a rough exterior, but a great heart. He was one of the nicest guys I ever met. When I came to the Warriors, I didn't know if I could make it or not. But the man had great integrity, and he showed it when he kept me and cut Pickles Kennedy, a second-round draft choice from Temple. He was white and a big hero in Philadelphia, and I was black and unknown. But he kept me, even though he always wanted to have local players on the team. I thought that was about as honest as anybody could get."

Ultimately, as more and more young black athletes filled the urban courts as well as the high school and college teams, basketball became a black man's game, just as it had been a Jewish man's game many years earlier. In 1956, there were only 22 black players in the NBA. By 1990, 75 percent of the NBA players were black. The number was up to 77 percent in 2005.

Black players had come a long, long way since the early days of pro basketball. Despite his original stance, Gottlieb had helped to pave the way.

CHAPTER 13

One Year at the Top

lthough there had been some changes in the NBA as the 1955–56 season began, none of them could really be called monumental. The Milwaukee Hawks had moved to St. Louis. New York Knicks legendary coach Joe Lapchick had retired, as had Max Zaslofsky, one of only two players remaining from the original BAA. Not much else had changed. To most observers, it looked like just another season.

Eddie Gottlieb knew otherwise. One year earlier, his Warriors had missed the playoffs for the third straight year. But this season was going to be different. This season was going to be the one in which the Warriors erased the word "mediocre" from their description. Gottlieb could sense it, even if nobody else could.

Gotty had figured out what made the 1954–55 team play less than .500 ball. "We need a shooting guard," he said. "But we don't have one."

The Mogul had tried an assortment of young players at the position. Rookie Gene Shue out of Maryland had been given a shot, but Gotty had given up and traded him during the season to the Knicks. Another freshman, Niagara's Larry Costello, was tried and also found wanting. Yet a third newcomer, George Dempsey from King's College, was called up from the SPHAS and put to the test, but Gottlieb told him to concentrate on defense even though he had always been a high scorer.

The answer to the problem resided almost in the shadow of Gottlieb's paunchy figure, the one that Red Smith had once described as "about the size and shape of a beer keg." Up on the north side of Philadelphia at 20th Street and Olney Avenue, Tom Gola had put little La Salle College on the basketball map with such stellar play that he had made the All-American team three years in a row.

Rejecting the chance to play at Duke, North Carolina State, or any of numerous other basketball factories, Gola had moved virtually from one building on one side of the street to another across the street as he attended La Salle High School on the same campus as La Salle College. While becoming one of the top players in the country, Gola led the unheralded Explorers to the NIT championship as a freshman in 1952, then sparked his team to the NCAA title in 1954, beating vaunted Bradley in the final game.

Playing for Ken Loeffler, who had been coach of the St. Louis Bombers and the Providence Steamrollers in the early years of the BAA, Gola averaged more than 20 points per game for his four varsity seasons at La Salle. What's more, standing 6 feet, 6 inches, he played center, forward, and guard. "He had the strength and timing to rebound with the biggest centers, the ball handling and passing and outside shooting to play back-court with the best of them, and the speed and inside moves to play All-American forward," wrote basketball writer Neil Isaacs.

Gottlieb saw Gola as the solution to his search for an all-around guard who could shoot. Thanks once again to the territorial draft, the Warriors would soon learn whether one of the city's finest players of all time was the answer.

Seeing Gottlieb walking down the street, one would be reluctant to classify him as the owner of a professional sports team. His dour appearance, jowly face, sorrowful eyes with big circles around them, and baggy eyelids made him look more like a St. Bernard than a mogul. His clothes, none of which appeared to have just rolled out from any of New York's finest fashion houses, did nothing for his image, either.

Gottlieb always wore a suit and tie—in the office, to games, at dinner. In earlier years, he wore a regular necktie. Later, he leaned more toward bow ties. His suits, which he'd buy six at a time, were usually plain, dark colors. His dress shirts were either solid white or gray-blue, and he bought them five or six at a time, although in the summer, he was sometimes seen wearing sport shirts. Because his feet often hurt, Gotty's shoes were of the soft-soled variety.

"His clothes were always rumpled," said Frank Dolson. "He looked like any guy you'd meet on the street. From his appearance, you wouldn't think of him as the business tycoon he was."

But he was. And he was a good one, too. "He was a very, very bright guy," said Michael Richman, "probably one of the brightest men I've ever met in my life. He had a unique ability to see things other people didn't see. I don't think you could discuss Shakespeare or Einstein's Theory of Relativity with him, but sports were different. He was brilliant."

The 1955–56 season gave Gottlieb the chance to put his considerable sports—and business—acumen into practice. The foremost job was putting together a team that could win.

The Warriors already had the nucleus of a winner with Neil Johnston at center, Paul Arizin and Joe Graboski at forwards and Jack George at guard. Now, the team had added Gola. It also had an exceptional bench with Ernie Beck, Dempsey, Jackie Moore, Walter Davis, and Larry Hennessy, a first-year man from Villanova. Of this group, all but Johnston, Graboski, and Davis had either played locally or—like Dempsey, a native of Merchantville, New Jersey—were from the area. It was a team that not only had the potential to be good, it was—in keeping with Gotty's ongoing theory that the more local players he had, the more fans the team would put in the stands—a highly appealing club that would surely bring out the fans.

"The team had good balance," Dempsey recalled. "It had good unity. Everybody did what he had to do. And we had a deep bench. Moore was a good rebounder. So was Davis."

The 1955–56 Warriors were also a team for which the radio announcers were Bill Campbell and Chuck Thompson. Dr. Si Ball was the team doctor and Mickey McLaughlin was the trainer.

The team trained as usual at Hershey. Gottlieb scheduled 14 exhibition games. One was a doubleheader at Convention Hall in which the Warriors met the College All-Stars in one game and the Harlem Globetrotters faced Red Klotz's Washington Generals in the other skirmish. Because of the ever-changing schedules at facilities where they played, the Warriors were slated to appear in only 16 of their 72 regular-season games at Convention Hall. Other home games were scheduled for Lincoln High School, the Camden Armory, and the Arena. The Warriors also practiced on occasion at a gym at Fourth and Shunk Streets in South Philadelphia.

Gola broke his hand in the second exhibition game, played at Houlton, Maine, and Dempsey took his place. Despite the loss of Gola, once it

All-American Tom Gola out of La Salle College was just what the Warriors needed
to fill out the 1955 team. *(Courtesy of Rich Westcott)*

was evident that Gottlieb had put together what could be an exceptional
team, the Warriors became the pre-season favorites to win the Eastern
Division title.

The Warriors' home opener was held November 9 against the Minneapolis Lakers. Incredibly, the game was played at Lincoln High with
the Warriors winning, 117–106.

The following night, a record crowd of 18,245 jammed Madison
Square Garden to see the Warriors thump the Rochester Royals in the

first game of a doubleheader in what was billed as a battle between Arizin and Maurice Stokes.

Gola made his debut on November 17. The hometown phenom had originally wanted a contract for $17,500, but Gottlieb offered $11,500. Gola took the offer. (During the season, Gottlieb made up some of the difference by staging a night for Gola at which the rookie from North Philadelphia received a new car, clothes, and other gifts.) Now, he was finally in the lineup, and he wasted no time making his value apparent when he registered 15 assists, part of a team record 48, during a victory over the Lakers.

Warrior highlights continued as the early season progressed. Johnston scored 37 points in a game with Syracuse. George sank two foul shots to beat Syracuse for the team's seventh straight win. Hennessy set a career high with 18 points in a loss to the Boston Celtics, then came back two nights later to beat New York with a high, arching shot in the last minute of play. Beck scored nine points in the fourth quarter in a win over Fort Wayne. And on December 29, a record crowd of 11,236 battled through rain and sleet to watch the Warriors down the Nats.

The Warriors had become the best team in the league. "We had become an excellent team," Arizin recalled. "We played well together. We all got along well. We were eight or nine players deep. We knew the fundamentals. And we played good defense. We were very good."

It helped, of course, that Gola was playing superbly. "Tommy is living up to everything we expected of him and he will get better as he goes along," Hugh Brown quoted Gotty in an *Evening Bulletin* article. "Sure, he isn't scoring heavily because he's willing to sacrifice his scoring for the good of the team. But a player's value doesn't just depend on his scoring."

Gottlieb usually sat at the end of the press table near the Warriors' bench, although sometimes he perched in the first row of the stands directly behind the scorer's seat. Gotty had made George Senesky the coach, but he wasn't about to remove himself from the action. He no longer had many conversations with players about their performances on the court, but he did confer regularly with Senesky, a quiet person who said he spoke as little as possible because a professor at St. Joseph's had once told him, "Those who talk a lot, show people how stupid they are."

Although he still screamed at the referees—and occasionally overly critical fans—Gotty denied reports that he was the de facto coach, although he frequently gave instructions to Senesky. He insisted that Senesky, inex-

When he became coach in 1955, George Senesky (center) inherited standout players such as Paul Arizin (left) and Jack George. *(Courtesy of Rich Westcott)*

perienced as he was, was fully in charge of the team. "He needs to learn," Gottlieb said. "He can't learn if he doesn't do it himself."

Nonetheless, Gottlieb was never reluctant to insert his own views, as Beck illustrated. "If we were losing a game, and he had a big crowd, even though he was no longer the coach," Beck said, "he would come into the locker room at the half. You made sure you were not the first guy he saw because he would start screaming at whomever he saw first. He wouldn't holler at Paul. He never hollered at Paul. But he would holler at the rest of us, maybe Graboski, maybe me, maybe somebody else. It was funny in some ways because here he was the owner of the club hollering like that.

"I remember one game at Convention Hall," Beck continued. "We had a big crowd, and we won the game. But there was a young boy in charge of the towels. Eddie started hollering at him. 'Where are the rest of those towels? You stole them.' That was Eddie. He ran the whole operation. He had his hand in everything."

Campbell was well aware of that. "After Gotty became the owner, he became very frugal," the broadcaster said. "He got our traveling party down to 10 players, Senesky, and me. We didn't have single rooms, so I roomed with George. Eddie would call every night after the game to talk to George. He would say, why did you do this, why did you do that, how come you didn't do this? We'd go back to the hotel after a game, go to the room, and George wouldn't even have time to get his clothes off before the phone would ring.

"One night we're playing in St. Louis," Campbell remembered, "and Bob Pettit had missed four foul shots in a row. Late in the game, he had two foul shots, and I said on the air, 'We have Pettit on the line, and he's usually an excellent foul shooter, but he's already missed four shots. If he misses here, we're in pretty good shape.' Pettit made both shots, and we wound up losing the game. After the game, Eddie called, and after yakking with George about what he did right and what he did wrong, he said, 'Let me talk to Bill.' George handed me the phone. Gotty said, 'If you'd have kept your goddamned mouth shut about Pettit missing those fouls, he might have missed two more. I'm holding you responsible for this game.'"

As the new year began, the Warriors were still operating at top speed. On January 2, they set a team record with 130 points as seven players scored in double figures in a victory over Rochester at New Haven. The next night, they beat Fort Wayne in a game about which *Evening Bulletin* writer Bill Dallas wrote that "Gola did everything but comb Gotty's hair." Graboski, who had joined the Warriors in 1953 after the Indianapolis club had folded, sank a 50-foot shot at the buzzer to beat the Knicks. In a game at Lincoln High, Clyde Lovellette slammed Beck in the head, sending the guard to the hospital for five stitches as the Warriors overcame a 13-point fourth quarter deficit to beat the Hawks. On Neil Johnston Night, the Warriors' center was given $7,000 in gifts, including a new car, and a basket of vegetables, plus an off-season job with a cleaning firm. Arizin sank two clutch field goals at the end as the Warriors downed the Celtics.

Through February and into March, the heated action continued. In one game, Celtics coach Red Auerbach complained about Senesky's kneeling in front of the bench. Gola quipped that George was actually praying. Referee Sid Borgia had to be escorted off the court after a game following a disputed call, and fellow refs Mendy Rudolph and Arnie Heft were pelted with eggs during another game. Johnston bagged 41 points as the Warriors routed Syracuse. Gola registered 20 points, 17 rebounds, and 10 assists in a win over St. Louis, despite Pettit's 46 points. Beck's tap-in with two seconds left to play beat the Nats. On March 7, the Warriors defeated the Knicks at Boston to clinch the Eastern Division crown. Then they finished the regular season with a 45–27 record, six games ahead of second-place Boston, climaxing the season with three straight wins, including one in which they scored 142 points against the Celtics. Arizin was second and Johnston was third in the league behind Pettit in scoring, and George was second in assists behind Bob Cousy. It was on to the playoffs for the Warriors.

Drawing a bye in the opening round, the Warriors played the first game of the division final on March 23 at Convention Hall. The opposition was provided by Syracuse, which had won a tie-breaking game over New York to finish third during the regular season, then beat Boston two out of three in the division semifinal. Always the promoter—although in this case, it's questionable whether he needed such extra fan inducement—Gottlieb scheduled a preliminary game pitting the Harlem Globetrotters and the College All-Stars.

Arizin's 29 points combined with Johnston's 24 rebounds to lead the Warriors to a 109–87 victory. The Warriors then lost, 122–118; won, 119–96; and lost, 108–104, before Arizin hit 10 of his first 12 shots to spark the Warriors to a 109–104 win and a spot in the final against the Fort Wayne Pistons.

The Pistons were a team featuring sharp-shooting George Yardley and Mel Hutchins, La Salle College graduate and South Philly native Larry Foust, and former Warrior standout Andy Phillip. Fort Wayne was coached by Charley Eckman, a colorful character who had been an NBA referee and would later become a controversial sportscaster in Baltimore. The Pistons had finished first in the Western Division during the regular season, placing four games ahead of the Lakers and Hawks with a highly average 37–35 record. In the playoffs, they reached the final round, beating St. Louis in a best-of-five semifinal series after losing the first two games.

In the series opener, Beck came off the bench to score 23 points as the Warriors won a squeaker, 98–94. In the second game, the Warriors arrived in Fort Wayne to find their cabs from the airport had been canceled. To add insult to injury, Yardley's two foul shots with 42 seconds to play gave the Pistons an even closer 84–83 verdict. A record crowd of 11,698 at Convention Hall saw Johnston and Graboski team for 32 rebounds to put the Warriors ahead with a 100–96 win. That was followed by a 107–105 Warriors victory as Corky Devlin's game-tying shot at the buzzer was ruled too late. The Warriors then wrapped up what for them had been a spectacular series with a 99–88 triumph at Convention Hall in a game in which Graboski, who could be a deadly shooter from the corner, sank 29 points and grabbed 16 rebounds. As the final buzzer sounded, fans streamed out onto the floor, paper showered the court, and in general pandemonium broke out.

The Warriors were now the toast of the town. With good reason, too. The city's other two major league teams, the Phillies and the Eagles, were both in the midst of a series of mediocre years. The Warriors were by far the best-loved, most respected team in town.

"It's great to be champs," Senesky told reporters as he applauded the work of his team, especially that of Arizin and Gola. "Arizin is the greatest marksman since Joe Fulks," the coach proclaimed. "And Gola was sensational. When he came, it changed our whole game. He didn't play like a rookie. He was a leader, and we had confidence in him."

As a reward for their victory, each player received $1,500 from the first place money of $15,000. In addition, Gotty gave each player an additional amount ranging from $400 to $1,000, depending on how well he had played. Players also received gold, diamond-studded rings in the shape of basketballs.

"It was just a tremendous year," said Moore. "Things just seemed to fall into place. We had a lot of local guys, and everybody knew each other. We were very close as a team. Everything seemed to gel."

"We knew we could win," Beck claimed. "Once you get that feeling and you have the talent to do it, you win. We had everything. Paul was a great shooter. Neil was strong inside. Tommy did all phases of the game well. Grabbo could shoot. George was the leader. We all came together at the same time."

Following the team's final victory, a joyous celebration was held, as it had been in 1947, at Sam Framo's King of the Shrimp restaurant at 23rd and Allegheny. An attractive young woman got up and sang, although not too well. Nobody, though, was about to say anything critical.

In a sharp departure from his previous escapades off the court, Gottlieb now had a steady girlfriend. Neither she nor the fact that he was dating were matters Gotty discussed. He kept them strictly to himself, as he did with all of his personal business. And if anybody dared raise the subject, that person was likely to incur the unbridled wrath of The Mogul.

That had happened before. In one memorable outburst in the 1930s, Gotty tore into Don Basenfelder, a writer with the Philadelphia *Record*. Basenfelder had come to Gotty's office to pen an article on The Mogul. During the interview, Basenfelder asked Gottlieb why he never married. Gotty flew into a rage, screaming at the innocent newspaperman that "it was none of his goddamned business." It was obvious that he didn't want any questions about his love life.

Everyone always said that Gottlieb was married to sports and didn't have time for wedded bliss. Gotty himself claimed that from a domestic standpoint, he was fully occupied taking care of his mother and sister, both of whom always lived with him. That did not mean, however, that he was opposed to an occasional dalliance. Gotty kept it undercover, but it was known that he and his pal Dave Zinkoff, a notorious womanizer, sometimes went on double dates. Bernie Brown knew that because while working in the SPHAS office, Gottlieb sometimes dispatched him with envelopes to take to a woman friend of the boss's who lived near 600 North Broad Street. Once, the woman appeared unannounced at the Warriors' office, only to be met by a tirade from Gotty. "I told you never to come here," he yelled. Suitably chastised, the woman fled the premises.

Then there was the lady from Spain. She was a singer/dancer whose name was Carmen C. Trejo, and she was more than a friend. Gottlieb met her during one of his summer trips to Europe with the Globetrotters and, suitably enamored, invited her to leave Spain and come to the United States. Although nearly 20 years younger than Gotty, she accepted and, going for some unknown reason under the name Alicia Romay, lived quietly in New York City, where Gottlieb paid her rent and often visited.

She rarely came to Philadelphia, although when she did, Gottlieb sometimes brought her for dinner to Ike Richman's house in Elkins Park. "She was a very nice woman," said Ike's son, Michael Richman. "When I was studying Spanish, she gave me some tips. But Gotty didn't want most people to know about her." Most people never even saw her with Gotty.

And even if they did, they either didn't know who she was or kept her presence unmentioned. But for some 20 years, she was a major part of The Mogul's life.

Trejo/Romay was the singer at the Warriors' victory celebration. It was a celebration that went on far into the early morning hours. For the Warriors, though, it would be their last one in Philadelphia.

In the spring of 1956, Auerbach and the Celtics made a move that would change the face of pro basketball forever. Boston traded center Ed Macauley and the rights to Kentucky star Cliff Hagen to St. Louis for a draft position that allowed them to pick center Bill Russell, who had led San Francisco University to the NCAA championship in each of the previous two seasons. The swap paved the way for the Celtics to win nine NBA titles over the next 10 years. And it effectively ended the Warriors' brief claim to league superiority.

The year 1956 had been a noteworthy one for the Warriors. So, too, had it been for the rest of the nation, although not everything was positive. Elvis Pressley made the charts for the first time, Grace Kelly married Prince Rainier, and Marilyn Monroe wed Arthur Miller. *My Fair Lady* opened on Broadway, Dean Martin and Jerry Lewis closed their act together, Chet Huntley and David Brinkley opened theirs, Dick Clark began *Bandstand*, and Don Larsen pitched a perfect game in the World Series. Elsewhere, the house of Martin Luther King, Jr., was firebombed, Nikita Khrushchev told the free world that the Soviet Union would bury it, and the *Andrea Doria* sank off Nantucket. President Dwight D. Eisenhower signed the bill that created interstate highways, the U.S. Supreme Court ruled that racial segregation on buses is unconstitutional, and the words "In God We Trust" became the national motto.

As this was happening, the Warriors, who had been feted in May at a gala dinner attended by more than 1,000 at the Bellevue-Stratford Hotel, headed back toward the abyss of the NBA. The team finished third in 1956–57 during the regular season and was knocked out of the playoffs in the first round by Syracuse. It placed third again the following year, and made it to the Eastern final before losing to Boston. In 1958–59, the Warriors wound up dead last.

It was not a pretty picture on the court or in the stands where attendance dropped steadily after the championship season. Aiding the bad news was the dilemma of the three Gs—Gola had to spend one year in the army, Graboski was on the decline, and George wound up getting

The Warriors won the NBA title in 1955–56 with (from left) Jack George, Larry Hennessy, George Dempsey, Ernie Back, Paul Arizin, Jackie Moore, Tom Gola, Neil Johnston, Joe Graboski, and Walter Davis. Coach George Senesky kneels in front of Gottlieb. *(Courtesy of Rich Westcott)*

traded to the Knicks. About the only good news was Arizin's second scoring title in 1956–57 and his continued ranking among the league leaders in that department.

Gottlieb had tried to remedy the situation. In 1956, he drafted a player named Clarence (Bevo) Francis out of tiny Rio Grande College in Ohio. A school with 96 students, Rio Grande played a schedule against regular four-year colleges as well as two-year ones. In 1954, the 6-foot, 9-inch Francis led the nation with an average of 48.3 points per game, even scoring 116 points in one game. But after taking a closer look at Rio Grande's watered-down schedule, National Association of Intercollegiate Athletics (NAIA) officials purged a number of the school's and Francis's records from the books. Francis quit school and joined the Boston Whirlwinds, one of the teams that played the Globetrotters. But when Gottlieb drafted him two years later, Francis refused to sign, instead quitting basketball and going home to Ohio to work in a steel mill.

Gottlieb made Temple's Hal Lear in 1956 and Guy Rodgers in 1958 the team's territorial draft choices, hoping the two local players would bolster the Warriors' sagging attendance. But at 5 feet, 10 inches, the flashy Lear was said to be too small to play pro ball. Senesky told Lear that Gottlieb said he wasn't ready for the NBA. Gottlieb told Lear that Senesky said he wasn't ready for the NBA. After all the doubletalk, Lear, an Overbrook High grad, was cut from the team in mid-November. Rodgers, on the other hand, turned into a solid 12-year NBA player, four of those years being with the Warriors while they were in Philadelphia.

But Gotty, whose office was now located in the Essex Hotel at 13th and Filbert Streets where he also maintained a room in which he sometimes spent the night, couldn't resist taking shots as his withering team. At one point early in the 1956 season, Gottlieb called four of the players on his team "deadheads." Without naming names, Gotty said the players were stricken with "championitis." He added, "They're not displaying the same hustle and aggressiveness that marked their title run a year ago."

Another time he said, "I don't know what's gotten into them. They're not playing like they can. I keep thinking maybe we'll straighten out. But it looks to me like they think they have it made." Then, after a particularly distressing loss, Gottlieb blasted Rodgers for his "indifferent play," adding that he "acted like a two-year-old, a juvenile without any pride."

The situation got so bad that during one game in 1957, Senesky ordered his team into a full-court press early in a game against the Knicks. Even though the Knicks won by 26 points, the coach was roundly criticized for his action by the New York press. "When you're going as badly as we are, you try anything," Senesky responded.

Gottlieb even got involved in a skirmish with Auerbach after complaining that Russell was blocking shots illegally. After batting away a shot by Arizin, Gottlieb said, "If this isn't goal-tending, I want somebody to tell me what it is." Gotty added that Russell tries to play zone defense instead of the required man-to-man. Auerbach labeled the charges as "sour grapes." But after Russell snatched 34 rebounds and held Johnston scoreless, Gottlieb filed a complaint with the league office. The charges were quickly dismissed. Later, Gottlieb told Russell: "I hope you're not paying attention to all that stuff about goal tending. It just helps to keep our seats filled."

The best seat at Convention Hall was still a bargain at $2.75. General admission was 75¢. One of the Warriors' biggest fans was concert violinist Isaac Stern. He attended Warriors games whenever he was in town. Once, Stern asked Gottlieb if he could switch a game to 11 a.m. because he had a concert that night at the Academy of Music. The request was denied.

Just like he was with Stern, Gottlieb could be tough with the media. He read all the local newspapers. He knew what everybody was writing. He seemed generally to like the writers and broadcasters who covered the team, but that was often because he agreed with what they wrote or said.

"Write something negative about his team or his league, and he could be tough," said Frank Dolson, who worked for the *Inquirer* for some 40 years, covering the team as both a reporter and columnist. "You'd parry back and forth with him. He had opinions on everything. If he didn't like what you wrote, he'd tell you off in a minute, even if he liked you. He wouldn't hold anything back. He was never reluctant to tell you something you wrote was crap. You would certainly know how he felt. But 20 minutes after he'd yelled and hollered, it would all be forgotten.

"He was completely open," Dolson added. "When you talk to owners today, half of them can't be believed. Many of them are very secretive. And when they do tell you something, you wonder whether it's for real or just self-serving. You never had that feeling with Gotty. He would tell you what's going on. If you asked him a question and he didn't want to answer or couldn't answer, he'd tell you. There was never any bullshit. I can't imagine him ever lying about something."

Jim Heffernan, the Warriors beat writer for the *Evening Bulletin* during the team's final years in Philadelphia, saw Gottlieb this way: "He had a great mind," he said. "He was from the old school. He wasn't the most beloved character. He'd chew you out if you wrote something critical. He was used to having his own way, and he wanted us to be cheerleaders."

Of course, then, as it is now in most cases—although not every case in Philadelphia—media people would rather swim in the Delaware River than be perceived as shilling for a team. But when Gottlieb decided to talk to the press, as he often did, a good story was usually forthcoming.

"You'd ask him a question, and you'd get an answer," claimed Ralph Bernstein, who covered sports for the Associated Press for more than 50 years. "And if you were looking for a story, he'd help you if he could. And if he saw something that was interesting, he'd call you. From my standpoint, he was super with the press. He acceded to anything it wanted."

"He was a very likable guy," said Campbell, a broadcaster from more than 60 years. "You never got a lot of bullshit from Eddie. He told it like it was. When he was mad at a player or a member of the press, everybody knew about it. If he disagreed with something you said on the air or something you wrote, he could jump on you pretty good. But he didn't carry any grudges. He'd say something, maybe call you on the phone, then it was over. He might buy you a beer later that day. You always knew where you stood with him."

Obviously, what mattered most in the way members of the media regarded Gottlieb was a person's own experiences with him. Not everybody had the same impression of The Mogul.

"He wasn't a real good interview," stated Heffernan. "But he always tried to be fair with everybody."

Stan Hochman, who served as a reporter then a columnist for the *Daily News* in a career that began in Philadelphia in 1958 and still continues, viewed Gottlieb this way: "He was very guarded with the media," Hochman said. "He was kind of an introverted guy. He didn't share a lot of his life with the press. He was not very anecdotal. He was strictly business. I seldom saw him with a smile."

Bernstein provided another take on The Mogul: "He wasn't a super friendly person," he said. "He was always very nice to me. Very courteous. But he was never close to any of us. He was a bit aloof."

Dolson had a vivid recollection of the first time he engaged Gottlieb. It was in 1959. "It was my first column," he said. "Wilt was still playing with the Globetrotters. They're playing over in Camden, and I went over there. Hughie Brown [from the *Bulletin*] was there. Brown was talking to Gotty. He says, 'Wait until you read what I have you saying tomorrow.' Gotty sort of smiles, and says, 'Oh, yeah, what?' And Brown reads him some lines from his story that were reasonably funny. Gotty says, 'That's great.' The stuff was all fabricated. Gotty didn't mind.

"I was getting ready to do an interview, and I said to Gotty, 'I don't make up lines. I want to hear it straight from your mouth. You make up the lines.' Gotty just laughed. He was fine with it, either way. That was Gotty. I always got along great with him. Some people did, and some people didn't."

Following the 1957–58 season, Gottlieb decided he needed a new coach. Under Senesky, the Warriors had gone steadily downhill as the nucleus of the title team continued to age. Draft picks such as Lennie Rosenbluth, a nonproductive former All-American from North Carolina University, failed to help.

The excuse given for Senesky's dismissal was that he was too nice a guy. George, who had been almost like a son to Gottlieb, didn't agree. "All the sudden I'm a nice guy," he told Bill McBride for a *Bulletin* article. "Last year, I couldn't find two people who liked me."

As he had done in 1956 with the Warriors and several times before that with the SPHAS, Gottlieb once again offered the job to his old friend

Harry Litwack, the head coach at Temple. Litwack, who had served as Gotty's assistant coach from 1949 to 1951 while also coaching the Temple freshmen (he did not usually go on long road trips with the Warriors), was not willing to travel. Once again, he declined the offer, despite his view that it was extremely attractive.

Deep down, Gottlieb knew what the Warriors really needed. They needed a fiery coach who could bring some sparkle back to the team. A tough guy. Somebody with enthusiasm. Somebody who could ignite the team. Somebody who didn't back down, who had coaching experience, who knew his way around the NBA.

Gotty found just that man in Al Cervi. Although he didn't attend college, Cervi was a high-level athlete who went to spring training one year with the Washington Senators as a combination shortstop-center fielder. He had also been invited to attend the Pittsburgh Pirates' camp, but threw out his arm and turned full-time to basketball. Cervi began his basketball career back in 1937 in the NBL. He played as a hustling, scrappy, no-nonsense player for nine years, the last four in the NBA with Syracuse. Once, when Cervi beat Gotty's Warriors, The Mogul was furious. "But I still would like him on my team," he said.

For much of his career, Cervi was a player-coach, serving from 1948 until 1956 as skipper of the NBL and then the NBA Nats. Dismissed early in the 1956–57 season, Cervi was working for a trucking company when Gottlieb called.

"He gave me one of the best contracts I ever had," Cervi recalled. "He was a very nice person and a very good person to work for. When we'd go on the road, he'd reach in his pocket and pull out all the money and the tickets for the trip. He kept his office in his pocket."

Gottlieb, however, had created one not-so-slight problem. He and Cervi were both strong personalities, and they didn't get along. At one point, the coach wanted to trade Graboski to the Pistons for Philadelphia native Larry Foust. Gottlieb was aghast. "What the hell do you want Foust for?" he bellowed. "You're getting Chamberlain next year for God's sake." By the end of the season, Cervi had had enough. He resigned after the Warriors landed in the Eastern Division cellar, winning 32 of 72 games. Despite a two-year contract, Cervi said he resigned to take a job as sales manager for the trucking company in his hometown of Rochester, New York.

"I can't believe I quit the job right before Wilt came," Cervi said many years later. "But the previous season we won only 32 games, losing four in overtime. I said to myself, 'What the hell are you doing here?' I hated coaching. I liked being a player-coach, which I had been in Syracuse, but I hated sitting on the bench and just being a coach. Yet, it was the best coaching job I ever had. I went back and forth. Finally, I said, 'The hell with it,' and went home."

Cervi's departure cleared the way for Gotty to make another unsuccessful offer to Litwack. He then gave the job to Johnston, the three-time NBA scoring champion with the Warriors. Johnston was a Philadelphia favorite who was the premier hook shot artist of his day. He had missed most of the previous season after going down with a cracked knee. When it appeared that his eight-year playing career was about to end, and even if it didn't, Johnston would lose his job to the soon-arriving Wilt Chamberlain, Gotty made him a sentimental choice as the new coach, telling him, "The job is yours. Sink or swim."

Why did Gottlieb choose a coach with no experience? "I just felt he deserved a crack at the job," Gotty told Heffernan. "He's been in the league eight years and knows the conditions which exist in the NBA. He knows the Warriors' personnel. And it's been his ambition to coach. Neither Neil nor myself can predict what will come about. After all, last year I hired a guy who was supposed to be the best in the business. Things didn't work out did they?"

At first, Johnston was thrilled to be taking over a team that included the highly touted Chamberlain. He readily admitted that he thought the Warriors were now in a position to loosen the Celtics' stranglehold on the NBA championship. "If Wilt does as many things as Eddie and I believe he can," Johnston said to Heffernan, "I see no reason we shouldn't be a contender."

The story changed, though, once the season began. It didn't take long for Wilt and his teammates to become disenchanted with Johnston's lack of experience. Gottlieb sat near the bench, looking straight ahead, but according to Al Attles, making loud comments such as "get that guy out of there." Chamberlain had no respect for Johnston, and for the most part ignored him. At one point, Johnston fined Wilt, who appealed to Gottlieb. The Mogul overruled his coach. Another time, Johnston and Chamberlain almost engaged in a round of fisticuffs. Wilt refused to play until Gotty intervened. He did, and from then on, the past and present centers never spoke.

Despite the dissension, the Warriors played well and drew even better. Attendance increased 56 percent at home, and it also skyrocketed on the road. It was so good at away games, in fact, that Gotty asked other teams to give him a piece of the gate. The request, of course, was denied. Although the Warriors eventually finished second with a 49–26 record before losing in six games to the Celtics in the division final, there was no particular joy in Phillyville. And the feeling carried into the following season.

It was, to say the least, a messy situation. Once again, Gottlieb had made a bad decision. Shortly after the 1960–61 campaign ended with the Warriors posting a 46–33 record, but getting knocked out by the Nats in the first round of the playoffs, Johnston resigned. "It was an unhappy and disappointing season for me," said Johnston, who shortly afterward landed a job as coach of Pittsburgh in the new American Basketball League. "I thought things would change for the better after last year, but they didn't. So, due to the situations and conditions that exist on the team and the belief that they will not improve, I thought it best for everyone that I resign."

Johnston readily admitted he made mistakes. "But this was a dead team," he said. "There was a complete lack of spirit."

Hardly unnoticed amid Johnston's comments was his long finger pointing directly at Chamberlain, despite his average of 38.4 points per game and second straight scoring title. The two did not agree on the way the team should be run. Wilt was not reluctant to voice his views. "He didn't know shit about basketball strategy or tactics or how to work with players or anything else a coach needs," Wilt said. "The team had no respect for him and neither did our opponents, and he lost control of us."

At the press conference announcing Johnston's departure, Gottlieb, who earlier had told Wilt, "I made a big mistake hiring him." was almost as harsh. "Maybe the situation had something to do with Wilt," he said. "But if it did, Neil should have talked to me about it. Maybe he feels he did, but he never came to me with any problems. When a superstar like Chamberlain joins the team, adjustments certainly have to be made. Maybe a 10-year coach could have coped with the situation better."

Gottlieb, though, was not immune to some blame himself. He had hired the wrong man for the job. To make matters worse, Gola said that "the players did not know who was running the team, Neil or Gotty." Gotty told reporters: "When I gave Neil the job, I let sentiment run away with my judgment. He lacked the coaching know-how and he couldn't handle men."

When Gottlieb hired Frank McGuire away from the University of North Carolina for the following season, the problem seemed to be resolved. The players liked McGuire, who had been the coach in 1957 when North Carolina beat Kansas and Chamberlain, 54–53, in triple overtime in the NCAA final. Wilt liked him. And the man, who had originally turned down Gotty's offer for the job, knew how to run a team.

Once again, Gottlieb had with no uncertainty carried out his role as a team owner. It was a typical move for a man who made all the decisions by himself and who operated with both strength and wisdom.

"He was a hands-on owner," said Michael Richman. "He was not like the owners of today who sit up in a box, fan themselves, tell somebody to send up popcorn, and fire this guy or that guy. He ran the whole franchise by himself."

Referee Norm Drucker called Gottlieb "the leader of all owners. He'd tell the other owners what they had to do. He had a heavy voice in practically all aspects of the league. Plus, he knew more about the history of basketball than any person I ever met."

Gottlieb gave the *Evening Bulletin*'s Frank Brady some insight into the job of owning a team. "There are only two reasons owners get involved," he said. "First, he can get his name in the papers because he couldn't get a name for himself in his own business. Second, it's to get tax relief. In the old days, people [owners] got into sports because they wanted to and because they had to make a living."

The Mogul claimed that it was more difficult to be an owner in the early days of pro basketball. "We had to work harder because we had to bring in paid customers," he said. "In recent years, they just came in by themselves."

As the end of the 1950s arrived, however, there were other matters weighing on Gottlieb. He was still peripherally involved in promotional activities. On October 10, 1959, he joined with former baseball player Sid Gordon to promote a game at Connie Mack Stadium between American and National League all-stars. Willie Mays and Mickey Mantle both participated in the exhibition.

All the while, Gottlieb was still living on the corner of Salford and Upland Streets in the upper floor of a duplex where a garage in the back housed his Cadillac. Ironically, looking southwest from the house, it was possible to see Overbrook High School looming off in the distance.

Although he had lived there with Leah and Belle since 1949, few knew a prominent sports figure resided in the neighborhood.

"He didn't mix with the neighbors," said attorney Dan Promislo, whose parents owned the building and lived in the first floor apartment. "He just came and went. Sometimes, he looked like he'd been up forever. He never seemed too happy. And he looked preoccupied all the time. He always looked busy, although he was always very nice when you approached him."

Gottlieb frequently gave Promislo, who became at outstanding basketball player at Drexel, tickets to Warriors games. Except for frequent visits by Zinkoff, that was the only tangible evidence that the man in the upper duplex had any connection with sports.

"A guy who owns an NBA team today certainly wouldn't live in a place like that," Promislo said. "I think he only paid about $250 a month rent."

Away from sports, Gottlieb was confronted with a far different situation. His mother, Leah, was in increasingly poor health. Eventually, it became necessary to move her into Rest Haven Convalescent Home in Broomall.

While there, Leah Gottlieb died on December 25, 1959. She was buried at Har Nebo Cemetery in Northeast Philadelphia.

• • •

CHAPTER 14

The Dipper Comes Home

During more than six decades in sports, Eddie Gottlieb enjoyed a career that was peppered with noteworthy achievements. Many had such a lasting effect that they are still very much in evidence.

But none of the accomplishments in Gottlieb's life came close to matching the one when he made Wilt Chamberlain a member of the Philadelphia Warriors. It was the defining moment in Gotty's career. And the feat allowed him to climb to the summit of Philadelphia sports success stories.

Reaching that point was an arduous task. It required perseverance, guile, guts, aggressiveness, intelligence, and possibly even a little bit of deception. After all, Chamberlain was no ordinary basketball player. He was the pick of the litter, an almost supernatural figure who was on the verge of becoming the most widely heralded player ever to participate in the game of basketball.

There was, of course, never anything halfway about Chamberlain. Even later on, whether it was his size, his ego, his salary, or his phenomenal scoring feats (a category that can be measured several different ways), Wilt was larger than life. It was like that almost from the day that somebody pulled out a yardstick when Wilt was in third grade and found out that the skinny youngster with the unforgettably long arms and legs already stood 5 feet, 10 inches tall.

By the time he was a college freshman at Kansas, Wilt Chamberlain had already been drafted by the Warriors. *(Courtesy of Rich Westcott)*

One of nine children—three boys and six girls—Chamberlain grew up in a four-bedroom corner house at 401 North Salford Street in West Philadelphia. Ironically, although the houses were a number of blocks apart, it was the same street where Gottlieb lived for many years.

By the time he was attending Shoemaker Junior High School and was already an ardent proponent of physical fitness, lifting weights and performing all kinds of strenuous exercises, Chamberlain had started to attract serious attention that extended far beyond his West Philly neighborhood. That attention spread even farther when as a 6-foot, 11-inch sophomore at Overbrook High School, Wilt scored 24 points in his first varsity game, then, averaging 31 points per game for the season, led his team to the Public League championship.

During the next two years, Wilt propelled Overbrook to two more league titles as well as two city championships over the Catholic League winners. In one game during his senior year, Wilt scored a then-state record 90 points during a 32-minute game in an incredible 123–21 victory for Overbrook over Roxborough High School, which alternated 6-foot, 5-inch twin brothers in a futile attempt to stop the big kid's barrage. After averaging 47 points per game in his senior year, Chamberlain finished his high school career with a 37 point per game average over three years. Overbrook posted a 56–3 record during that time.

Now called Dip, Dippy, or Dipper by his friends because he always seemed required to duck under doorways, trees, and anything else that mere mortals would've ignored—he always hated the nickname "Wilt the

Stilt"—Chamberlain had understandably attracted the attention of Gott-lieb. Nothing in Philadelphia basketball ever escaped Gottlieb's notice. But a local player with Wilt's talent and future? Gotty, who in 1950 had made the statement that "the little man is through in basketball," would practically break out into a nervous sweat every time he contemplated Chamberlain wearing a Warriors' uniform and packing people into the stands to watch him perform.

In the interest of carving a few inroads, Gottlieb helped during the summer of Wilt's junior year to secure him a job as a bellhop at Kutsher's Country Club, a prominent resort in the Catskill Mountains of New York where Gotty often spent parts of his off-seasons and was a good friend of the owners. Chamberlain made $13 a week plus tips. But more impor-tantly, during the two summers he spent at Kutsher's, he played against some of the nation's top college players in a fast-paced league sponsored by the hotel that for several decades was highly regarded and heavily attended by the nation's basketball intelligentsia.

By then, Chamberlain was foremost in the minds of virtually every col-lege coach in the country who purported to have a basketball program of even the slightest merit. UCLA, North Carolina. Michigan, Indiana, Cin-cinnati—all the top basketball schools—plus little ones and, of course, all the Big Five colleges in Philadelphia, came after Wilt with the vengeance of a tsunami. It was estimated that, in all, 160 colleges had an interest in the giant schoolboy.

The madness did not escape the attention of Gottlieb.

Even in its early years, the league had a rule that said if a player attended a college within 60 miles of a pro team, that team had the right to draft the player at the end of his four-year college eligibility. The rule had played a prominent role in Warriors' selections over the years with All-Americans such as Paul Arizin from Villanova (1950), Bill Mlkvy from Temple (1952), Ernie Beck from Penn (1953), Tom Gola from La Salle (1955), Hal Lear from Temple (1956), and Guy Rodgers from Tem-ple (1958), all having been chosen by the Warriors as territorial picks (which preceded the regular draft).

Gottlieb had a special affinity for the rule. In the basketball-rich city of Philadelphia, where the college game was more popular, especially after the formation of the Big Five, it not only gave him the rights to out-standing players, but it allowed him to stock his team with players who already had a strong following in the city. Moreover, with fierce competition for publicity among the city's major sports teams, press coverage was likely to be better when local players were involved.

Gotty, who could often be seen scouting players at college games and who regularly attended even high school games, had always been partial to local players anyway. His first Warriors team in 1946 had three local players (Howie Dallmar from Penn, George Senesky from St. Joseph's, and Angelo Musi from Temple) in the starting lineup. Early Warriors teams were always well stocked with locals, including players such as Chink Crossin (Penn), the team's first draft pick in 1947, Jerry Rullo, Ike Borsavage, and Nelson Bobb (all from Temple), Matt Guokas, Sr. (St. Joseph's), Jackie Moore and Jack George (both from La Salle), and Larry Hennessy (Villanova). The 1955–56 championship team had no less than seven local players on the roster. Indeed, Gotty's strong belief in the merits of selecting local players was regularly displayed throughout his draft choices each year. In 1950, for instance, he picked five local collegians in the draft. He chose five more in both 1952 and 1955, and four in 1953.

"His philosophy was that the fans would come out to see the local players, " Arizin recalled. "The people already knew them. They boosted the gate. Eddie believed that people come out to see the game and the players. They don't come out to see the side shows. He would've died back then if anybody had suggested having cheerleaders."

Of course, it helped considerably if the team was a winner. With Chamberlain, Gotty figured, that would be a sure thing. Now, the trick was to make sure Wilt became a Warrior.

The territorial draft gave Gotty the ammunition he thought he needed. Gottlieb would talk Chamberlain into attending Penn (although he decided later that if Wilt attended a local college, Warriors attendance would suffer). Meanwhile, Boston Celtics' coach Red Auerbach, a regular in the basketball crowd at Kutsher's, tried to persuade Chamberlain to enroll at Harvard. Other NBA teams had similar ploys.

Auerbach was especially relentless in his pursuit of Chamberlain. Saying that Wilt was comparable to the best college players he had ever seen, the wily Celtics coach drilled the young giant on the finer points of the game in specially arranged workouts at Kutsher's. So enthralled was Auerbach with Wilt's ability and hustle that he urged Celtics' owner Walter Brown to give Chamberlain's parents $25,000, a bribe if there ever was one, if they made sure their son went to college in Boston. To his credit, Brown saw the scheme for what it was, and firmly demurred.

Gottlieb, meanwhile, insisted that Chamberlain would play for the Warriors. "If that kid even thinks about blowing town for Boston," he informed Milt Kutsher, "I'll turn your joint into a bowling alley."

Despite his brave talk, it became readily apparent to Gotty that he needed to play a stronger card. And then in the spring of 1955, just before Wilt was to graduate from Overbrook, it came to him.

"There was a question as to what college Wilt would finally attend," Gottlieb said in an article he wrote in 1971 for a publication called *Inside Basketball*. "That's when I suggested a change in the territorial rule— allowing a high school player in his senior year to be a first territorial choice four years later, which would have to be exercised whether he was able to play or not. This could backfire on a club if the player selected did not want to play pro ball, wasn't good enough, or was injured."

That was a chance Gottlieb was more than willing to take. He was firmly convinced that as a Philadelphian, Wilt should play nowhere else but in Philadelphia. And so, with visions of Chamberlain wearing a Warriors uniform four year hence, Gotty took his idea to the other NBA owners. After some preliminary skirmishing, the proposal passed by a vote of seven to one. Curiously, the Celtics backed the plan. Auerbach said later that the Boston people didn't like the deal, but the team was not willing to take the chance that Wilt would still be the same paragon four years hence. The New York Knicks were the lone dissenter.

Some said the other owners passed the proposal as a reward to Gottlieb for his long years of service to the league. Others claimed that with the Warriors in the midst of a downward spiral, especially at the gate, Gotty's colleagues felt sorry for him and readily acquiesced. A few thought it was just another case of a backroom deal being made, as in "you scratch my back, I'll scratch yours." Whatever the case, Gotty had surely put one over on the other NBA chiefs.

"The other owners must have been asleep," said longtime Gottlieb sidekick Harvey Pollack. "Nobody seemed to think too much about it. They acted like they really didn't know what Gotty was thinking. Then, when they realized what had happened after he drafted Wilt, they wondered, 'What the hell did we do?' It didn't take them long to figure it out. And soon afterward, they rescinded the rule."

It was too late, though, to prevent Chamberlain from his eventual move to the Wigwam. In the spring of 1959, four years after graduating from Overbrook, he would become a Warrior. Just to make sure there were no flaws in the plan, Gottlieb campaigned vigorously for Chamberlain to attend the University of Kansas and play under legendary coach Phog Allen. With Wilt at Kansas and no pro team within 60 miles of the Lawrence campus, Gotty reasoned that his choice of Chamberlain would then be totally without a challenge.

In September 1955, Chamberlain enrolled at Kansas. Allen, was ecstatic. "With Wilt, we can win the national championship with two Phi Betas, and a pair of coeds," he told Dippy's mother, Olivia. By then, standing more than seven feet tall, he would play one year of freshman ball, then two years on the varsity, astounding anyone who was paying attention with his magnificent skills on the court.

Chamberlain, who, as it turned out, would never play for Allen because the coach was forced by the university to retire at age 70, just before Wilt's first season, averaged 30 points per game and was twice named first team All-American during his two years on the Kansas varsity. During that time, Kansas won 42 of its 50 games, reaching the NCAA final in Wilt's junior year where it lost to North Carolina, coached by Frank McGuire, in triple overtime.

After his junior year, Chamberlain had seen enough of college life. Despite the territorial rule that Gottlieb had pushed through and Wilt still one year away from being eligible for the NBA draft, Chamberlain said in his autobiography, *Wilt: Just Like Any Other 7-Foot Black Millionaire Who Lives Next Door*, written in 1973 with David Shaw, that the Warriors owner tried to circumvent his own territorial draft rule by offering Wilt a $25,000 contract as a hardship case. The NBA owners refused to allow it. Ultimately, the most highly acclaimed player in college basketball history signed to play with the Harlem Globetrotters for a staggering salary estimated to be at least $65,000.

Wilt spent one year with the traveling comedy team, playing more than 200 games around the world and substantially boosting the Globies' attendance wherever they played. Although the experience vastly improved the Dipper's ball-handling skills and he said he enjoyed the experience immensely, he yearned to join the pro ranks. Or so it was thought, anyway.

As planned, Chamberlain was the Warriors' territorial pick in the 1959 draft. But Wilt's joining the team was by no means automatic. Numerous obstacles blocked Chamberlain's path back to Philadelphia, not the least of which was his own obstinacy and the perceived value his ego placed on his services.

Chamberlain played one year with the Harlem Globetrotters before joining the Warriors in 1959. *(Courtesy of Rich Westcott)*

Having already learned not only the basics of negotiating but also about the luxuries provided by money, Wilt let it be known that he was thinking about returning to the Globetrotters. In an attempt to make that happen, Gottlieb's old friend and Globies owner Abe Saperstein offered Chamberlain a new contract that was said to pay considerably higher than his previous salary with the team.

Feeling he might lose the battle and thus jeopardize the financially strapped Warriors' diminishing chances of survival, Gottlieb persuaded the other NBA owners to increase the salary cap of $25,000. He then offered Wilt $27,000, which the Dipper promptly rejected.

In desperation, Gottlieb turned to one of his closest associates, Philadelphia attorney Isaac (Ike) Richman. The highly respected Richman was the lawyer for both Gotty and the Warriors and would later become Wilt's attorney and lifelong friend. What better person to try to negotiate a settlement?

Richman set up an appointment with the reluctant phenom. He summoned his 17-year-old son, Mike, to help.

"My father hated to drive," recalled Richman who became an attorney himself and also served 20 years as a judge in Philadelphia. "We had a big, tan Cadillac, and whenever my father and I went out together, I drove. At the time we were living in Elkins Park.

"One night we were sitting around, and my father said, 'Mike, I need you.' Now, there are only three people in my life who I never asked why—Eddie Gottlieb, my former rabbi, and my father. So, when he said, 'I need you,' I said, 'OK.'

"We got in the car, and he said, 'Drive me to 4700 North Broad Street.' I drove down York Road to Broad Street. When I got to the address, he said, 'Make a U-turn and pull over.' A few minutes later, a big, white Cadillac convertible pulled up. My father told me he'd be back in half an hour. He got out of our car and got into the convertible. I pulled away and rode around the neighborhood for about a half hour. Then I came back and pulled over. A few minutes later, my father got out of the other car and got in ours.

"He looked over, and said, 'Mike, I just worked harder than I ever worked in my life.' I said, 'What did you do?' He said, 'I just convinced Wilt Chamberlain to play professional basketball with the Warriors.'"

It was said that the affable Richman could talk birds out of trees. In the midst of his persuasive effort, he had come up with one particular reason for signing with the Warriors that hit the family-oriented giant right in the heart. "You don't want to play somewhere where your parents can't see you, do you?" he said. It was the hook that clinched the deal.

On May 13, the Warriors held a press conference at the Sheraton Hotel in Center City to announce the results of Richman's work. Just one month after his contract with the Globies had expired, Wilt became a Warrior. Although the actual figure was not revealed, it was said that Wilt's new salary would be in excess of $30,000, and he would also get bonus money, royalties, and fees for endorsements. The salary alone put Wilt's pay at $5,000 higher than Boston's Bob Cousy, previously the league's highest-paid player whose earnings placed him at the top of the NBA's maximum allowance.

"He's getting more money than I paid for the whole franchise," Gotty said. He added that he thought that Wilt "was one of the few who could play in the pros right out of high school."

Saying that his total earnings probably compared favorably to the $100,000 that made baseball's Ted Williams the highest-paid athlete in the land, Chamberlain noted that he'd just purchased for his parents a deluxe, 13-room house at 6205 Cobbs Creek Parkway at a cost of $15,000 and had bought $10,000 worth of furniture. "It's nice that the money will enable me to do and have many things that otherwise would have been out of the question," Wilt said. It had always been his ambition to play in the NBA, he added.

Gottlieb was ecstatic. He said, "Chamberlain has more potential than anybody who ever came into the NBA. He can do anything Bill Russell can, and he'll score more. Wait until the people at Convention Hall see Wilt dunking that apple." And, Gotty added, "I think he should raise our gate by $100,000 next season."

No question about it, Philadelphia basketball fans were already speculating the benefits of Wilt's presence. The city pulsated with excitement. Dipper was already being placed on a pedestal that was occupied by the legends of Philadelphia sports.

"People were saying, 'Oh boy, with Chamberlain, they're not going to lose a game," longtime *Inquirer* columnist Frank Dolson remembered. "'What a great team this is going to be!' But Gotty was a bit more reserved. He said, 'I know the Globetrotters never lost a game when he was there. But I got news for you. They never lost a game before he was there, either.' Gotty refused to be suckered in by all the excitement."

Gotty did surrender to one unusual condition, though. Wilt said he wanted to wear number 13 on his uniform. No one was more superstitious than The Mogul. There was no way he was going to allow such a blatant act of frivolity. Wilt persisted. Finally, as is so often the case in an owner-superstar dispute, Gotty gave in. Chamberlain got his way, wearing a number that would adorn his jersey for the rest of his career.

Soon after the contract was signed, Gottlieb left on his usual summer tour with the Globetrotters. Chamberlain joined the team in July, and at one point, the Globies drew 130,000 in nine games in Moscow.

Back in the States in August, Wilt made it clear that Gotty had made the right decision when he mortgaged the franchise. Chamberlain was playing in the annual Maurice Stokes benefit game at Kutsher's with a group of NBA stars that included Cousy, Jack Twyman, Dolph Schayes, Richie Guerin, Tom Heinsohn, and a host of others. The opposing team started with 7-foot Walter Dukes at center, then switched to 6-foot, 9-inch strongman Larry Foust, and finally clever Johnny Kerr. None could stop Wilt as he scored 20 points and grabbed 15 rebounds. Afterward, one player was heard to say, "He'll revolutionize the game."

In September, Gottlieb scheduled an unheard of 31 exhibition games for the Warriors. He also arranged team scrimmages at various locations. In every case, he made sure he received the major share of the ticket sales.

Wilt's first NBA game took place on October 24, 1959, in Madison Square Garden against the Knicks. It was as stunning a debut as any player ever made. Chamberlain scored 43 points, snatched 28 rebounds, and led the Warriors to a 118–109 victory.

"There is no way you can stop him from getting the ball," Knicks' coach Fuzzy Levane told beat writer Jim Heffernan of the *Evening Bulletin*. "We tried to collapse, but it didn't do any good. Sometime, he might hit 90 points in a game."

"He's better than George Mikan," Knicks guard Carl Braun proclaimed. "This fellow's astounding."

One week later, the Warriors played their home opener against the Detroit Pistons. "It was absolutely bedlam before the game," remembered Ken Berman. "Eddie called and asked me to come early. I helped control the ticket line. There were so many people we could only let two in at a time."

The 23-year-old Chamberlain went on to average 37.6 points and 27 rebounds per game during the season, while setting eight NBA records and winning both the Rookie of the Year and Most Valuable Player awards. Warriors attendance increased 56 percent. Wilt attracted huge crowds everywhere he played. In fact, so great was his drawing power that Gottlieb insisted that other owners give him a share of the gate when the Warriors were on the road. The suggestion never got off the bench.

After finishing second during the regular season—a spot they would hold in each of the next two years, too—the Warriors lost to the Celtics in six games in the Eastern Division final, Wilt made a stunning announcement right in the midst of new contract negotiations in which Gottlieb had reportedly offered him a three-year deal worth $100,000: He was considering quitting the Warriors and returning to the Globetrotters "I'll never play in the NBA again," he said. "It's over."

Earlier in the season, Wilt had suggested to *Daily News* beat writer Jack Kiser that he might want to leave basketball to pursue a secret ambition to become a world decathlon champion. Despite being an outstanding track star in high school where he excelled as a high jumper (he could leap 6 feet, 8 inches), shot putter, and in the 220, 440, and 880, few doubted that the Dipper was really serious.

"I expect him to continue with the Warriors," Gottlieb responded. "Wilt is already a pro. Where else would he compete?"

"The whole story was a bunch of baloney," Heffernan recalled. "After Kiser wrote it, Gottlieb called me into his office and gave me the story that Wilt was staying. The story made front page headlines."

But the Globies? That was different. That seemed like serious stuff. But wasn't it also an early version of been there, done that?

Gottlieb was furious. "It's very upsetting," he said. "Frankly, if I had known last year that he was going to play only one season, I wouldn't have gone after him."

Not only was Gotty mad at Wilt. He was outraged by the apparent attempt of his old friend Saperstein to lure the 7-foot, 2-inch dominator away from the Warriors with an annual salary that was rumored to be in the $100,000 range.

As it turned out, the situation would eventually lead to a rift between Gottlieb and Saperstein that was never fully mended and that, for another reason, became a permanent split a few years later. Their relationship was badly damaged, and in 1960 for the first time in five years, Gotty refused to travel abroad in the summer with the Globies.

Gottlieb also had to deal with one other issue with Saperstein. That was the matter of Warriors stock. The Globetrotter owner had become a small stockholder in the team when Gottlieb bought it in 1952. Now, Eddie wanted no part of his ex-pal.

While Chamberlain again toured Europe with the Globies and pondered the contract that Saperstein had offered him, Gottlieb continued to fume. "We're not accepting Wilt's statement as final," he groused.

Eventually, after a considerable amount of discussion, Gottlieb prevailed. In August, soon after Chamberlain returned from Europe, he persuaded Wilt to sign a three-year contract calling for a yearly stipend said to be in the range of $85,000. Wilt was back in the fold and the Warriors—or so Gotty expected—were headed to the top.

They didn't get there. But Chamberlain did. While the team failed to get past the first round of the playoffs, losing to the Syracuse Nats in three straight games, Wilt averaged 38.4 points per game in his second year. And in his third year, while his ability to attract fans had fallen off and Warriors attendance was dwindling, he etched his name among his sport's immortals by scoring 100 points in a single game.

It happened on March 2, 1962, before a slim crowd of 4,124 at Hershey, Pennsylvania, where the Warriors trained and occasionally played regular-season games because they weren't drawing all that well at home. The opposition was the Knicks.

Chamberlain scored 23 points in the first quarter, 18 in the second, 28 in the third, and 31 in the fourth. With 10 minutes left in the game, Wilt had scored 75 points, just three less than the NBA record he had set three months earlier in a three-overtime loss to the Los Angeles Lakers.

"When Zink [public address announcer Dave Zinkoff] announced that Wilt had 85 points," remembered Tom Meschery, an outstanding forward on that Warriors team, "everything changed. Wilt went after it. The atmosphere was really electric. The Knicks tried to foul other Warriors as soon as we got the ball. But our players would get the ball and throw it down court to Wilt. Nobody told us to feed him. But we all were doing it. I couldn't believe my eyes. Everything Wilt did was golden."

The Knicks tried to stall, but when they did, the Warriors fouled them. Three Knicks centers fouled out trying to guard Wilt. When it was finally over, Chamberlain had shot 36 of 63 from the floor and 28 of 32 from the foul line. Al Attles was the Warriors' second-highest scorer with 17 points. The Warriors won by the staggering score of 169–147. And, according to Bill Campbell who broadcast the affair, "That game really helped to put the NBA on the map because it brought so much attention to the league.

"To me, the first tipoff that Wilt was going to do something spectacular was when he started making all his foul shots," added Campbell. "He was an atrocious foul-shooter. Worse than Shaquille O'Neal, which is pretty bad. A lot of people said the rims were soft. I don't know about that. I just know he had a helluva night, although I think it became more of an exhibition after you saw guys like Paul Arizin and Tom Meschery passing up good shots and Guy Rodgers getting 20 assists."

By the end of the season, Chamberlain had averaged 50.4 points per game. He was playing virtually every minute of every game. Gottlieb, who had called Wilt, "Babe Ruth all over again," a term he had once used to describe Joe Fulks, had exactly what he had wanted.

"Gotty always wanted Wilt to score three zillion points because that's what translated into an increased gate," Dolson recalled. "It's because of Gotty that Wilt scored those 100 points at Hershey. Around then, Wilt was having those fantastic years when he was averaging around 50 points.

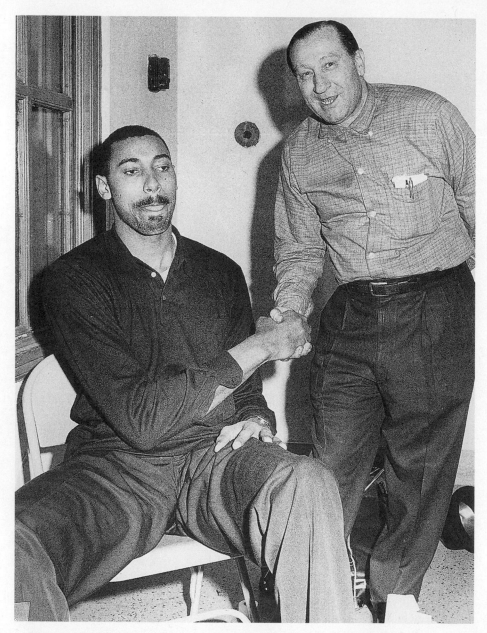

Mike Iannarella congratulates Chamberlin after a tough win over the Boston Celtics. Iannarella was an associate of Gottlieb's for 48 years. *(Courtesy of Ed Iannarella)*

That's because Gotty made sure he had the ball. Wilt shot whenever he damn pleased. And if he didn't shoot enough, Gotty wanted him to shoot more. He told other players to get him the ball."

It was all part of Gottlieb's strategy. "Gotty always wanted to have the high scorer in the league," said Ernie Beck. "He wanted Paul to lead the league. When Neil (Johnston) came up, he wanted him to be the high scorer. He wanted Wilt to lead the league. That's not the way to win championships, but Eddie always thought it would be the selling point that would bring people out to the games. And to him, that was a more important thing than winning a championship."

One time, Tom Gola was spotted before a game standing outside the locker room at Convention Hall, throwing a ball against a wall. Asked what he was doing, Gola said, "Practicing our offense. Throw the ball to Wilt and stand there." But, Gola also said, "No one ever dealt with the kind of pressure Wilt did. He was expected to be perfect."

"Wilt was so good that you had to get the ball in to him," said Arizin. "He was just a tremendous player. I think they bent the rules with Wilt a little bit. And people talked about him missing practices. But in the three years I played with Wilt, I never remember him missing a practice."

Wilt was far from being a one-dimensional player. Sure he could score, rebound, block shots, and defend when he was so inclined. But one year (1967–68), he wanted to prove that he was really a more versatile performer than he was thought to be. Instead of shooting at his usual rate, he focused on assists. The Dipper wound up leading the league in that category, averaging 21 assists per game.

"His aim," Gottlieb told Alan Richman for an article in the *Evening Bulletin*, "was to show he could do anything he wanted on the basketball court as well as or better than anyone else. And I don't believe that you can doubt his determination."

Gottlieb and Chamberlain had a special relationship. Each had a considerable amount of respect for the other. And they liked each other as people, although there was seldom any socializing between the two away from the arena.

There was no doubt that Chamberlain was Gottlieb's special pet. After all, Wilt was his drawing card, and Gotty didn't want to lose him. Many accused Gotty of spoiling his superstar. Whatever Wilt wanted, Wilt got. Gotty saw to that. "At halftime, Eddie would even go out and get him a soda," Beck said. "He knew dollar signs and what Wilt was doing for the team. He made sure that Wilt was happy."

When Chamberlain needed to be defended, Gottlieb was always quick to come to his aid. It was said that Wilt sometimes missed practices. "He never missed a single practice when he was with the Warriors in Philadelphia or San Francisco," Gotty told Alan Richman. Wilt was criticized for shooting too much, for not playing defense, for failing to pass the ball, for all kinds of transgressions, both real and imagined. Whenever such complaints arose, Gottlieb grabbed his sword and stood up for his star player.

For his part, Chamberlain was not reluctant to share his opinion about Gottlieb. "Eddie Gottlieb was a first-class owner," he said in his autobiography, "the only real basketball man who's ever owned a club I played for."

When Wilt scored his 10,000th career point, Gotty bought him a special trophy. It stood well over 7 feet high, a few inches taller than the Dipper himself.

There was one element of Wilt's game, though, that bothered Gottlieb: Chamberlain's poor foul shooting, which hovered in the 40 percent range through much of his career. Once, Gotty hired Cy Kaselman to coach Wilt in the fine art of foul shooting. Kaselman, who had been a magnificent foul shooter with the SPHAS, once sinking 247 of 261 free throws, often had put on exhibitions shooting blindfolded at the Broadwood Hotel. He helped Wilt improve to 65–70 percent from the line.

As they were throughout the parts of their careers that overlapped, Wilt's battles with Boston's Bill Russell ranked among the most memorable—not to mention fiercest—clashes in professional sports. Chamberlain, the scoring and rebounding wizard, and Russell, the magnificent defender, were friends off the court but bitter rivals on it. Although Russell is usually credited with having held the upper hand in their on-court debates and somewhat overshadows Wilt because of his team's 11 NBA titles to the Dipper's two, few who saw them will ever forget the sight of number 6 and number 13 pounding the daylights out of each other.

The 1961–62 Warriors lost to the Celtics in seven games in the Eastern Division final. Soon afterward, Gottlieb delivered a blockbuster announcement. He had sold the Warriors to a group that was moving the team to San Francisco.

Chamberlain went with the team to the West Coast and had two and one-half outstanding seasons. Then in 1965, one and one-half years after the Syracuse Nats had become the Philadelphia 76ers, Wilt came back to his hometown in a stunning trade that gave the Warriors Connie Dierking, Lee Shaffer, Paul Newmann, and cash. According to Berman, one of the reasons San Francisco was willing to trade Wilt was because the team had given him a physical exam and found a previously undetected heart problem. "They were afraid he'd have a heart attack, and they'd get stuck with him," Berman said. "So, they agreed to trade him."

It was said that Chamberlain wasn't overjoyed about coming home.

At the time, former Nats star Dolph Schayes was the coach of the 76ers. "Larry Merchant [of the *Daily News*] called me at 3 a.m." Schayes recalled. "I said, 'What the hell are you calling me for?' He said, 'The 76ers just traded for Wilt.' I sat straight up in bed.

"I remember Wilt was absolutely against the trade," said Schayes. "He did not want to come back to Philadelphia. He wanted to make a deal with the [Los Angeles] Lakers and go there."

Instead, along with giving him a salary reportedly of $375,000, Ike Richman, the 76ers' co-owner, made a special deal with Wilt. "When Wilt came back from San Francisco, Richman told him he'd get him a piece of the team," said Pollack. "But Ike died in Boston Garden soon after that. The following year the Sixers won the title, and Wilt told Irv Kosloff [the team's remaining owner] that Ike had said he was going to get a piece of the team. Koz said, 'I don't know anything about that.' Ike had never told him. Koz said, 'Why should I give a piece of the team to a player?' He and Wilt talked about it all the next season. Finally, Wilt said, 'If you're not going to fulfill the promises made to me, I don't want to play here anymore.'"

On July 9, 1968, the 76ers traded Chamberlain to the Lakers for Archie Clark, Darrall Imhoff, and Jerry Chambers. Wilt's long, brilliant, and sometimes stormy Philadelphia career was over. But not before he had paid a special tribute to the man who had helped to make him a superstar.

When Chamberlain scored his 20,000th career point on January 2, 1966, he mounted the game ball on a silver plaque and presented it to Gotty. An inscription on the plaque read, "Your foresight into the future of basketball gave me the needed inspiration to drive on to goals like this. Thanks, Dip."

Chamberlain played five years with the Lakers, teaming in 1971–72 with Jerry West and Elgin Baylor to lead LA to the NBA championship. When he retired after the 1972–73 season, he had career averages of 30.1 points and 22.9 rebounds per game. He had scored 31,419 points and led the league in scoring seven straight times and in rebounding 11 times (and never fouled out of a game). He was the only center in NBA history ever to lead the league in assists, while compiling a career total of 4,643. He once got 22 points, 25 rebounds, and 21 assists in a single game (1968). He had won four MVP awards, set 55 regular-season records, and 118 times had scored 50 or more points in a single game.

"Wilt was the greatest player who ever played the game," Gola once told *Evening Bulletin* sportswriter Frank Bilovsky. "He dominated it. He could do it in every phase—scoring, rebounding, defense, assists. You name it, he could do it."

And he immeasurably rewarded Gottlieb's brilliantly successful effort in the distant past of altering the territorial draft, thus changing the course of basketball history. "When Wilt signed, I knew the game would never be the same," Gottlieb told Kiser some years later. "And I knew Wilt was going to make everybody money, and I knew he was worth any amount he asked."

That view was beyond dispute. Likewise, the act of putting the Dipper in a Philadelphia Warriors uniform and then watching him perform like nobody in the NBA has ever done before or since unquestionably ranks as Gotty's greatest achievement.

CHAPTER 15

• • •

Going to San Francisco

It was often said that money was what motivated Eddie Gottlieb. Everything had dollar signs on it. If a venture couldn't put some cash in his pocket, he wasn't interested. Gotty's bank account was the most important thing in his life.

Gottlieb always accounted for every dollar. He knew the attendance of every game and how much money that it would produce. He knew how much everything cost. He knew how much he was willing to pay for an item—or for a player's salary—and he wouldn't give a dime more.

Gotty watched his dollars like a hawk watches a mouse. It was said that he walked around with all his money in his pocket. He saw where every cent came in and where every cent went out. And nobody ever ripped him off. One time at Convention Hall, Gotty even chased a kid who was trying to steal a basketball.

The impression Gottlieb gave was that he was cheap. He was described as a penny-pincher, a tightwad. He was a guy who, when he doled out money, always asked for the change, no matter if it was only a few cents. Once in New York, he drove around and around a block until it was 6 p.m. after which it was not necessary to put money in a parking meter. An executive from another team asked Gotty one time for a ticket to a game, and The Mogul told him to bring a chair. When a player asked Gotty if he could take a basketball home, he was told it would cost him $25. The Warriors never had any assistant coaches before he got to the NBA. And the team doctor was an ear, nose, and throat specialist who got the job because he was a friend of Eddie's.

Gottlieb's penurious traits were especially conspicuous on road trips. At times, when the team had an out-of-town game, it would run out of adhesive tape and would have to borrow some from the other team. Players had to wash their own uniforms in hotel room sinks. Trainers didn't go on the road with the team. Once, when the team was coming home from New York on a chartered bus, Gotty tried to sell the empty seats to fans who were at the game. Often, when the team was traveling, The Mogul had it fly home after the game so he didn't have to spend money for hotel rooms. Most of the hotels that the team stayed in were pretty dismal, anyway.

When the team did stay in a hotel, Gottlieb knew the charge on every bill. "He made sure you paid for any extras you used, such as room service, telephone, things like that," said Tom Meschery. "You didn't get away with anything."

On the road, Gottlieb also knew the whereabouts of all the low-priced restaurants that served edible food. When leaving Madison Square Garden on the way home, for instance, he would tell the bus driver to go through the Lincoln Tunnel and head to Union City, New Jersey. where a restaurant served tasty steaks at reasonable prices.

"That stop was mandatory," said David Richman, Ike's son and Michael's brother.

The stories about Gottlieb's spending habits are legendary. Former Penn publicist Bob Paul remembered the time he saw Gottlieb standing on a street corner at 11:30 at night during a national amateur basketball tournament in Denver. "I said, 'Eddie, what are you doing out this late?' He said, 'They don't have a room for me at the hotel, so I'm going to sleep in the airport.' There was plenty of room in the hotel. He just didn't want to spend the money."

Al Attles recalled a two-day road trip that the team was about to take. "He gave everybody $14 for meal money," Attles said. "When he got to me, he asked if I had any ones. I told him I didn't, so he gave me three fives. A month later, he called me over and told me to give him a dollar. I said, 'What dollar?' He said, 'You remember, I gave you $15 on that road trip. You owe me a dollar.'"

George Dempsey had a similar experience. But in his case, the amount was even less. "I borrowed a couple of bucks from him on a road trip," he said. "I paid it back, but I still owed him 12¢. He didn't forget, and a whole year later, he asked me for the 12¢ I owed him."

Publicist and super statistician Harvey Pollack (left) and public address
announcer Dave Zinkoff were long-time friends and associates of Gottlieb's.
(Philadelphia Jewish Sports Hall of Fame, Adolph and Rose Levis Museum)

When Bill Mlkvy played with the Warriors while attending dental
school, he only appeared in uniform at home games and at a few nearby
away games. One road game was in New York. Mlkvy took the train to
Penn Station, thinking the game was at Madison Square Garden. "But I
found out the game was really in Kingston, so I took a cab to get there,"
Mlkvy said. "I got a receipt, and later when I went to get reimbursed,
Gottlieb look at it and laughed. 'Look at the big shot,' he said to Mike
Iannarella. Then he turned to me, and said, 'We don't take cabs.' He
gave me one dollar for what would've been subway fare."

Gottlieb could taketh away other ways, too. There was a time when he
decided to buy all the players handsome, navy blue sports coats with the letter W on the lapel. Gotty wanted the team to wear the jackets on road trips.
But when the team had an extended losing streak, he canceled the order.

Sometimes, Gottlieb was accused of being too stingy to rent a first-class
office or to hire a full complement of employees as would befit a professional sports team. His offices were always small and cluttered, noisy, with
phones ringing and voices yelling. Aside from Iannarella, Dave Zinkoff,
and Harvey Pollock, the latter two being part time, the size of the staff

was seldom bigger. It was often said that Gotty ran his office out of his hat, although The Mogul insisted that he rarely wore a hat.

Despite all the vignettes and jokes about the way Gottlieb handled money, there was another side to his financial practices. Quite simply, Gotty wasn't a rich man, and he didn't have money to fling around carelessly. He operated the team from the money he made from gate receipts, and if he didn't have it, he didn't spend it.

"The money was not as plentiful as it is today," said Paul Arizin. "I think Eddie was hustling just to get by. He was in basketball, not to get rich, but because he loved sports. That's why he was always so tough. He had to fight for every penny."

For Gottlieb, it was a fight for survival. "We had to make money or get out of the business," he once said. "We earned what we could, and we paid out [to players] what we could afford."

Mlkvy recalled the way Gottlieb paid players. "We were paid once a month," he said. "You always had to arrange an appointment to get your paycheck. I remember going into his office. I'd sit in a chair across from him. He'd say, 'Before I give you the check, let's review your stats. When you played against the Knicks, you played 10 minutes, and you didn't do crap. You were useless. I put you in, and you go out there, and you miss your first three shots. What's going on?' I'd listen, then he'd give me the check, and say, 'Now let's improve and work on this.'"

Negotiating new contracts each year was a ritual that few players enjoyed. "Eddie always made three points," Arizin said. "Either he felt you didn't have a good year, or he felt the team didn't have a good year, or—and you could never prove or disprove this because you could never look at the books—he didn't make any money. He would always hit you with one of those, and that would deter you from trying to get much of a raise."

Neil Johnston met Gottlieb one year to discuss a raise. Having just led the NBA in scoring, Johnston asked Gotty to at least double his $6,000 salary. Gottlieb reached into his pocket and handed the hook-shooting center the keys to the office. "Here," he said, "if I give you that kind of money, you'll own the team."

When Jerry Fleischman asked for more money one season, Gottlieb turned him down. "I own you," he said, "so you're not going anywhere."

After leading the league in scoring in his second season, Arizin joined the Marines, then returned to the Warriors two years later. "I'd earned $10,000 before I went, and when I came back, I said, 'I think I deserve a raise,'" Arizin said. "Eddie said, 'I don't know whether you can play any-more.' But finally I got a $1,500 raise, and I was happy."

"His word was as good as his bond," said Jerry Rullo, "but if a guy was holding out for more money, he would say, 'How many tickets can you sell?' If you weren't a big gate attraction, it would be hard to get more money. But he was fair. If he promised you something, you got it."

Following a superb first year, during which he had made the All-Star team, Meschery asked for a $15,000 raise. "See that window," Gotty said. "Before I give you that much money, I will jump out."

"Once a player came to see Eddie to negotiate a contract," recalled Attles. "Eddie listened to him, then the player said, 'Well, what do you think?' Eddie said, 'You'd better tell that to another team because I just traded you last night.' He was a very slick businessman. He had a rough exterior, but he had a big heart. I honestly believe he could not afford big contracts. His whole philosophy was, how do you fit in as a player and as a draw? He paid you on the basis of what he could afford and what he felt you could do for the team."

Even his players and close associates, never knew Gottlieb's real finan-cial condition. He figured his finances were nobody else's business, and he refused to divulge any details. "He kept his business activities pretty close to the vest," said Ernie Beck. "We never really knew anything about those things. Eddie was very close-mouthed about his business interests. I think he thought that the less people knew, the better it was."

As owner of the Warriors, Gottlieb, unlike many of his peers, never had any sources of income other than his team. And in those days, a team's financial situation depended solely on attendance, and small payments from radio and television for the rights to broadcast games. There were no signage, no super boxes, no licensing agreements, no money from parking or concessions, no selling the rights to a perfectly named stadium to some carpetbagger who would give the venue a company name—all modish practices that today put millions of dollars into a team's treasury.

Gottlieb had no choice but to run a tight ship. As part of that, he paid his bills on time, he scheduled games wherever he thought he could make some money, and he paid himself a minimum salary—it was esti-mated never to have exceeded $15,000. Warriors partners received no dividends and no bonuses. Their main perks were free tickets—and good seats—at home games.

"Dollar for dollar, I made a lot more money with the SPHAS than I did with the Warriors," Gottlieb told *Evening Bulletin* columnist Tom Fox.

"With the Warriors, we operated out of the receipts. I never ever spent more than I took in. I wasn't that daring. Of course, I never had a private plane or a helicopter. I never drove a Rolls Royce or a Mercedes-Benz, and I never had a multimillion television contract, either. I suppose that's why I never made a bank loan. I never had the collateral the owners have today."

"He was frugal," described Al Shrier. "He had to be. He didn't grow up a rich guy. He had to make his own way. But he knew what he had to do and he did it. That's what made him successful."

Pollock said that Gottlieb really wasn't a skinflint. "That description reflects the circumstances, not his personality," he said. "He just didn't have any money."

But he went anywhere to find some. Before he became a nationally prominent college and NBA coach, Jack Ramsay was a teacher and coach at Mt. Pleasant High School in Wilmington, Delaware, while also playing in the Eastern League. "The Warriors had fallen on hard times and badly needed income," Ramsay remembered. "Eddie called and asked if I could put together a game with an Eastern League team at the school. I couldn't get one team, but I put together an all-star team of eight guys. Eddie said, 'Make it seven, and I'll pay each one $50, the school will pay the expenses, and I'll keep the rest.' The gym was packed with 5,000 to 6,000 people. After the game, Eddie called the athletic director and me together, and said, 'What are your expenses?' He had all the money from the tickets in his pocket. He pulled out a roll, peeled off some money, and gave some to the athletic director for expenses, some to me for the players, plus $75 for my work. Then he said, 'Is everybody happy? Good.' And then he left."

In his personal life, though, Gottlieb, was well above the poverty line. He owned Cadillacs. He never ate at home. When he wasn't devouring a meal at Horn and Hardart's, he often dined at some of the best restaurants in the city. He had an active nightlife, frequently attending movies, as well as the top shows that came to town. He traveled. He attended Athletics, Phillies, Eagles, and Big Five games. He hung out with some of the city's most prosperous citizens.

Gottlieb had relatives in the area. One was a cousin, Rose Adler, who along with her husband, Charles, was a Russian immigrant. The family lived for many years with children Lillian and Gerald at 6216 Osage Street in a West Philadelphia community that was largely Jewish and that was just a few blocks from Gotty's longtime residence on Catherine Street.

One of The Mogul's close friends was NFL commissioner Bert Bell, a Philadelphian, too. Gottlieb and the one-time owner of the Eagles were often seen together at some of the downtown eateries.

Bill Campbell relayed the story of the night the two were on the same podium. In charge of putting together a sports night at a church in Wynnefield, Campbell asked Bell to attend and answer questions from the audience. "He agreed," said Campbell. "Several days later, I was in Gotty's office, and I told him about the event and that I was going to have Bert as a guest. He said, 'How come you've never asked me to appear at one of those functions?' I said, 'Why don't you come, too?' Sure enough, he did. And it turned out to be a night I'll never forget. They both spoke, and people were firing questions at them. The NFL commissioner and the owner of the Warriors on the same stage. It was the greatest speaking event I ever attended."

Gottlieb was never reluctant to help a friend in need. Even going back to his early days with the Warriors, Gottlieb showed a charitable side, although he never discussed it openly. "My second daughter was born with dislocated hips and needed extensive surgery," Ralph Kaplowitz recalled. "When Eddie found out about it, and without my asking, he offered to help with medical expenses. I had no insurance at the time. I was tempted to accept his offer, but I didn't. But I felt indebted to Eddie for his generosity."

Once, when an accident ended the career of a player, word got around that Gottlieb had bought the player a house. Gotty frequently helped retired players who had financial problems. "When no one was in trouble, his hands stayed in his pockets," wrote Jack Kiser in the *Daily News*. "But when you needed money, he took them out."

"He didn't socialize with players off the court," said Beck. "He never came to your house. But I remember one year when Neil bought his first home [in Broomall], Eddie loaned him the money for the down payment."

Gottlieb loaned Harry Litwack $50,000 to start a basketball camp in the Poconos. Many years later, he donated $7,500 to the Basketball Hall of Fame to establish a SPHAS display. He gave money to build a dormitory—named the Eddie Gottlieb House—at Orde Wingate School of Physical Education in Natanya, Israel. He helped to pay for a special memorial chapel at Congregation Beth Tovim at 59th Street and Drexel Road in Wynnefield, a synagogue he attended during his long years of residence on Salford Street. He helped to set up and contributed every

year to a scholarship fund to send worthy students from South Philadelphia High School to college. Once when a youth league in Camden
couldn't afford enough baseballs to finish its season, Gotty—unlike others who could've contributed—sent the group three dozen balls. When
Joe Fulks died, Gottlieb chartered an airplane to fly former teammates
and others to his funeral in Kentucky. And when Gotty reached the age
when he could no longer drive, he gave his car to a rabbi friend.

In his second year with the Warriors, Meschery was tapped by the
army. He was still serving when his father died back in California. "Gottlieb paid for my travel back and forth to San Francisco," Meschery said.

"He really cared about people," said Frank Dolson. "He was a very
thoughtful person. Sure, he was a terrific businessman, and business and
basketball were always on his mind. And while he drove a very hard bargain, on the other hand, he could be tremendously generous."

D. Donald Jamison, once a partner of Ike Richman's as a Philadelphia
lawyer before going on to serve as the presiding judge in the Pennsylvania Supreme Court, was a good friend of Gottlieb's for many years. "He
was the ultimate generous guy with friends," Jamison said. "He wanted to
be known for taking care of his friends."

At Christmas, Gottlieb always sent cards to friends. He gave out gifts
each holiday season, usually boxes of Hershey chocolate bars, which he
bought by the case, or a bottle of whiskey, which he also gave to his favorite writers. In his later years, he also sent friends a newly minted coin.

One of the most enlightening stories about Gottlieb's generosity
involved his good friend Dave Zinkoff. The story began when The Zink,
on one of the first of his countless trips to visit the sick and the less fortunate, called on an orphanage to talk to the children about the Warriors.
"I wasn't too experienced," Zink told Gaeton Fonzi for *Greater Philadelphia Magazine*, "and I started feeling sorry for all these kids listening to
me with such interest. Before I know it, I've invited all 30 of them to be
guests of the Warriors at a basketball game.

"When I come back and tell Gotty what I did, boy, you ought to have
seen him turn white. 'Why the hell did you do that?' he exploded. 'What
are you gonna do, invite every kid you meet to a ballgame? What do
you think we're doing here? This is a business. How are we gonna make
money if you invite everybody you meet to a ballgame?'

"Well, I really felt bad because I knew I really had no right to invite
those kids," Zink continued. "So I went home and wrote out a check for
the tickets for all 30 kids. Man, you think he was mad before, you should

have seen him when I gave him the check. 'What the hell is this?' he yells. 'What the hell are you, a wise guy? You invited those kids to see a ballgame, and they're gonna see a ballgame. To hell with your check.' And with that he rips up my check."

If a lack of money was ever a serious problem with Gottlieb, it ceased being an issue in 1962 when he sold the Warriors to a group that relocated the team to San Francisco. The selling price was $850,000, making Gotty a wealthy man for the first time in his life.

The events leading up to the sale were somewhat bizarre. Before he sold the team, Gottlieb had bought out the shares of both Lou Glazer and Abe Saperstein, leaving Jules Trumper and his sons, Alan and Jerome, as the only other stockholders. The buyout of Saperstein was rather acrimonious.

Abe and Eddie had been friends since the 1930s and had spent several decades aiding and abetting each other's interests. Gottlieb even went each summer with Saperstein and his Harlem Globetrotters on their annual trip to Europe. But when Gotty lured Wilt Chamberlain away from the Globies in 1959 and Abe tried to coax Wilt back to his team the following year, a rift began to appear. It widened one year later when Saperstein expressed an interest in obtaining the Minneapolis Lakers franchise and relocating it to the West Coast. When that did not happen, Saperstein blamed Gottlieb for not making a strong enough effort on his behalf. The friendship deteriorated even further, and in the summer of 1960, Gotty refused to accompany the Globetrotters abroad for the first time in five years.

"I have too much to attend to here," he claimed. When asked what would happen to Saperstein's stock in the Warriors, Gottlieb said, "Abe and I will work something out."

Saperstein no longer wanted the stock, anyway. He had his lawyers prepare the papers, and a suitable arrangement was made for him to relinquish his shares to Gottlieb.

Meanwhile, Gottlieb was reportedly trying to hatch his own idea involving the West Coast. As early as 1955, there had been reports that the NBA had an interest in placing teams in Los Angeles and San Francisco. In late 1960, rumors began to surface that it might be the Warriors who would move to Los Angeles. Gotty would sell the club and put a new franchise in New Orleans. He was also said to be angling to assume control of the New Orleans baseball team that played in the Southern Association.

That would open the way for Gottlieb to place a New Orleans team in the newly formed Continental League, the creation of Eddie's old nemesis, Branch Rickey, who had come to Gotty asking for help in putting the league together. Gottlieb denied the report, and, as it turned out, the plan never materialized.

Saperstein, all the while, was not finished with big league basketball. And in 1961, he formed the American Basketball League (ABL), a circuit that included a team from Hawaii and one called the Cleveland Pipers, which was owned by a budding 30-year-old tycoon named George Steinbrenner. Saperstein made himself the commissioner, ran the league out of his Globetrotters office, and installed the three-point shot, a 30-second clock, and a bonus shot after five team fouls. The ABL was almost an instant failure, and folded in January 1963, one and one-half years after it began.

Back in Philadelphia, the uncertainty surrounding the Warriors became more pronounced. Early in 1961, Gottlieb revealed that he had turned down an offer by a Los Angeles group to buy 51 percent of the team for $500,000 and move it to the southern California city. Gotty would have remained president of the team, but he rejected the offer because he didn't want to move to the West Coast.

Soon after that, Gottlieb fielded another proposal, this one from a 30-person group headed by Ambrose (Bud) Dudley, a prominent local sportsman who was president of the Philadelphia Ramblers ice hockey team and who the following year established a college football game called the Liberty Bowl that was held for several years at Municipal Stadium. Dudley, who was also attempting to purchase the Arena from Pete Tyrrell and his associates, made an offer for the team that was estimated to be between $350,000 and $400,000. Gottlieb countered with an asking price of $1 million. "I am not anxious to sell the Warriors," he said, "but I'm always open to a proposition." Dudley called Gottlieb's asking price "a little high." Again, no deal was made.

One deal that Gottlieb did make, however, was along the coaching lines. After Neil Johnston was dismissed, The Mogul enthusiastically pursued the University of North Carolina's highly successful coach Frank McGuire, offering him a three-year contract. McGuire first accepted the offer, then turned it down, and Gottlieb switched his attention to Memphis State's Bob Vanatta. But Vanatta also pulled out after saying that he wanted a three-year contract, while getting only a two-year offer from Gottlieb.

Gottlieb redirected his focus back to McGuire. This time, the three-time NCAA coach of the year accepted Gotty's proposal of a three-year

Gotty, guard Guy Rodgers (center), and coach Frank McGuire were award recipients at a basketball writers dinner in Philadelphia. *(Temple University Libraries, Urban Archives, Philadelphia, Pennsylvania)*

contract that called for a reported $20,000 per year. "I got the number one coach in America," chortled The Mogul. Gottlieb's only instructions to McGuire were to make sure Wilt got the ball so he could continue to score points by the bushel.

McGuire's tenure in Philadelphia was brief, but eventful. Once, the team, with McGuire, Gottlieb, and Ike Richman accompanying it, was returning to Philadelphia after a game in New York. Craving food, the team stopped along the way for dinner at a coffee shop that was not only crowded, but had just one waitress. Seeing the potential for a long delay, McGuire, Gotty, and Richman rolled up their sleeves, jumped behind the counter, and served dinner to the group.

The 1961–62 team compiled a 49–31 record and advanced to the division final before losing in seven games to the Celtics. But McGuire, a classy gentleman who wore starched white shirts, sharp sport coats, and silk ties, and rented a hotel room in Cherry Hill, New Jersey, during the season, found Gottlieb's thrift hard to deal with. One of the final straws came when the Warriors ran out of adhesive tape before a game in Syracuse. When the Nats' trainer refused to give tape to the Warriors, McGuire had to run to a nearby store and buy some. By then it was becoming apparent that Gotty was considering selling the team and moving it to the West Coast. With a son suffering from cerebral palsy, McGuire had no interest in moving. He quit the Warriors and returned to the college ranks at the University of South Carolina.

As the 1961–62 season moved toward a conclusion, the reports that Gottlieb was flirting with the possibility of unloading the Warriors became increasingly frequent. Gottlieb, it was suggested, was troubled by the escalating costs of operating an NBA team. He was particularly concerned with the rising level of players' salaries, not the least of which was the expected soaring salary demands of Chamberlain, who would soon be negotiating for a new contract. And he was adamant in his dislike for players' agents, a group that he rightfully felt was about to have a major impact on professional sports.

Gottlieb was also having trouble getting good dates at Convention Hall. Meanwhile, the highly popular Big Five was selling out almost every night, thus siphoning off much needed dollars from the Warriors' coffers. Along with that, Warriors attendance had been declining the past few years, dropping from an average per game of 8,000 in Wilt's first year to about 5,600 by 1961. Just 161,000 fans paid to see the Warriors play at home during the 1961–62 season. "Apparently, the novelty of seeing Wilt stuff the ball in the basket is wearing off," wrote Herb Good in the *Evening Bulletin*.

"He saw the handwriting on the wall," said Pollack. "He knew, with salaries increasing by such big amounts, that he was getting to the point where he wouldn't be able to operate the team. Financially, he couldn't compete. After all, his only source of income was the team."

There seemed to be other reasons, too. "I think Eddie might have been getting a little tired," said Alan Trumper. "He might have been a little down on players. He wasn't used to that. When he started out, what he said was it. Nobody ever gave him any back talk. As players started to get stronger, once in a while they would say something that he didn't care for. I don't know the exact reason he wanted to sell, but I think these were some of the things that fed into that decision."

Gotty was also aging. He was now 64 years old, and the long years of hard work had begun taking a toll on him. This was an opportunity to make some real money, which he was not likely to make elsewhere. Having financial security for the first time in his life would also be a welcome change, Gottlieb felt.

To add emphasis, Arizin, who had originally announced his plans to retire after the 1960–61 season, then was persuaded to return for one more year, said that he was retiring for certain after the 1961–62 campaign. The All-Star forward said that he was leaving basketball to accept a sales position with International Business Machines (IBM).

"Most of us, including myself, looked upon the game not as something we were going to do all our lives, but as something we would do for a few years, then get out," Arizin remembered. "It wasn't life-dependent, and we weren't making enough money to say, 'well, I don't have to work the rest of my life.' So we got out when we felt like getting out and went to work in the real world. That's the way I saw it, and that's why I retired."

The loss of Arizin delivered a severe blow to the Warriors organization, not to mention made Gottlieb angry about his star player's decision. And it fueled the widening view that the Warriors were about to leave Philadelphia.

As late as January 16, 1962, Gottlieb was still denying his interest in selling the team. "We expect to remain in Philadelphia," he said. "We are not planning to sell or move the franchise."

A few weeks later, Gottlieb admitted that he had fielded nearly one dozen offers for the team from local and out-of-town groups, including one from San Francisco. "But I haven't talked to these people," Gotty told United Press International. "Maybe my attorney has, but whether he did or didn't, I wouldn't know. I'm not considering anything until the end of the season, and I can't say that I'll consider anything after the season."

Soon afterward, another story began making the rounds. Maurice Podoloff was rumored to be resigning as commissioner of the NBA, although he still had two more years left on his contract. Podoloff's successor was rumored to be Eddie Gottlieb, assuming he was no longer affiliated with a team in the league.

Podoloff, the only commissioner since the league began, agreed that Gottlieb would be a logical choice as his successor. "But I have no present intention of resigning," he said. As for Gottlieb, Podoloff said, "You can't tell what he'll do."

One thing Gottlieb had decided to do for sure, despite his earlier denials, was to sell the Warriors. He realized that the highest purchase price for an NBA team was the $250,000 paid for the Rochester Royals in 1957. He knew the Warriors would command a much higher amount. Moreover, there was a strong desire in the NBA office to place a second team in California, now that the Lakers were already there.

"Bob Short had said he wasn't making any money in Minneapolis and moved the Lakers to Los Angeles," said Dolph Schayes. "Then the NBA said it needed two teams on the West Coast and asked Danny Biasone if he wanted to move the Syracuse team out there. He wasn't interested in moving the Nats from Syracuse. So the focus switched to the Warriors."

Gottlieb was approached by New York City businessmen Matty Simmons and Leo Mogel, two executives of the Diners Club, a worldwide credit card company. Simmons and Mogel represented a group that included Marshall Leahy, general counsel of the National Football League. Having seen how well the Lakers had done in Los Angeles, the pair wanted to buy the team and move it to San Francisco. They were convinced that a team in San Francisco would do well. They felt that their club would form a natural rivalry with the Lakers. And they were smitten by the notion of having Chamberlain on their team. They offered Gotty $850,000 for the Warriors.

When word got out that Gottlieb was entertaining serious offers to sell the Warriors, a sizable public outcry arose. A local radio station even launched a campaign to "keep the Warriors" and received 1,500 cards and letters. "A lot of people were upset," recalled Campbell. "The main reason Eddie wanted to sell the Warriors was because people never came to games. But these were the same people complaining about his selling the team. I remember Gotty saying, 'If all these people had bought tickets and come to games, we wouldn't be selling the team.' There was a lot of resentment, but Eddie didn't let it bother him."

Gottlieb had a bigger problem, anyway. He needed approval from the league to move the team to San Francisco. But despite earlier claims by the league that it wanted a second team on the West Coast, Gotty's plans hit a snag. At a lengthy meeting that lasted until 11:30 p.m. at the Roosevelt Hotel in New York, old friends and fellow owners Ned Irish of the Knicks and Walter Brown of the Celtics adamantly opposed the move. A major reason was that the switch would leave Philadelphia, despite decreasing attendance in recent years, without a team and the league without an important—and highly visible—charter member. Jim Heffernan speculated in the *Bulletin* that another reason for the rejection was that Eastern teams' attendance would suffer "since Wilt Chamberlain would not make as many appearances in New York and Boston" because the relocated Warriors would reside in a different division.

"I don't know how anybody could agree with it [the proposed sale]," Brown was quoted in the *Inquirer* as saying. "I have no case against Eddie. I'm only doing what I think is best for the league. I feel as though Eddie has some obligation to the league, too."

Gottlieb argued that he intended to remedy that problem by placing another team in Philadelphia. His original plan was to convince Biasone to bring the Nats to Philly, but the Syracuse owner declined the invitation. Then, at the urging of the other owners, Gotty tried to swing a deal for first the Detroit Piston, then the Chicago Zephyrs. Both attempts failed.

Gotty then said that he would start a new team that would be manned mostly by local players such as Arizin, Tom Gola, Hubie White, Wayne Hightower, and others. When the other owners couldn't settle on a viable plan to stock the new team and wouldn't agree to sell or trade to Gotty some players of their own, that idea fizzled, too. And with it went Gottlieb's attempt to relocate the Warriors to San Francisco. Two days after the meeting, he withdrew his proposal to sell and move the team.

"It was a bitter disappointment for Gottlieb," Good reported in the *Bulletin*. "It would have been a fantastic, unprecedented deal if he had been able to pull it off. But the other league owners weren't inclined to let The Mogul have his cake and eat it, too. Gottlieb went to New York in high spirits under the impression it wouldn't take more than half an hour to get the sale approved and to get permission and help to get started in business all over again. He returned to Philadelphia downcast from missing out on his golden opportunity. But he did his best to shrug it off as one of the breaks of the game. 'I'll make the best of it,' he said. 'I suppose everything will work out all right. I'll still eat and I'll still sleep.'

"'If they had agreed to my plan, Philadelphia still would have had a strong team,' he lamented. 'It might not have been as strong as the present club, but it would have made a good showing and everyone would have been happy. As it turned out, I killed my own deal to make sure Philadelphia had a strong team.' Gottlieb said he probably could have had the sale approved if he had been willing to settle 'for 10 rinky-dinks on a new team. But I couldn't consider putting a team in the league that wouldn't have been a representative one. So I gave up the whole idea.'"

The idea, though, wasn't completely dead. Gottlieb continued to talk with the other NBA owners. And just two weeks after getting vetoed at the New York meeting, Gottlieb announced that the league had reversed its earlier decision and had approved the sale of the Warriors and the club's transfer to San Francisco by a seven to two vote. Again, Brown and Irish were the two dissenters.

With the approval, Gottlieb agreed to sell the team for $850,000, some $825,000 more than it had cost to purchase the club in 1952. John Dell reported in the *Inquirer* that Gottlieb received $425,000 up front and would be paid the balance in installments over a period of several years. "Selling was a very good deal for me," Gottlieb joyfully told the press, "because I put in so many years in basketball, and I got to think about retirement. It was a once in a lifetime chance."

When asked by Heffernan how it felt to give up a team with which he had such a long involvement, Gottlieb was upbeat. "I have strong feelings for Philadelphia," he said, "but I don't think it's up to me to carry the burden."

Nevertheless, the deal surprised some and perplexed others. "What in the world is Gotty going to do with himself now?" asked Neil Johnston. "He has done what his head's been telling him to do for several years, but his heart wouldn't let him."

Gottlieb, however, was far from through with basketball, or, for that matter, the San Francisco Warriors. Because the new owners had no previous contact with professional basketball, Gotty's experience was desperately needed. He was given a one-year contract at a reported pay of $35,000 to help run the team. His title was officially a consultant, although his job resembled that of a general manager. In effect, Gotty was hired to run the team.

The new owners also made another smart move. Realizing that the team's ownership group had no visible local representation, Franklin Mieuli was offered stock. A native Californian, Mieuli had attended the University of Oregon where his roommate was Dick Whitman, later an outfielder on the 1950 Phillies National League champions. He had become a radio/TV producer in San Francisco where he also owned small interests in both the Giants baseball team and the 49ers football team.

"They needed a local face," Mieuli said, "so they offered me a piece of the team. I wound up with 10 percent."

There was one other issue that needed to be resolved. It involved the players: Who was going to San Francisco and who wasn't? Arizin said he was not interested in moving to the West Coast, preferring instead to work full-time at IBM. Tom Gola also expressed a desire not to relocate to California, suggesting that he might retire to pursue other interests in the Philadelphia area. Chamberlain—a major key in the deal—first refused to switch coasts, then changed his mind after he and Gottlieb negotiated a lucrative new contract. The Warriors' other Philadelphia natives, Guy Rodgers and draft choice Hubie White, readily agreed to move. (Later, Gola also agreed to go to San Francisco, but as previously promised was traded back to an Eastern Division team [the Knicks] after one year there. Arizin stayed home and played three years with the Camden Bullets of the Eastern League.)

The Warriors' first year in San Francisco proved to be a disaster. After McGuire decided not to accompany the team to the West Coast, Bob Feerick, a player in the early years of the BAA, was named coach. But he proved to be incapable of coaching a pro team. The Warriors played in an ancient relic called the Cow Palace, which had a capacity of 14,000, but most of those seats were never occupied. Although Chamberlain averaged 44.8 points and 24.3 rebounds pr game, the team finished next to last with a disappointing 31–49 record.

"It was a terrible year," remembered Mieuli, who, once the club moved, had been named its president. "We didn't draw. On a good night, we'd draw no more than 7,500. People out here didn't know the pro game. They only knew the college game. And Wilt would dunk one ball after another, but that was too dull for the fans. They didn't come to see that. He'd score 40 points, and we'd still lose. Once he scored 73, and we lost. The Cow Palace was a bad place to play. We couldn't get good dates, and we wound up playing home games in San Diego, San Jose, and various other locations. We thought we would win, but we didn't even make the playoffs."

Mieuli said that the team lost $250,000 in its first year. "After that, the Diners Club guys wanted out. They sold the team to me, making me the majority owner."

Gottlieb, who was supposed to stay in San Francisco for just one season, was asked to return for another year. Gotty, who lived at the Jack Tar Hotel during the season, but moved back to Philadelphia for the summer, living with Belle at 2201 North Salford Street, agreed. This time he was labeled Mieuli's special assistant and was the owner's representative on the NBA's Board of Governors.

"He ran the team," said Mieuli, who owned the club until 1986, long after it had been renamed the Golden State Warriors. "He made trades, sold tickets, he even hired the coach. We worked very closely together, and he became one of my best friends. I didn't have any experience in basketball. I was a student at his knees. He taught me everything, how to run a team, the rules, even where to buy uniforms. He was wonderful. If it wasn't for him, today there'd be no such thing as the Golden State Warriors."

One of Gottlieb's most important actions was to dump the old coach and hire a new one. In Gotty's eyes, Feerick was a dismal failure. "He does not know the score," Gottlieb stated. "He does not know how to run the team. He's just a nice guy. But his ideas on the game are ass backwards." Feerick was then named the Warriors' general manager.

Gottlieb soon found the coach he wanted. His name was Alex Hannum, a journeyman NBA performer who, as a player-coach of the St. Louis Hawks in 1956–57, had pushed the Boston Celtics to the seventh game of the NBA final before losing the deciding game by two points in the final seconds of overtime. Hannum, who had piloted the Syracuse Nats for three season from 1960 through 1963 and who later coached the 76ers to the 1966–67 NBA title, immediately justified Gotty's choice by guiding the Warriors to first place in the Western Division. The Warriors then defeated St. Louis in seven games in the Western final, but lost, four games to one, to the Celtics in the championship round.

"We still weren't drawing well," said Meschery, who had moved with the Warriors back to his native state and become one of San Francisco's most effective players. "The owners were determined to make a go of it, but it took a while for us to catch on. Wilt saved the franchise, and then after that, Nate Thurmond and Rick Barry came along to help keep it alive. Hannum helped, too, because he was such a charismatic coach."

Even Hannum couldn't do much during the 1964–65 season—his second of three with San Francisco. Unwilling and unable to pay Chamberlain his reported $85,000 salary, Mieuli traded him to the 76ers during the season, and the Warriors plummeted to a 17–63 record. It was one of the worst marks in NBA history, and it sent the team back down to the bottom of the list of fan preferences for sports entertainment. It remained there until Thurmond and Barry became high-level players.

The Warriors' dismal season wasn't helped by that year's draft. Hannum had urged the Warriors to select Barry Kramer instead of Mel Counts, Gottlieb's choice. Gotty did not hesitate to criticize the selec-

After Gottlieb sold the Warriors to a group that moved the team to San Francisco, he was joined at his Hall of Fame induction by (from left) Ben Kerner, Franklin Mieuli, Danny Biasone, and Walter Kennedy. *(Naismith Basketball Hall of Fame)*

tion. Then the following year, after Kramer had been a major disappointment, Gotty took Hannum for a walk around the block the night before the draft. "You blew it last year," Gotty said. "If you want to keep your job, you better take [Rick] Barry." Hannum heeded the advice and chose the future NBA All-Star.

By then, Gottlieb had fulfilled his obligations in San Francisco, and then some. He was still due nearly half of the balance of the Warriors' selling price. (Mieuli said that in lieu of payments, he gave Gotty stock in the team, which he held until 1965, by which time he had paid off the remaining debt.) Gotty longed to be back in Philadelphia. The Warriors gave Gotty the title of "Eastern Representative"—which meant he represented the team at league meetings in New York—and he came home to stay.

The 76ers Arrive

When Eddie Gottlieb shipped the Warriors to San Francisco after the 1961–62 season, Philadelphia was left briefly without a professional basketball team. An attempt was made to fill that spot in 1962 by the Philadelphia Tapers, a team that had begun the previous season in Washington, then moved during the campaign to Long Island, New York.

Part of Abe Saperstein's one-year-old American Basketball League, the Tapers were staffed mostly by NBA rejects and pro ball wannabes and were coached by a basketball unknown named Mario Perri. Playing at Convention Hall, the Tapers averaged 700 fans per game, a figure that was matched by—and in rare cases exceeded—the attendance of most of the other teams in the league. With such lack of fan support and an estimated $2 million in debt, the league disbanded midway through the 1962–63 season.

The Tapers, though, weren't the only group that tried to fill the void created by the Warriors' departure. From California, Gottlieb made a similar attempt.

Gottlieb was already working quietly to have another NBA team placed in Philadelphia. Chicago and Detroit were originally considered possibilities, but were no longer in the picture. The most likely candidate was the Syracuse Nationals, whose majority shareholder was Danny Biasone, like Gotty, one of the pioneers of the league.

"Danny was losing money," recalled Dolph Schayes, who as a Nat at that time was one of the league's leading players. "They'd raised the rent at War Memorial Arena [the Nats' home in Syracuse], the team wasn't drawing, and Danny was worried about rising salaries. Gotty told him, 'I have a couple of investors. If you ever want to sell the team, let me know.'"

The potential investors were Ike Richman, longtime lawyer for Gottlieb and the Warriors, as well as Wilt Chamberlain, and Irv Kosloff, owner of Roosevelt Paper Company, a business he had launched in 1932 and turned into one of the nation's largest suppliers of printing paper. Both Richman and Kosloff were devout Warriors fans. They were both South Philly natives, attended South Philadelphia High School together, and were for many years acquaintances of Gottlieb's. In fact, Gotty had been Kosloff's basketball coach back in the late 1920s at George Thomas Junior High School.

Always one step ahead of everybody else, Gottlieb realized that giving the Nats some exposure in Philadelphia would not only show Biasone that the city would be a good place to ship his beloved team but would also help make the club more familiar to fans as well as to potential buyers. Accordingly, Gotty promoted several doubleheaders involving the Nats at Convention Hall. He even bought the balls for the games. Later, he instructed Mike Iannarella, who handled the ticket sales for the games, to make sure each time that he sent Biasone a check for $10,000.

Biasone, who, during the 1962–63 season, expected to lose some $100,000 playing in Syracuse, was never far from Gottlieb's sights. The Nats' owner had promised that he would talk first to Gotty's friends when the time came to entertain thoughts of selling the team. From San Francisco, Gotty talked regularly with Biasone.

"We are working quietly, trying to do something for next season," Gotty wrote to Iannarella in a letter from San Francisco dated January 2, 1963. Ken Berman confirmed The Mogul's role in bringing the Nats to Philadelphia. "He was working behind the scenes to make it happen," he said. "Eddie was calling all the shots to arrange the move."

In May, Biasone got in touch with Gottlieb's friends Kosloff and Richman. As reconstructed by Irv Kosloff's son, Ted, neither man had enough money to purchase the club outright, so they decided to find 10 investors who would each put up $50,000. But when no one answered the call, Kosloff and Richman decided to borrow the money and buy the team themselves.

An agreement was finally worked out, and Syracuse stockholders by a vote of 165½ to 7½ agreed to sell the club to Kosloff and Richman for $500,000. Compared with the money Gottlieb got for the Warriors, the price was a bargain. (Who would have dreamed that in 1996, the very same team would sell for $130 million, and by 2005 was estimated by *Forbes* magazine to be valued at $350 million?)

Biasone, who had made most of his money operating a bowling alley, said he was sad to see the team leave Syracuse. "I feel very badly that this had to come about," he said. "But because of the increase in costs of operation, it is impossible to operate."

When the sale was announced on May 15, 1963, rumors immediately began to circulate that Kosloff and Richman were actually fronts for Gottlieb. Gotty, it was said, was the real owner of the team. He, of course, denied the claims. "I am not involved in this deal," he told Jim Heffernan of the *Evening Bulletin*. Gottlieb, still a driving force in the NBA, added that he had agreed to remain with the Warriors for at least another season. "But I am glad to see Philadelphia back in the NBA," he said. "I did everything I could to help the local interests." Gottlieb also denied reports that he would become general manager of the new team.

The truth of the matter was that Kosloff and Richman each owned 50 percent of the team and that Gottlieb had no involvement in the everyday affairs of Philadelphia's new NBA entry.

Although he was still spending his winters in San Francisco with the Warriors, Gottlieb didn't desert the new team once the deal was made to bring it to Philadelphia. He was determined to have a voice in matters involving the transplanted Nats. After all, he had an opinion about everything. So why should he stop now?

Once the team was ensconced in Philly, one of the first items of business was to give it a nickname. The owners decided to hold a contest in which fans could make suggestions. Some 500 names were suggested.

Gottlieb threw his weight into the debate. In a letter penned July 27, 1963, and sent to Iannarella, who was now selling tickets for the new team, Gotty made his views known. "Don't select Dolphins (after Dolph Schayes) or any name connected in any way with coach, player, etc., as they will not be with the team always," he said. "Get something representing the city or a symbolic name that can last forever. Quakers is a lousy name, and does not represent the city today, although it may have in revolutionary days. You can see that the name Dolphin does not reflect me, as I would not give it a thought."

Gottlieb's obsession with Dolphin was appeased when the name 76ers was chosen from the entries submitted. In keeping with the patriotic theme, red, white, and blue were selected as team colors and circular pattern of 13 stars was included on uniforms.

In the same letter, Gottlieb attempted to dictate ticket prices. He also made a reference to getting Paul Arizin to play with the new team. Arizin had decided not to go to San Francisco with the Warriors and had taken a full-time job with IBM. He played on weekends with the Camden Bullets of the Eastern League. Now, Gotty thought he should return to the NBA.

"As for Paul, I will try to talk to him again when I get back in the middle of next month," he wrote. "Ike's trouble here is that he is being guided too much by the Syracuse angle, and they do not realize the importance of some local talent. I am certain he can still play and would be a big help." (In an earlier letter, Gottlieb had expressed his concern that Arizin might play in the ABL. "I don't want him playing in the ABL under any condition," he wrote.)

Gottlieb's two-page, July 27 letter was packed with other pronouncements. He critiqued articles written in the *Daily News* by Larry Merchant and Jack Kiser. He made sure Iannarella knew that Richman was "a dynamo." He wrote about his role in getting the Nats to Philadelphia: "After all, would the team be in Philly without my efforts?" he claimed. And he commented about the 76ers' hiring Schayes, who had never coached before, as the team's first pilot.

"If Schayes wanted the coaching job, he certainly deserved it above anyone else, considering his knowledge of the Syracuse players, the years of service he gave them and the league, and the nice press he has always given the league," Gottlieb wrote. "Dolph should do a good job, as he knows more about the game than Senesky and Johnston, has had more experience handling people than they had at the time they became coaches, and has a much better personality and can get along with people much better."

Quite obviously, the overall perception provided by the letters Gottlieb wrote while he was in San Francisco revealed a man who was not content to sit on the sidelines. Gotty had to be near the action.

New Philadelphia 76ers owners Ike Richman (left) and Irv Kosloff (right) signed Dolph Schayes as the team's first coach. *(Temple University Libraries, Urban Archives, Philadelphia, Pennsylvania)*

Whether it was the West Coast, Philadelphia, or the NBA, he had to have his finger on the pulse of all that mattered, and he had strong opinions on everything.

Much of the correspondence that survived the years was with Iannarella. In the two seasons that he spent on the West Coast, The Mogul sent nearly 30 letters to him. The letters showed a man who had not left his heart in San Francisco.

In a letter written December 14, 1962, he had this to say about Wilt Chamberlain's apparent lack of enthusiasm: "You know Wilt and his moods. Unless we are winning, he won't change."

Few issues involving the new 76ers escaped Gottlieb's attention. Gotty read all the articles about the team and often made comments to Iannarella, such as, "I think you should send poison pens to Merchant and [Frank] Dolson." He also asked Iannarella to "give Delaney [Ed Delaney was a sportswriter with the *Evening Bulletin*] a bottle, but let him come to the office for it so no one else knows."

In one letter, Gottlieb told Iannarella to "keep Ike [Richman] dynamic," and in another he advised his friend to tell Dave Zinkoff, who had been hired by the 76ers as the team's public address announcer, that he should conduct himself with "no high jinks or no wise guy stuff." In his letters, Gotty frequently mentioned phone calls from Frank McGuire and often commented about the Phillies and how well he thought they were or weren't playing. Once, he reminded Iannarella to make sure he bought new sweaters for Richman, Harvey Pollack, and himself. Having once tried to set 76ers' ticket prices, Gotty usually asked about attendance, too.

Two recurring themes in Gottlieb's letters involved money and his sister, Belle, who at the time was still living in Wynnefield. The Mogul nearly always asked Iannarella, who handled Gotty's business affairs in Philadelphia, how much money was in his account. At times, he requested payment of certain bills and asked for checks to be sent to his girlfriend, Alicia. Almost always, Gottlieb asked about Belle's welfare and commanded Iannarella to call her to say hello and to find out how she was doing.

Sometimes in his letters, Gottlieb strayed from sports, money, and family. In one, he editorialized about the assassination of President John F. Kennedy. "What goofs the Dallas police are," he wrote. "How Jack Ruby could kill [Lee Harvey] Oswald in full view of the Dallas police is beyond me. What a tragedy that our president could be assassinated in an American city."

After a one-year absence, the NBA returned to Philadelphia for the 1963–64 season. Gottlieb was still in San Francisco, but he kept a close watch on the city's new 76ers, the transplanted Syracuse Nats.

The 76ers played at Convention Hall and in their first home game drew a mere crowd of 6,850. Soon afterward, attendance fell sharply, and although it made a spurt back upward as the 76ers finished in third place in the Eastern Division before losing in the first round of the division playoffs, the shallow response to the new team was a huge disappointment. Even with players such as Hal Greer, Chet Walker, and Johnny Kerr, the 76ers finished a distant seventh in the league with an average attendance of 3,600. At one point during the playoffs, only 4,255 showed up for a game with the Cincinnati Royals.

A major part of the reason for the small crowds at 76ers games stemmed from the lack of coverage given the team by the *Inquirer* and *Daily News*. Both newspapers were part of Triangle Publications, the company owned by Walter Annenberg. A local tycoon of considerable wealth and influence, Annenberg, of course, had a previous connection with professional basketball when his company owned the Warriors.

This time, though, Annenberg's relationship with the sport was quite different. Instead of standing behind the 76ers as they tried to build a successful franchise, Annenberg was now out to destroy them. And his actions had ramifications throughout the city of Philadelphia and the entire NBA. In fact, an article on the 76ers' very first home game was buried on the second page of the sports section.

"Annenberg was pissed at Gottlieb for selling the Warriors," Schayes related. "He called him a carpetbagger. Then Eddie was supposed to be the general manager of the 76ers, and Ike Richman said, 'I can't make you GM. We won't get any coverage.' So Eddie never got the job." And the 76ers had to look for somebody else to be their general manager.

In 1961, WFIL, the Annenberg-owned top-rated radio and television stations, had hired a broadcaster away from WINS in New York, bringing him to Philadelphia to serve as the station's sports director. His name was Les Keiter. A big, jovial man, Keiter, who had broadcast New York Giants, Titans, and Knicks games, as well as boxing matches and college basketball games at Madison Square Garden, quickly became a popular figure in the city. (In 1965, his popularity would skyrocket with his broadcast of the legendary bomb scare at the Palestra when he delivered commentary for 40 minutes from the booth high atop the ancient arena while the rest of those in attendance were evacuated from the building.)

WFIL outbid its rival stations—WCAU and KYW—to win the rights to televise Warriors games. Soon after he arrived in Philadelphia, Keiter began to broadcast the games, even traveling on the road with the team. He became acquainted with the local pro basketball intelligentsia, including Gottlieb who he called "a beloved individual who was highly regarded by the whole community." Later, he developed a friendship with Kosloff, the new co-owner of the 76ers.

"We were on a flight to Detroit, and Irv came up to me and asked, 'What's wrong with this city?'" Keiter recalled. "'Nobody comes out to see the team. We've spent all this money to bring a team here, but we're losing our shirts.' I told him, 'First, you need to get local players. Guys like Matty Guokas, Wally Jones, Billy Melchionni. That's why the Palestra always sold out. Fans come to see local guys playing. You don't have anybody like that with a local impact. You have to get some on your team.' Then I said, 'Second, you need a basketball man to run the day to day operations of the team. You don't have that. You need somebody who knows basketball.'

"A few weeks later," Keiter continued, "I was walking through the lobby at Convention Hall and Irv was standing there waiting for me. He said, 'Remember that conversation we had a few weeks ago? Well, we decided to do what you suggested. It's you.' I said, 'What the hell do you mean? I'm not a basketball man. I don't know anything about running a team.' Kosloff said, 'We checked all around and decided you'd be a natural to take over the team. Who should we talk to at WFIL?'"

Keiter suggested Tom Jones, the station's program director who had hired him away from New York. "Kosloff went to Jones," Keiter said, "and told him, 'We're going to steal Les Keiter from you.' Well, that set off a furor. One thing led to another. It [the discussions] went through George Kohler, through Roger Clipp [both WFIL executives] all the way up to Walter Annenberg. He made an announcement that said, 'As of this moment, Les Keiter will not mention the 76ers on the air. He will not travel with the team.' He said that the papers would run two paragraphs if the 76ers win, and three if they lose. That left the *Bulletin* as the only local paper covering the team."

Dolson, working at the *Inquirer*, remembered the incident from the vantage point of an insider. "One day, the beat writers and some of the other sportswriters all received notes," he said, "telling us the new rules on coverage of the 76ers. After that, some guys used to write some pretty long paragraphs. At the time, we never really knew why this was happening. We thought it was because Gotty sold the team to San Francisco, and Annenberg was mad at him for that. Years later, we found out the real reason. Why Keiter as general manager? Because he was very popular at the time. He didn't have a background in basketball, but the 76ers were looking for a name."

Shortly after the boycott began, Keiter went to a luncheon. "John Quinn of the Phillies was there," he said. "So was Joe Kuharich of the Eagles. Everybody was asking me what I was doing. I was the bad guy. Then after a couple of weeks, Kosloff went to see Annenberg. The team was not drawing. Irv said, 'You're killing me.' Annenberg said, 'Get out of my office. I don't want to see you.'"

According to Pollock, the 76ers' public relations director, the boycott lasted throughout the first season and into the second one. Then, without any advance notice, it was lifted, and coverage by Triangle Publications resumed, ending what had been one of the most disgraceful episodes in Philadelphia journalism.

After Gottlieb permanently returned to Philadelphia following the 1963–64 season, he dissolved Philadelphia Warriors, Inc., on November 25, 1964. The company had originally been formed July 8, 1952. At the time, Gotty was still employed by the San Francisco Warriors as the team's Eastern Representative. Despite that connection, various reports continued to suggest that he had a financial interest in the 76ers. As late as January 1965, Fred Byrod tried to link Gotty with the new team in a column in the *Inquirer*.

Gottlieb offered a rebuttal. "I'm still a stockholder with the Warriors," he said. "That's a matter of record. The league wouldn't let me have an interest in two clubs at the same time." He added, "Get it straight. I never had any money in the 76ers. I don't have any money in them now. And the way things are, I never expect to have any money in them."

The reason Gottlieb was still a "stockholder in the Warriors" was somewhat circuitous. When Franklin Mieuli had assumed control of the team, Gottlieb was still owed one-half of the original sale price. As compensation, Gotty was given stock in the club. He retained the stock for a short time even after the debt was settled several years later.

That did not mean, however, that Gottlieb avoided the 76ers. He came to many of their games, usually sitting in the lower level directly below the press box. He interacted with the team's owners and others with the club. He even used the 76ers ticket office at the Sheraton Hotel at 18th and JFK Boulevard where he'd arrive around noon, then spend the rest of the afternoon kibitzing with Zinkoff, Iannarella, and Pollack and talking on the phone.

"But he had no input with the team," said Jack Ramsay, the team's general manager beginning in 1966 and later the coach of the team for four years starting in 1968. "He'd come into the office around 5 p.m. almost every day. He came late because he was a night person. Ike Richman ran the team from his law office."

Richman and Gottlieb had been good friends for many years, dating back to the days when the former was a student at South Philly High. Over the years, they were often together, Gottlieb frequently visiting the Richman house for dinner. "When we were kids and he came to the house," Ike's son, Michael, said, "he would give my brother David and me lessons in sports. He would pretend he was the quarterback and hand the ball off. He taught us how to dribble. When he'd go to Europe with the Globetrotters, he'd leave his car with us, which meant I had a car to drive around. My father and Gotty were the best of friends. There was a certain reverence my father had for him. When Gotty would call, my father would drop everything. Whatever Gotty asked or needed, my father would do it."

Michael Richman, who often attended Warriors games with his father—once when he was five or six years old, even jumping out of the stands and putting his hands in a huddle with the players—said that Gottlieb, usually accompanied by Zinkoff, who drove The Mogul's 1959 Cadillac, frequently visited his father at the family's summer home in Longport. "They always stayed out late and slept until noon. Then they'd get up and my mother would make them breakfast," Richman said. "My father explained to me that that was their lifestyle. Gotty and Zink liked to go down to this little burlesque theater called the Globe on the board-walk in Atlantic City. Once in a while, Gotty would go to the beach. Zink would key on the girls. In that respect, they were very similar. Gotty was a womanizer, too. But he was very quiet about it.

"Gotty was very private about his personal life," Richman added. He cited the time when Gottlieb, Jules Trumper, and his father, Ike, were driving to a game and stopped for gas. Trumper had to visit the men's room. "After he came back, a guy came over to the car and said, 'Hey, Mr. Gottlieb. Good luck tonight.' Gotty got furious. 'How did he know who I was?' he yelled. Jules said, 'I told him.' Gotty said, 'Why would you tell him that?'

"Another time," Richman recalled, "Gotty was sitting by himself in the stands at the Arena, waiting for the game to start. A guy came along and took a picture of him. Next day, it was in the paper. It showed Gotty with his head kind of down in his hands. The caption read something like, 'Eddie worries about the crowd.' I told Eddie I had seen the guy taking the picture. 'Why didn't you tell me?' he yelled. 'If you had I would've ducked down.' He never wanted publicity about himself. But he always wanted as much as he could get for the team."

On December 3, 1965, while sitting on a chair at the end of the 76ers' bench during a game in Boston, Ike Richman collapsed and died of a heart attack. He was 52 years old, and his passing left a deep hole in Gottlieb's life that couldn't be filled.

Although he and Kosloff disagreed on some things, Gottlieb maintained close ties to the 76ers. He was even shown the plans for the new Spectrum before it was built and subsequently opened in 1967.

"He took one look at those plans," remembered Michael Richman, "and he said, 'There aren't enough urinals.' And he said that the ones they had, 'were in shitty places.' Gotty was never one to mince words. He was a very lovable guy, and he never gave you any reason to dislike him. But he always said what he thought and never held back."

Apparently, at times Gottlieb had a hand in selecting 76ers personnel, too. Pat Williams, who would become the 76ers' general manager in 1974 before going on to an extensive career in the NBA, recalled how he landed his first job with the team in 1968 while he was working as a youthful general manager with the Phillies' farm team at Spartanburg, South Carolina.

"Jack Ramsay called and asked if I'd be interested in running the front office of the 76ers," Williams related. "So, I came up from Spartanburg, and he offered me the job." But soon after Williams returned to South Carolina, he was summoned back to Philadelphia to meet Kosloff. "I had to meet him, his banker, his accountant, everybody under the sun, then I had to go through a battery of tests," said Williams. "Then I had to meet Gottlieb in his office at the Sheraton. I went in cold turkey. I was a little confused, a bit on edge, and I was wondering, 'Why am I going through all of this?' I was alone with Gotty for about an hour. Afterward, Kosloff drove me to the airport and told me I had the job. I guess Gotty must have liked me, and he had enough influence to suggest that they hire me."

Since the formation of the BAA in 1946, Gottlieb had played a major role at the operational level of pro basketball. He was a member of the Board of Governors. He was a friend and confidant of league commissioners from Maurice Podoloff (1946–63) to Walter Kennedy (1963–75) to Larry O'Brien (1975–84). And in his most visible and widely acclaimed role, he made up the schedule for the entire league.

Gottlieb also performed another hugely important function with the league. That was to serve as chairman of the rules committee, a job he held for 26 years. He began the job in the first year of the BAA and was still chairman for the NBA 10 years after he had sold the Warriors. Even when he died in 1979, he was a member of the committee.

"He knew the rules better than anyone else in the game," said Norm Drucker. "And his sole interest was in the prosperity of the league. He knew which rules were good for the league and which ones weren't."

During his tenure with the committee, nearly every innovation and rule change was either initiated or influenced by Gottlieb. With every change or new rule, Gotty was always motivated by the desire to speed up the game, a condition that he thought would maintain and increase fan interest in pro basketball. Does the rule make the game more appealing? Does it improve the way the game is played? These were questions he would always ask. Over the years, the questions that produced affirmative answers resulted in dozens of major changes.

"I probably was responsible for more rule changes in pro basketball than any other man," Gottlieb wrote in a 1971 issue of *Inside Basketball*. "I always felt that college and pro rules should be somewhat different because pro fans want a faster and slightly more physical game, and in my opinion, would not tolerate a slowed-down game."

Gottlieb had an uncanny ability to connect past and present basketball. "I'm the only one who knows why this rule was put in or that one was thrown out," he said. Some of the rule changes that Gottlieb either proposed or supported were accepted. Others were rejected. Gotty was the originator of the territorial rule that allowed teams to draft high school players within a 60-mile radius of their home base. That was the rule that landed Wilt Chamberlain for the Warriors.

Gotty was also one of the first and staunchest supporters of the 24-second clock, an innovation devised by Biasone in 1954. The Syracuse owner was concerned that the slow pace of games, with teams stalling and holding the ball for long lengths of time, thereby drastically reducing scoring, was destroying basketball. (In one game in 1950, the Fort Wayne Pistons beat the Minneapolis Lakers, 19–18, with the winners outscoring the losers, 3–1, in the fourth quarter.)

"He was right," Drucker said. "Teams would sit on the ball, and people would start leaving. Basketball was headed for doomsday."

Biasone figured out that the average game lasted 2,880 seconds and 120 shots were taken by the two teams. Dividing 2,880 by 120, he concluded that a shot was taken every 24 seconds. That, he thought, should be often enough to keep the pace moving quickly. Biasone demonstrated his theory to a group of NBA luminaries, including Gottlieb, Red Auerbach, and Ned Irish, by holding a scrimmage with his Nats and some col-

Guarded by Nate Thurmond, Wilt Chamberlain faced his old team, the San Francisco Warriors, after his return in 1965 to Philadelphia. *(Courtesy of Rich Westcott)*

lege players at a high school gym in Syracuse. A man on the sidelines kept the time by shouting the seconds.

The group of observers was suitably impressed by the speed of the game. One month later, at a meeting in New York, club owners voted on a proposal that would require teams to shoot within 24 seconds each time they brought the ball up court. The motion was unanimously approved. And with that vote, the game of pro basketball was changed forever.

"We were huffing and puffing," Schayes, one of the participants in the experimental game, recalled. "It was all running. There wasn't any standing around. But it made the game more fun to play. None of us realized at the time, but it became the most important rule change in the history of the game. Without it, I think pro basketball would have disappeared."

While Gottlieb played a major role in the use of the 24-second clock, he lost some other battles. He fought against widening the lane from six feet to 12 feet—a move that was designed to curtail the scoring of Chamberlain—but lost. He proposed playing a game by "innings" with one team having the ball for two minutes, then the other for two minutes, rotating back and forth throughout the game. That idea was voted down, too, as was his suggestion that that no free throws be taken from fouls committed outside of an "attacking zone," which would be an area from the out-of-bounds line behind the basket to 25 feet out on the court, although personal fouls in that zone would be counted. He also offered a proposal in which all free throws would be shot at the end of the quarter, except in the final period when the shots would be taken after the fouls were called. That idea was also vetoed.

At the very least, it could certainly be said that Gottlieb was innovative. He never sanctioned the status quo, always looking for new ideas. At one meeting, he wanted to make a rule that divided the court into two offensive zones with a neutral zone in the middle. A player having possession of the ball when fouled in his own offensive zone would get two shots regardless of whether or not he was in the act of shooting. The idea had minimal support.

When a proposal surfaced in the late 1970s that would give a shooter three points if he sank a shot from 25 feet or more away from the basket, Gottlieb fought vehemently against the idea even though it eventually was passed. If a baseball batter hit a ball that traveled 300 feet into the stands and another hit a ball 500 feet, they both counted as home runs, Gotty reasoned. Why should different distances matter in basketball? Gottlieb felt that three-point goals would mainly help inferior players. "He couldn't understand why you would get three points for a shot like that," recalled Drucker. "He was much more in favor of layups."

Early in the BAA's existence, Gottlieb championed a proposal in which a shooter would not be credited with a shot when fouled if he didn't make the shot. "After that change was made, shooting percentages improved considerably," said Pollack, the NBA statistical wizard. Another change initiated by Gottlieb and inserted into the rulebook was to keep track of turnovers. "Auerbach fought to the bitter end against that one," Pollack said.

Another change that Gottlieb initiated in the early years was to increase the number of personals needed to foul out of a game from five to six. That shift came following a situation in which a Warriors' opponent (Providence) had five players foul out, leaving the team with only four men to finish the game.

Gottlieb was always trying to improve the game and to make it more interesting for spectators. Shifting his roots away from the old-time game, he was anxious to make modern basketball faster, higher-scoring, more entertaining. He fought vehemently against zone defenses, ultimately getting the procedure banned (until it was reintroduced many decades later). "Fans love to see the ball dropping through the basket, and they love the speed of play," Gotty told Hugh Brown in the *Evening Bulletin*.

Because of his role on the rules committee, as well as his duties putting together the league's schedule, Gottlieb spent at least two days every week working in the NBA office in New York from the mid-1960s through the mid-1970s. Until 1965, he was still listed as a consultant with the Warriors. But once that position ended, his attention was mainly focused on his work with the league for which he also served as a consultant to NBA commissioner Walter Kennedy.

Traveling to New York, of course, gave Gottlieb the opportunity to spend time with Alicia, whom he visited whenever he was in town. It also gave him the chance to work in an office with an exceedingly more professional setting than the seat-of-the-pants, vest-pocket operation that Gotty had always known.

By 1970, the NBA had stretched to 17 teams spread across four divisions, making Gottlieb's work as a scheduler considerably more difficult than the eight-team circuit for which he had set dates in much of the 1950s. And, with the game getting faster, bigger, and more technical, much of his time was spent dealing with new or proposed rules, too. All in all, Gotty was a valuable addition to the bustling NBA office in the heart of midtown Manhattan.

"You had to take advantage of somebody with his experience," said Matt Winick, a member of the NBA staff since 1976. "He was a brilliant man. He was extremely knowledgeable about basketball. He knew the league history. He knew all the rules and procedures. People leaned on him for his basketball knowledge, and he shared that with everybody. He was certainly easy to talk to. I don't know of anybody who didn't have a good relationship with him."

In the later years that Gottlieb worked in the NBA office, Schayes also had a job there as supervisor of referees. More than a few times, the former Nats star and 76ers coach saw the humorous side of Gotty.

"One time we went out to lunch together," Schayes recalled, "and a fan came up to us. He says, 'Schayes, are you still living in Syracuse?' Gotty said, 'Yeah, he doesn't know any better.'"

Another time, Schayes, Gottlieb, and Ben Kerner drove to an NCAA playoff game in College Park, Maryland, to scout some college players. With Schayes driving Gotty's Cadillac, the trio arrived at Cole Field House about 45 minutes before game time. Schayes let his passengers out, then drove around until finding a parking space.

"With a couple of minutes left in the game, one team was up by about 10 points," Schayes related. "Gotty said, 'Let's get out of here and beat the crowd.' Walking out of the building, I said, 'Oh, shit, I forgot where I parked the car.' It all looked the same. We walked around, and Gotty was going nuts. Finally, he says to Kerner, 'Are you sure this guy's Jewish?'"

Throughout his adult years, Gottlieb was never known to have any hobbies. He didn't play golf. He didn't collect stamps. He didn't paint, play the piano, or write poetry. Except for frequently attending shows and movies, Gotty's whole life revolved around sports. "That," said Dolson, "was all he ever talked about."

In the strictest definition, Gottlieb was not a particularly religious man, although he became more so in his later years. He observed Jewish high holidays, belonged to synagogues in the neighborhoods in which he lived, made financial contributions to them, was good friends with more than one rabbi, and sometimes ate kosher foods. But he did not attend services on a regular basis. And he seldom talked about religion. Gotty never hinted that religion played much of a role in his everyday activities.

While living in Wynnefield, Gottlieb had become a member of the congregation of nearby Temple Israel. When Congregation Beth Tovim opened in 1964, he joined that synagogue, sometimes attending services with Jules Trumper or Dave Zinkoff. Eventually, he made a sizable contribution toward the establishment of a memorial room, which became known as the Eddie Gottlieb Chapel and contained bronze plaques commemorating the lives of Gotty, each member of his family, and many other former members of the congregation.

"He was very Jewish at heart," said Rabbi Amiel Novoseller, who succeeded his father, Sherman, at Beth Tovim and who as a youth knew Gotty and often was given tickets to Warriors games. "He was not devoutly religious, but he was a dedicated Jew."

Rabbi Novoseller saw a side of Gottlieb that was not generally observed by others.

"Eddie never forgot where he came from," he said. "He always remembered his parents and the concept of charity that they had taught him. He was a gentleman's gentleman. He was sincere. He had a desire to be kind. He was not a show-off, and he didn't care for status symbols. He was definitely not a bells and whistles person. There was something exceptionally unique about Eddie."

To those who associated with him through sports, Gottlieb was superstitious. He could be gruff. He could be aloof. He was stubborn. He never hesitated to exercise his displeasure by scolding an offender or berating someone with whom he disagreed. "There was no BS about Eddie," Campbell said. "He was loud. He was blunt. A lot of people didn't react well to that. If you didn't know him, I can see why you'd be turned off by him."

Marv Bachrad portrayed another side of Gottlieb: "If you knew him, he was your friend. But he was not a real up-front guy. He'd sit back and observe. He was very guarded. He never said much unless you knew him. And if he did a favor for somebody, he'd say, 'Don't tell anybody.' He backed a lot of things that he didn't want people to know about."

Without question, Gottlieb ran the show, no matter when or where it was. He even ordered meals for people, as Campbell discovered one morning in Atlantic City. "We were down there for an exhibition game, staying at one of the hotels, and he bangs on my door and says, 'I'm going to take you to breakfast,'" Campbell said. "It was the middle of winter and we had to walk about six blocks up the boardwalk. The wind is blowing like crazy. I'm freezing. We get to a Jewish delicatessen and go in. Eddie says he wants two orders of lox and bagels. I hated them. But because he ordered them, I had to eat them."

"Eddie was a person you either liked or disliked," said Arizin. "There was no in between. He was just very, very forceful."

Tom Meschery said that he "always thought that Gotty was a guy who wanted to create an image as a stern person. But he was actually a very big-hearted guy." Schayes said Gotty "was a basketball lifer who was one of the big people in the NBA from the very beginning." Pat Williams said, "If something ever happened to Eddie, you always had the feeling that the NBA would cease to operate."

Bill Mlkvy observed that Gottlieb was a person who liked to impose his will on others. "He wasn't the kind of person who'd just sit and listen," he said. "He was very dominating. He liked to take over the conversation. But I think he was fearful of failure. And I don't think he was a real happy guy."

"I felt like a daughter to him," Estelle Litwack claimed. "He'd come to the house, and we'd sit and talk for hours. Basketball was his true love, but we'd talk about all kinds of things."

Accountant Alan Levitt said that Eddie "was fascinating to work with. He was a whiz with mathematics. He was very argumentative, very persuasive. I always thought he would've made a good lawyer."

Gottlieb liked to walk, especially when he lived in San Francisco, and didn't like to drive, even though he always owned a car. He'd spend countless hours on the telephone, although potential callers had instructions not to call him before noon because he slept late, seldom having gone to bed before 2 a.m. the night before. Once, when Mlkvy entered the office, he found Gotty on the phone. Abruptly, The Mogul hung up. "I'm so glad you came in," he said. "I've been on the phone for five hours. I've got to take a rest."

A way from the office or the arena, one of Gottlieb's favorite activities was to make an occasional wager. Although not known to be a high roller—or if he was, his friends and associates never knew it—Gotty's fondness for gambling dated back to the days when he was one of the guys placing bets at Phillies and Athletics games. Of course, SPHAS games always enticed a crowd of small-time gamblers, too, and at least one player—Red Wolf—was said to indulge heavily in sports betting, sending his wife to New York to place his bets. Another player, Petey Rosenberg, became a well-known local bookmaker. But nothing suggests that Gottlieb ever wagered on his own teams.

"He bet a lot. He bet on everything," said SPHAS player Butch Schwartz. "But I'm sure he never bet on his own team, though."

In later years, gambling scandals circled the perimeter of Gottlieb's workshop. New York City was the gateway to sports betting in those days, and basketball was the preferred game of the gamblers, most of their wagers dealing with point spreads. In 1945, basketball players from Brooklyn College were found to have fixed games. A few years later, a much larger scandal surfaced when it was learned that between 1949 and 1951, basketball games in 22 cities, involving 33 players, six colleges, and 49 games had been fixed. The scandal brought down U.S. Olympic players Alex Groza and Ralph Beard, who had formed an NBA team in Indianapolis, as well as star college players such as Sherman White and Jack Molinas.

Although it benefited from the college betting scandals by luring fans to what was perceived as the "cleaner" pro game, the NBA was not unblemished. Gambling was common at Madison Square Garden when the Knicks played. In 1951, a referee was charged with taking a bribe in an unsuccessful attempt to fix a game between the Washington Capitols and Minneapolis Lakers. Equally futile was an attempt to bribe him to fix two Warriors games.

Gottlieb stood far above such improprieties. "I know he gambled sometimes," recalled Dolson. "People said he was pretty good at it, especially in his younger days. But I never saw him do anything that was unlawful."

Alan Trumper went one step further. "I never saw any evidence of Eddie being a gambler," he said. "At least, not when I knew him. I never heard anything from my father, either. And he was certainly in a position to know."

Gotty, of course, had ample opportunities to associate with the seedy side of society. When in public, even just walking down city streets populated by gamblers, he always tried to avoid them. No one doubts that he didn't have more than a few acquaintances in the "Jewish Mafia" that operated out of South Philadelphia. And surely he rubbed an occasional elbow with some others involved in "the rackets." "Being in the area of sports that he was, he almost had to be involved with people who were involved in the rackets," said Dolson. "But I think that's as far as it went. I don't think he broke any laws or anything like that."

He almost did, though, on at least a couple of occasions. At about 2 a.m., the Warriors were traveling in three cars across upstate New York when they were stopped by a state trooper. Claiming that he clocked the cars going 80 miles-per-hour, the trooper led the caravan to a nearby farmhouse, where the local justice of peace resided. "He read the riot act to us for speeding, then he laid a heavy fine on us," Ernie Beck remembered. "All we wanted to do was get out of there, but Eddie had to pay and while he was counting the money, he screamed at the guy. 'When I get back to Philadelphia, I'm going to get a couple of guys and they are going to come up here and eliminate you. I have friends who will do that.' Down deep, I think he did have contacts who could've done that."

Gottlieb is also known to have clobbered fans and others for their improprieties—once before a SPHAS game, he raced down the street after a scalper who was selling $2 seats for $1 and knocked the guy halfway to Market Street. Another time, during a Warriors game at the Arena, he went after a fan who had told him to "drop dead." And at a Warriors game in Moline, Indiana, he jumped into the stands intent on administering physical harm to a loudmouth who was razzing Gotty about his clothes. "I think he would've killed the guy if some of the players hadn't grabbed him," Arizin said.

In the documents at the Court of Common Pleas in the Criminal Justice Building in Philadelphia, however, there is no record of Gottlieb's ever having been arrested.

In his later years, Gottlieb became a familiar figure around local racetracks. He, Zinkoff, and Jules Trumper frequently traveled together to watch the nags at places such as Delaware Park and Atlantic City. Gotty also went to Liberty Bell where he sometimes sat in Mlkvy's private box when the Owl Without a Vowel and his brother, Bob, owned horses.

Writing in the *Daily News* for which he also covered the sport of kings, Jack Kiser noted Gottlieb's frequent visits to Liberty Bell and Brandywine to see harness racing. "He was one of the few men I knew who won money," Kiser wrote. "He bet small, but wisely. I guess you could call him frugal, but he was highly intelligent about it."

Bachrad, who followed a radio career with public relations jobs at several local racetracks, remembered Gottlieb's special betting formula. "Gotty liked Wilt an awful lot," Bachrad said. "And Wilt wore number 13. So when Gotty came to the track—usually with Jules and Zink—he played the one-three double. When the exacta came into being, he played the one-three exacta."

Once in a while, the one and three horses would even pay off. And Gotty would go home happy. Without the daily hassle of running teams, merely sitting in the stands and watching, it was one of the most enjoyable times of his life.

· · ·

CHAPTER 17

The Final Years

For Eddie Gottlieb, the early 1970s were quite unlike anything he had ever experienced. In one of the more ironic twists of his life, it was a time when Gotty made a significant connection with halls of fame in two different sports.

One, of course, was basketball. The other was baseball. In basketball, it was Gottlieb who was honored. In baseball, Gotty's role was to make sure others were honored. In each case, Gottlieb would be widely acclaimed for the contributions he made to the sport.

Gottlieb's lifelong contributions to pro basketball were almost too numerous to count. He was a pioneer, an innovator, a driving force in a sport that might have failed without him.

Harry Litwack once said that Gotty "is just as important to the game of basketball as the basketball." Some called Gottlieb a giant in the game. Others called him "Mr. Basketball." "If you want the father of pro basketball," said Frank Dolson, "it would be Eddie Gottlieb. There's no question about it."

"To me," Dolson continued, "he *was* basketball. He was the guy who started the league more than anybody else. He was more instrumental in making the league survive than anybody else. The other early owners couldn't come close. He worked like hell on basketball. That was his passion. That's what he cared about. He was simply remarkable."

Angelo Musi said that without Gottlieb there would have been no NBA. "Gottlieb was the driving force behind the formation of the league," he said, "and he was largely responsible for what the league became. No one contributed more to the sport."

Such glowing descriptions were all parts of Gottlieb's portfolio when it was announced that he would be inducted into the Naismith Basketball Hall of Fame in Springfield, Massachusetts. Gotty was scheduled to enter the Valhalla of basketball at a ceremony April 20, 1972, along with Bob Douglas, owner and coach of the New York Renaissance, Paul Endacott, a two-time All-American at Kansas and college player of the year in 1923, Marty Friedman, a 5-foot, 8-inch star in early pro leagues, Cliff Wells, winner of nearly 900 games as a high school and college coach, and Ed Dibble, a highly successful coach at Western Kentucky.

The February 7, 1972, press release that accompanied the announcement called Gottlieb "a man ahead of his time." NBA commissioner Walter Kennedy was quoted as saying, "I have been a part of the national basketball picture, man and boy, for more than 40 years. I know of no one—and I mean no one—who has contributed more to all phases of basketball than Eddie Gottlieb. He is the most respected man I know in basketball."

At the ceremony in April, numerous friends, former players, and members of the local media were in attendance. It was a festive occasion, and no one was in higher spirits than the 74-year-old basketball patriarch. "The thrills always come from winning," Gottlieb said. "But being put in the Hall is the ultimate thrill."

Stan Hochman quoted Dave Zinkoff in his *Daily News* column: "Of all the things Gotty has done," said Zink, "I guess his greatest achievement has been getting harmonious relationships out of warring factions. You get owners sitting there with knives at their throats and when all the shouting dies down, Gotty somehow creates some harmony."

In an article in the *Inquirer*, Gottlieb made additional remarks to John Dell. "I've been in every facet of the game—in every stage of it," Gotty said. "I've seen the game grow. And it's going to keep on growing bigger and bigger."

No one was more responsible for that growth than Gottlieb. His induction into the Hall of Fame clearly supported that point.

L ess than one year before his own induction into the Basketball Hall of Fame, Gottlieb had attended another hall of fame ceremony. This one was in Cooperstown, New York, where baseball holds its annual ritual of honor.

This time, Gottlieb was not there to be inducted. He was there to see the results of his—and others'—work on a very special project finally become a reality. The ceremony marked the first time that players who performed primarily in the Negro Leagues were admitted to the baseball shrine.

Reaching that point had been a long process. For many years, there had been a growing clamor for the admission of Negro League players. Before 1970 only two African Americans—Jackie Robinson in 1962 and Roy Campanella in 1969—had been elected to the Hall, and both of them were voted in because of their performances as major league players.

By 1970, however, it had become increasingly apparent that major league baseball was way out of step with the times. The recognition of old Negro League players was long overdue. Few in baseball agreed, but one who did was commissioner Bowie Kuhn.

Early in 1970, Kuhn called a meeting in his New York office to discuss the situation. Those present included National League president Ford Frick, Hall of Fame president Paul Kerr, several members of Kuhn's staff, including Monte Irvin, and Dick Young and Jack Lang from the Baseball Writers' Association.

In his book *Hardball: The Education of a Baseball Commissioner*, Kuhn described the session. "The meeting was heated and unpleasant. Frick and Kerr took the negative position. Young was passionate and unrelenting in support of admitting black players." Kuhn added that since the opposition was so formidable and that he could not muster enough votes of support from the Hall of Fame's board of directors, he would "slip around their flank and look for an opening." That opening, he decided, would come in the creation of a committee of "Negro League experts" whose assignment would be to identify the best Negro League players and to recommend that they be honored accordingly by the Hall of Fame.

"A predictable furor ensued," Kuhn wrote. "Cries of 'Jim Crow' were heard; we were again treating players separately, putting them through a back door in Cooperstown. Jackie Robinson, the NAACP, and all sorts of activist groups spoke out in protest. I was placed under personal attack for putting forth the idea."

Kuhn, however, prevailed. And in 1971, he named a committee to carry out the assignment. The voting members of the committee consisted of ex-players Campanella, Irvin, Judy Johnson, Bill Yancy, and Eppie Barnes; writers Sam Lacy and Wendell Smith; and three who were described as "organizers," Frank Forbes, Alex Pompez, and Eddie Gottlieb.

As the first recommendation of a special committee that included Gottlieb and was formed by Bowie Kuhn (right), Satchel Paige entered the Hall of Fame in 1971. *(National Baseball Hall of Fame Library, Cooperstown, New York)*

Why Gottlieb? "We felt that Eddie had good, in-depth knowledge of Negro League baseball," Kuhn related some 35 years later. "The fact that he was connected to basketball was beside the point. Eddie was the owner of a club in the Negro Leagues, and he was considered a very intelligent guy with a wide range of interests. He was well qualified to be on the committee."

Gottlieb, who also served at the time on the Basketball Hall of Fame selection committee, looked at his appointment as a chance to correct a small part of society's past mistakes. "I have considerably more sympathy for men who should have been able to make what money there was available to athletes in the old days than I do for so many of the spoiled kids today who play almost casually because they've got the big cash," he told Bob Broeg of the St. Louis *Post-Dispatch.* "Even those of us who watched and enjoyed them [Negro League players], did not realize how many deserved to be in the major leagues. I say that on the strength of how many blacks came to the fore once the opportunity was granted them."

During its first year, the committee met about once a month. Eventually, the group picked ageless pitcher Satchel Paige as its first nominee.

"Gottlieb knew a lot about Satchel," Irvin recalled. "In fact, Eddie made a sizable contribution to our committee. He had extensive knowledge about Negro League history, and he gave us all kinds of good information."

Paige was inducted into the Hall of Fame on August 9, 1971. In the ensuing years, more nominees of the committee were inducted: Buck Leonard and Josh Gibson in 1972, Irvin in 1973, Cool Papa Bell in 1974, Johnson in 1975, Oscar Charleston in 1976, and Martin Dihigo and John (Pop) Lloyd in 1977. By then, the committee had completed its mission. But the inductions of Negro League players into the Hall of Fame continued, and over the years, many more players and others, including 17 in 2006, were inducted at the annual ceremony in Cooperstown.

In the early 1970s, Gottlieb was showing no signs of slowing down. Along with his halls of fame work, he was still chairman of the NBA's rules committee and was drawing up the league schedule that ultimately encompassed 22 teams. He was working in the NBA office in New York two days a week. He was scouting college referees for the NBA. In 1975, Gotty even flew in a snowstorm to Salt Lake City to testify for the defense in a contract dispute in which the Utah Stars had filed suit against Bill Sharman and the Los Angeles Lakers. And he had numerous local duties. "He had so much energy," said Dolson. "His energy was limitless."

In 1969, Gottlieb had moved to Center City where he took up residence in a co-op apartment at the Kennedy House at 19th Street and JFK Boulevard. On September 12 of the following year, Gotty's sister, Belle, her eyesight virtually gone, died at the age of 74. Gottlieb had taken care of her for virtually her entire adult life.

When he wasn't in New York, Gottlieb usually walked the few blocks to the 76ers ticket office at the Sheraton Hotel where he told stories, worked the phones, and parried with his old pals Mike Iannarella, Harvey Pollack, Zinkoff, and whoever else dropped in. Gotty's stories about the SPHAS, the old Negro League days, and the by then mostly forgotten Warriors were usually spiced with humor and always found willing listeners.

"You could always have a lot of fun with him" Al Shrier remembered. "Depending on the situation, he had a great sense of humor. And when he was with Zink, it was like going to a side show. They could be hilarious."

Eddie Iannarella remembered Gottlieb as "an imposing figure. His frank, sometimes loud dealings with my father," he said, "scared me as a kid." But Iannarella also saw Gotty from another angle. "I was extremely heavy as a youngster, and frequently I got free weight counseling from Mr. Gottlieb. Whenever I'd go to work with my dad at the Sheraton Hotel, I always got called into the inner sanctum [Gotty's office] for an evaluation. It was always the same verdict, always delivered with his characteristic belly laugh. 'Eddie, you're eating too many potatoes,' he'd say."

Gottlieb's humor was not always evident. He could be gruff. And extremely serious. Often, his comments would begin with, "Listen, I've got news for you." He neither smoked nor drank and objected to those who did. And when asked once how he was doing, he growled, "What's it to you how I'm doing?"

He seldom told jokes. "He wasn't really funny," Pollack said. "He didn't laugh too much. But every once in a while he came up with some funny lines. One day, I walked into his office and said, I thought this was the way to do whatever it was. He said, 'Stop thinking. You'll weaken the team.'" Once, Gottlieb was asked to identify a person. "I don't know him from a bag of peanuts," he said.

Alan Levitt noted that Gottlieb was an accomplished practical joker. "If you shook hands with him, you'd often get a shock," he said. "And he also had a pen with invisible ink. He liked to spray it on people's suits. One time he sprayed a guy wearing a herringbone coat. It took three-quarters of an hour for the ink to dry out."

Gotty's personal life in Philadelphia had many facets. He had legions of friends without whom he was seldom seen. Much of the time, he had Jules Trumper and Zinkoff with him. "Everybody knew him," said Marvin Black. "He had a following that really idolized him." Many of Gotty's friends were wealthy—far more wealthy than he was. "But," said Paul Arizin, "regardless of who they were, Eddie was still the boss when he was with them. Everybody respected him, and you might say kowtowed to him."

Gottlieb regularly bought a table at the annual banquet of the Philadelphia Sports Writers' Association (PSWA). He was the honorary president of the Jewish Basketball Alumni, a post he held for 40 years. He served on the board of directors of the U.S. Committee of Sports for Israel. He spoke frequently to local organizations. By his own estimate, he attended 80 to 100 basketball, baseball, and football games each year, watching—but not rooting for—different teams simply because he loved

The 76ers honored Gottlieb at a special night in 1976. Franklin Mieuli (upper left) took part in the event. (*Naismith Basketball Hall of Fame*)

sports. Occasionally, Gotty went to Clearwater, Florida, to see the Phillies in spring training. He even attended at least one Super Bowl.

"But you never had the feeling that he was a VIP or a big shot," Dolson said. "He was totally down to earth. Gotty came off as being just one of the guys. You would never know whether he had a nickel or $50 million. He was simply the kind of person you felt comfortable being around. He was instantly likable. I never met anybody who didn't think he was a great person."

After he became owner of the 76ers, Fitz Dixon often hounded Gottlieb for permission to stage a testimonial for The Mogul. Dixon's plan was to hold a gala affair at the Spectrum with hundreds of well-wishers in attendance. Indicative of his modesty and desire to avoid self-serving publicity, Gotty always refused the offer. "Testimonials are like an automatic last testament," he said.

Gottlieb finally relented in 1976 when Dixon scheduled an event that ostensibly was held to honor the 1955–56 championship Warriors team. The stated reason for the affair disguised its real purpose—to celebrate the career of The Mogul. It was a joyful evening, especially because most of the players from the title team were there. The best line of the night came when Gotty surveyed the three-piece suit and affluent appearance of Walter Davis, the one-time Warrior who became a sheriff and then president of a bank in Texas. "Did I pay you that much that you could open a bank?" Gotty wanted to know. "You never paid anybody enough," Tom Gola responded.

Honors and awards were also coming Gottlieb's way. In 1970, B'nai B'rith Sports Lodge gave Gotty an award designating him as "the Philadelphian who had made the greatest impact on the sports world in the last 50 years." Gottlieb's old friend, Chickie Passon, made the presentation. Another honor, conferred in 1976, was the John B. Kelly Award as the city's outstanding sportsman. And in 1979, the Basketball Hall of Fame named Gotty the recipient of the John W. Bunn Award, an annual honor bestowed on a person who has made "outstanding contributions to the game."

Special honors, of course, were nothing new to Gotty. As long ago as 1944, the U.S. Treasury Department had issued a certificate signed by secretary Henry Morgenthau Jr., that saluted Gottlieb "for patriotic coop-

Former SPHAS and Warriors standout Jerry Fleishman stood with the SPHAS exhibit that Gottlieb underwrote at the Basketball Hall of Fame. *(Courtesy of Jerry Fleishman)*

Among many honors Gotty received over the years, here's one he got from the City of Philadelphia. Participating in the presentation were (from left) Michael Richman, Jules Trumper, Mayor Frank Rizzo, and Dave Zinkoff. *(Courtesy of Alan Trumper)*

eration rendered in behalf of the War Financial Program." In 1955, the United States Service Organizations (USO) cited The Mogul "in recognition of distinguished service to the men and women of America's Armed Forces through the United States Service Organizations." Over the years, Gottlieb was also honored by the PSWA, the Philadelphia Basketball Writers' Club, and many other local groups.

One of Gottlieb's pet projects involved placing an exhibit commemorating the SPHAS at the Basketball Hall of Fame. Up to that point, one of the leading pioneering teams in pro basketball had gone without recognition. Gotty changed that by contributing $7,500 to establish an exhibit.

"I drove up with him for the unveiling," Dolson remembered. "He was so excited. And he was bursting with pride. He really wanted people to see the exhibit. He got really emotional about it."

In his final decade, Gottlieb often reminisced about his career. "I would do nothing different if I had my life to live over," he told Bill Livingston for an article that appeared in *The Sporting News*. "There's nothing as satisfying as being involved in sports. You associate with young people, and that sort of helps keep you young. One thing I'm really proud of, is that I've gone along with the times. I think I've tried to give people the type of game they wanted. And I think pro basketball now is the best game that's ever been played. Say, if I didn't change with the times, I'd be a dead bird now, wouldn't I?"

Gottlieb always looked nostalgically back at his days with the SPHAS. "We had more fun in those days," he once told writer Jerry Izenberg. "Take the business of rivalries. When the new league [BAA] was formed, we lost a lot of that. They thought we should be like college guys and shake hands after each game. Hell, I wanted to guarantee a fight a night."

After SPHAS games, Gottlieb said to Sandy Grady, "I'd put $500 or $600 in my pocket, and go home." Conversely, he told the *Evening Bulletin* columnist, he lost money with the Warriors every year except the championship season in 1955–56.

Frank Brady penned a piece in the *Evening Bulletin* in which Gottlieb talked about being an owner of a pro team. "There are only two reasons why owners get involved now," Gotty said. "First, he can get his name in the papers. Second, to get tax relief. In the old days, people did it because they wanted to and because they had to make a living."

By 1979, Gottlieb's health was starting to decline. He tried to keep busy, but maintaining the rapid pace he had kept for most of his life became increasingly difficult. Eventually, Gotty was hospitalized briefly. When he was released, he needed special care. Fortunately, Shrier, who had grown up at 60th and Catherine just across the street from Gotty's apartment, also lived with his wife, Ruth, at the Kennedy House, just two floors below The Mogul.

"After he got out of the hospital," said Shrier, then the director of sports information at Temple University, "Ruthie made him dinner every night. At one point, she made a different meal for him 31 nights in a row. He always liked something sweet at the end of a meal, and every night she made sure he had a little dessert. She was working and had a long trip each day. Gotty said, 'I don't know how you did it.' He was just amazed.

"We had a place at the shore, and at one point decided to go down for a weekend," Shrier added. "Ruthie set everything up. She made dinners, everything he needed, then laid it out for him. All he needed to do was warm it up. So we left, thinking he'd be fine. Then we came back home and called him. I said, 'How are you doing?' He said, 'Not so good. I have a problem.' Here he'd gone into the kitchen, took a plastic container with food in it, and put it right on the stove. Gotty was never the domestic type. He never cooked. He ate almost every meal out. He didn't know you had to take the stuff out of the container and put it in a pot before you heated it up. We spent a whole night cleaning out the stove."

On November 10, 1979, Gottlieb was admitted to Temple University Hospital with stomach problems. One week later, the NBA issued a press release stating, "Eddie Gottlieb is recuperating following intestinal surgery." The release was merely a hopeful plea.

Eddie Gottlieb, 81, the patriarch of pro basketball, died in his sleep on December 7 at Temple Hospital. The Certificate of Death, issued December 14 by the Commonwealth of Pennsylvania, listed the immediate cause of death as "cardiac and respiratory failure," which was caused by "post-operative chronic bowel disease."

Gotty had battled to the very end. The day before he died, he asked Zinkoff to make sure the Super Bowl tickets he had ordered for friends were delivered and that his annual gifts of one-pound boxes of Hershey bars or bottles of whiskey reached the people on his holiday list. A day or so earlier, he had asked The Zink, a daily visitor, to hand him a notepad so he could jot down a few ideas that applied to the NBA. It was also reported that Gotty was working on the league schedule for the next season.

"I visited him shortly before he died," recalled Marv Bachrad. "It was a very cold day. He told me to open the window. Actually, he commanded me to do it. He was that kind of guy. When he said something, you'd better respond. He didn't take no for an answer, even right up to the very end."

Within hours after he died, the tributes began arriving. "Eddie was truly Mr. Basketball," claimed NBA commissioner Larry O'Brien. "He dedicated his life to basketball, and I can think of no one who has made a greater contribution. I found him to be an astute advisor and counselor. He was a close personal friend, and will be sorely missed by all those who knew him."

"He was like a second father to me," said Gola. "He seemed like part of my family," claimed Bill Sharman, once a standout player with the Boston Celtics. "I lost a true, dear, loving friend who I consider the most important man in the whole country in basketball," declared Abe Pollin, owner of the Baltimore Bullets. "I take it as a personal loss. He was a very fine human being," stated Jerry Colangelo, general manager of the Phoenix Suns.

Said the New York *Times*, "His mental powers were extraordinary, and his memory faultless. He remembered the scores of games, the gate receipts, the attendance, and even the weather." Livingston wrote in the *Inquirer* that Gotty's "credentials were awesome. His vision helped take the game from a preliminary attraction at dance halls to its current base at multi-million dollar facilities." In the *Daily News*, Jack Kiser said that as a sports promoter, Gottlieb was the equal of "Hillary as a mountain climber or Einstein as a thinker." Jim Haughton, writing in *Basketball Weekly*, proclaimed that Gotty "has to rank as one of the great names in American sports. He can fit into the same category as Branch Rickey and Connie Mack; Bert Bell, Art Rooney and George Halas."

Zinkoff, who would later call for a moment of silence before a 76ers' game at the Spectrum, a task he admitted brought tears to his eyes for the first time behind a mike, informed Dick Weiss of the *Daily News* that Gotty was "like a grand uncle to me, a daddy, and a father confessor." When asked by other reporters what Gotty meant to him, Zink, who had been The Mogul's faithful sidekick for 43 years, had a heartfelt response. "How close is close?" he said. "We'd eat together and go to a movie together. I was his driver for a long time. Year in and year out, I was at the wheel of the car that took us to Springfield. We'd make our annual chocolate bar haul up to Hershey where he'd buy cases and cases. How much closer can guys get when if there was a vacation, or a 10-day break in the schedule, the two of us would go to Florida? Except for spending most of my waking minutes with him, day in and day out for so many years of my life, I don't know how to say how close Gotty and the Zink were."

The funeral was held on December 9, 1979, at the Joseph Levine and Sons Funeral Home at 7112 North Broad Street in Philadelphia. Zinkoff, Shrier, and D. Donald Jamison handled the arrangements. It was suggested that contributions be made in Gottlieb's memory to the Basketball Hall of Fame or to the donor's charity of choice.

According to funeral director Samuel Brodsky, who still holds that position, several hundred mourners attended the funeral. There were many former Warriors in the group, including Wilt Chamberlain, Arizin, Gola, and Al Attles, plus Billy Cunningham, Pat Williams, Dolph Schayes, Sonny Hill, Harry Litwack, and Jocko Collins; various old SPHAS and Stars players; NBA figures such as O'Brien, Red Auerbach, Franklin Mieuli, Ben Kerner, and Danny Biasone; and other notables, including Joey Bishop, Max Patkin, and Zack Clayton.

Everyone had a special Gottlieb story or comment. "He gave me my first start," said Bishop. "He's the only reason I'm in this business," declared Patkin. "His temper could explode like a volcano, then it would subside into good humor," recalled Collins, a noted basketball referee. "He gave me my second pair of sneakers when I played with the Rens," said Clayton, a prominent boxing referee. "He was the Connie Mack of his day," praised Williams.

"It was the most memorable day involving Gottlieb, other than the trip to Springfield for his induction ceremony," said Dolson. "It was just a remarkable affair. From the dignitaries to just the regular people who came to the service, it was something that anyone there will never forget."

Following the service conducted by Rabbi Sherman Novoseller of Congregation Beth Tovim, Gotty was laid to rest at Har Nebo Cemetery just off Oxford Circle in Northeast Philadelphia. There, he rejoined his mother, Leah, and sister, Belle, who were buried in the same plot. Also interned in the cemetery was another South Philadelphian, Louis Fine, who was better known as Larry Fine of the old comedy group known as The Three Stooges.

Today, the surrounding area is somewhat rundown, but thousands of graves surround the site where Gottlieb and his family are buried. Plain gravestones, noting only their names and dates of births and deaths, mark the spot. Without knowing, one would hardly realize that a towering figure lies beneath the slightly tilted marker.

Following his death, Gottlieb was the recipient of two special honors. One was the NBA's decision to name its Rookie of the Year Award "The Eddie Gottlieb Trophy." His contributions to the NBA "should never be forgotten," said O'Brien. "It is fitting to name the rookie award after him because, throughout his years, he always maintained the enthusiasm of a young man, and was constantly on the lookout for future NBA stars."

The first recipient of the award was the Celtics' Larry Byrd.

Gottlieb was also inducted into the Jewish Sports Hall of Fame. Other inductees were Litwack, baseball star Al Rosen, Pittsburgh Pirates owner Barney Dreyfuss, announcer Mel Allen, and football great Marshall Goldberg.

On the legal side, Gottlieb's estate was valued at $574,133.29. The bulk of that amount was contained in stocks and bonds, including $133,875 in school district bonds, $31,000 in stock in Anheuser-Busch Brewing Company, and $25,000 each in Texas Instrument and Teleprompter Corporation.

Gottlieb's will, originally dated November 2, 1977, and amended on November 13, 1979, specified a gift of $50,000 to the Basketball Hall of Fame. Gotty's girlfriend, Carmen Trejo, also known as Alicia Romay, then living in Majorca, was willed $35,000, while Rose Adler, Gotty's cousin, received $30,000. Litwack and his wife, Estelle, were the recipients of $25,000, and $20,000 each went to Zinkoff and to Al and Ruth Shrier.

Gifts of $10,000 apiece were awarded to Mike Iannarella, to David Lee Smoger, to Shelley and Jeff Smoger (members of the Litwack family), and to Congregation Beth Tovim Synagogue in Wynnefield. Amounts of $5,000 were distributed to the Philadelphia Department of Recreation, Congregation B'nai Abraham in Philadelphia, the United States Committee of Sports for Israel, Bea Sharpe, and another cousin, Bea Fein.

Bequests were given to the United Way of Philadelphia; the Federation of Jewish Agencies of Greater Philadelphia for the Allied Jewish Appeal; Rabbi Novoseller; Nathan (Shooey) Sisman, who worked long ago for the SPHAS and Warriors; and Nat (Feets) Broudy, a friend and former timekeeper at Madison Square Garden (each $3,000) and to the Bob Greasy Fund at Temple University, the Charles Baker Basketball League, the Jewish Basketball League Alumni, and the Philadelphia Police Athletic League (each $2,000). Gifts of $1,500 or less were designated to go to the South Philadelphia High School athletic fund; South Philadelphia High School scholarship fund; Congregation Temple Israel of Wynnefield; the City of Hope in Denver, Colorado, in memory of his mother; the National Jewish Hospital, also in Denver, in memory of his father; Friends Hospital, in memory of his sister; the Herb Good Basketball Club; the Bill Markward Basketball Club; the Basketball Old Timers' Association; and the Hotstovers' League.

Gottlieb's will provided a revealing glimpse of the man and his personality. It offered a final look at the inner workings of The Mogul and his regard for the special people and institutions in his life.

The will suggested that Gottlieb was loyal, that he cared about people, and that he did not forget or ignore those who had helped him and been his friends. It said that he was willing to honor the organizations that had honored him and that he was charitable, generous, and especially aware of those to whom even the smallest amount was important.

In its final reading, the will silently proclaimed that Eddie Gottlieb had lived a celebrated life that was both full and productive. And in a very special way, it recognized, perhaps for the first time publicly, his generosity and his loyalty.

Acknowledgments

Many, many people covering a wide area of expertise contributed in various ways to this book. All did it with enthusiasm and without the slightest hesitation. Without their help, there is no chance that a book of this kind could have been written.

I especially want to thank the people who participated in personal interviews, many of whom allowed me into their homes or offices for considerably more hours than they had originally anticipated. Many of them were subsequently subjected to frequent phone calls and follow-up questions, too, in every case responding helpfully and enthusiastically.

To my considerable sadness, three of the interviewees who were among those who provided the most information have since passed away. Paul Arizin, Ralph Bernstein, and Frank Dolson were all good friends and will be sorely missed. I could not have done this book without their information, help, and limitless encouragement.

Especially helpful, too, were Marv Bachrad, Ernie Beck, Ken Berman, Marvin Black, Bernie Brown, Bill Campbell, Bill Cash, George Dempsey, Red Klotz, Alan Levitt, Bill Mlkvy, Harvey Pollack, Michael Richman, Jerry Rullo, Al Shrier, Alan Trumper, and Pete Tyrrell, Jr. In the process of making themselves available for extensive interviews, they provided not only indispensable information, but also wonderful stories. And, many of them, were also willing to answer additional questions after the initial interviews.

Many others also granted interviews and supplied valuable information that could be found nowhere else, including Al Attles, Sam (Leaden)

Bernstein, Al Cervi, Norm Drucker, Mahlon Duckett, Jerry Fleischman, Harold Gould, Stanley Green, Jim Heffernan, Sonny Hill, Stan Hochman, Eddie Iannarella, Monte Irvin, John Isaacs, D. Donald Jamison, Ralph Kaplowitz, Les Keiter, the late Bowie Kuhn, Bob Levy, Estelle Litwack, Maje McDonnell, Tom Meschery, Franklin Mieuli, Jackie Moore, Angelo Musi, Amiel Novoseller, Bob Paul, Jack Ramsay, Dolph Schayes, Ossie Schectman, Butch Schwartz, Pat Williams, and Matt Winick.

Thank you one and all for all the helpful information you provided and for being such an integral part of this volume.

In addition to those listed above, countless others played major roles in this extremely difficult and lengthy process. I especially want to cite my good friend, Jim Rosin, for being so helpful and supportive in so many ways. Jim, the author of *Philly Hoops: The SPHAS and Warriors*, was truly an important part of this project. Two other major contributors were Sam Carchidi of the Philadelphia *Inquirer* and Courtney Smith, author of a marvelous master's thesis on the Philadelphia Stars entitled "A Faded Memory." Both helped in ways that couldn't be duplicated.

Matt Zeysing of the Naismith Basketball Hall of Fame, Brian McIntyre and Zelda Spoelstra of the NBA, Raymond Ridder of the Golden State Warriors, and Tim Wiles of the Baseball Hall of Fame were also extremely helpful. Warren Weiner of the Sportsters and my nephew, Andy Dallin in San Francisco, also provided help and information that I could not have done without. Alex Holzman of Temple University Press contributed astute guidance and understanding.

Numerous others helped in many different ways. They include Rebecca Alpert, Barbara Allen, Frank Bilovsky, John Bossong, Samuel Brodsky, Kit Crissey, Bea Doyle Daily, Don Davis, Parry Desmond, Gene Dias, Don DiJulia, Mike Elkin, Bill Esher, Joe Ferrante, Jimmy Gallagher, Simcha Gersh, the late Bucky Harris, Chuck Hasson, Lawrence Hogan, Donald Hunt, Joe Juliano, Ted Kosloff, Dan Lanciano, Norman Macht, Selma Neubauer, Rich Pagano, Nahja Palm, Dan Promislo, David Richman, Jennifer Robbins, John Rossi, Adam Salky, Jack Scheuer, Lois Sernoff, Bobby Shantz, Sarah Sherman, Alice Smith, Carl Smith, Marty Stern, John Thompson, Richard Watson, and Brenda Wright. I am extremely grateful to each person.

Last but far from least, I want to thank my wife, Lois, not only for reading and critiquing every word herein but also for her unbending patience, support, and understanding—sometimes even in the middle of the night when an inspiration surfaced—during this elongated project.

Sources

PRINCIPAL SOURCES

Chapter 1

Special contributions were made to this chapter by sources that included the U.S. Census Reports, Philadelphia Street Directories, and South Philadelphia High School yearbooks. In addition, extremely helpful material on Jews and Jews in Philadelphia was gleaned from *A History of Jews* by Paul Johnson, *Philadelphia Jewish Life* edited by Murray Friedman, *South Philadelphia: Mummers, Memories, and the Melrose Diner* by Murray Dubin, and *Philadelphia: A 300-Year History,* edited by Russell F. Weigley. Other sources were *Ellis Island to Ebbets Field: Sports and the American Jewish Experience* by Peter Levine, and *Cages to Jump Shots: Pro Basketball's Early Years* by Robert Peterson, plus articles by Frank Deford in *Sports Illustrated,* by Bill Ordine, Alan Richman, and Edgar Williams in the Philadelphia *Inquirer,* and by Jon Entine in the *Jewish World Review.*

Chapter 2

Books that were used as reference material for this chapter included ones listed in the previous chapter by Robert D. Bole and Alfred C. Lawrence, by Peter Levine, and by Robert Peterson, as well as *Hank Greenberg: The Story of My Life.* Articles to which references were made included the ones listed above by Deford, Ordine, and Entine, and others by Paul Gallico in the New York *Daily News,* S. O. Grauley, Cy Peterman, Bill Dallas, and John Dell in the Philadelphia *Inquirer,* Ron Avery and Steve Cohen in the *Jewish Exponent,* Gaeton Fonzi in *Greater Philadelphia Magazine,* and Robert Strauss in *Philly Sport.* Also contributing to this chapter was material from *Wikipedia.*

Chapter 3

An especially valuable source was *Philly Hoops: The SPHAS and Warriors* by James Rosin. Among other worthy books were *Luckiest Man: The Life and Death of Lou Gehrig* by Jonathan Eig, and ones mentioned above by Robert D. Bole and Alfred C. Lawrence, by Peter Levine, and by Robert W. Peterson, Also, articles previously cited by Ron Avery, Steve Cohen, Frank Deford, Jon Entine, Gaeton Fonzi, Bill Ordine, and Robert Strauss as well as ones in the Philadelphia *Inquirer* by Frank Fitzpatrick and Laurie Hollman, and in the Philadelphia *Daily News* by Ted Silary. Highly relevant material was also provided by Parry Desmond and by Tim Kelly.

Chapter 4

For this chapter, a critical source was once again Jim Rosin's book on the SPHAS and Warriors. Other key sources included books already cited by Robert D. Bole and Alfred C. Lawrence, and Robert Peterson and *The Modern Encyclopedia of Basketball* by Zander Hollander. In addition to articles already listed, other articles by John Malone, Ed Pollack, and Bob Vetronè in the Philadelphia *Evening Bulletin* were also useful.

Chapter 5

Books used as references were *Blackball Stars: Negro League Pioneers* by John B. Holway, Sol White's *History of Colored Baseball* with an introduction by Jerry Malloy, *Fair Dealing and Clean Playing: The Hilldale Club and the Development of Black Professional Baseball, 1910–1932* by Neil Lanctot, and *Sandlot Seasons: Sport in Black Pittsburgh* by Rob Ruck. Special articles providing references were authored by Bill Livingston in the *Sporting News*, Randy Dixon in the Philadelphia *Tribune*, Bill Dallas in the Philadelphia *Inquirer*, Dick Weiss in the *Daily News*, Rich Pagano in *Town Talk*, and the *Temple News*. Material culled by Bucky Harris from the yearbooks of Philadelphia College of Textiles and Sciences (now Philadelphia University) was also extremely helpful.

Chapter 6

First and foremost, an invaluable source for this chapter was the master's thesis by Courtney Smith at Lehigh University entitled *A Faded Memory*. Written in 2002, it gives a detailed history of the Philadelphia Stars. A book that provided special information was Murray Dubin's *South Philadelphia: Mummers, Memories, and the Melrose Diner*, which gives an excellent view of early black baseball as well as the evolution of groups and neighborhoods. Another helpful book in this area is *Philadelphia: A 300-Year History*. Books that were particularly helpful with their coverage of black baseball in Philadelphia included *A Complete History of the Negro Leagues* by Mark Ribowsky, *Shades of Glory: The Negro Leagues and the Story of African American Baseball* by Lawrence D. Hogan, *Fair Dealing and Clean Playing: The Hilldale Club and the Development of Black Professional Baseball, 1910–1932* by Neil Lanctot, *The Integration of Baseball in Philadelphia* by Christopher Threston, *Blackball Stars: Negro League Pioneers* by John Holway, and Sol White's *History of Colored Baseball*. Other useful sources were the African American Museum, the Philadelphia *Tribune*, Philadelphia *Inquirer*, and the Delaware County *Daily Times*.

Chapter 7

As in the previous chapter, a major contribution was made to this chapter by Court-ney Smith, author of a master's thesis on the Philadelphia Stars. Other books that provided important information on black baseball included the ones listed for Chapter 6 by Mark Ribowsky, Lawrence D. Hogan, Neil Lanctot, Rob Ruck, Christo-pher Threston, and John Holway. Other helpful books included *Invisible Men: Life in Baseball's Negro Leagues* by Donn Rogosin, *Baseball's Great Experiment: Jackie Robin-son and His Legacy* by Jules Tygiel, *Only the Ball Was White* by Robert Peterson, *Sand-lot Seasons: Sport in Black Pittsburgh* by Rob Ruck, *The Biographical Encyclopedia of the Negro Baseball Leagues* by James A. Riley, *It's Good to be Alive* by Roy Campanella, and *The Negro Leagues Book* edited by Dick Clark and Larry Lester. Articles by Ed Harris and others in the Philadelphia *Tribune*, by Wendell Smith the Pittsburgh *Courier*, and in the Philadelphia *Inquirer* were also helpful.

Chapter 8

There are a number of sources that provided the information for this chapter, none more significant that the column by Red Smith in the New York *Times*. *The Phillies Encyclopedia* by Rich Westcott and Frank Bilovsky and *Philadelphia's Old Ball-parks* by Rich Westcott also played roles in the preparation of this chapter, as did articles by Ed (Dutch) Doyle entitled *Baker Bowl*, published in *The National Pastime* of the Society for American Baseball Research. Of special help, too, were Robert Levy and John Rossi of La Salle University.

Chapter 9

Material used in this chapter came from a variety of sources. Among those partic-ularly helpful were *The Official NBA Basketball Encyclopedia* and *The Modern Encyclo-pedia of Basketball*. Other important sources were *The Origins of the Jump Shot: Eight Men Who Shook the World of Basketball* by John Christgau, *The Philadelphia Story* by Frank Dolson, *24 Seconds to Shoot: The Birth and Improbable Rise of the NBA* by Leonard Koppett, and again Jim Rosin's *Philly Hoops*. Other material came from the origi-nal minutes of the BAA, a fascinating booklet assembled by Peter Tyrrell about his father, a defunct publication called *Inside Basketball*, and articles by Sam Goldaper in the NBA's *Hoop* magazine and Mike Lupica in the New York *Daily News*.

Chapter 10

The two basketball encyclopedias listed above were once again highly valuable sources for this chapter. So, too, were *The Rivalry: Bill Russell, Wilt Chamberlain and the Golden Age of Basketball* by John Taylor and *Cousy: His Life, Career and the Birth of Big-Time Basketball* by Bob Cousy. Books listed above by Robert Peterson and Jim Rosin again proved useful, as did articles by Ed Delaney in the *Evening Bulletin*, Fred Byrod in the Philadelphia *Inquirer*, *Inside Basketball*, *Basketball Illustrated*, and by Frank Deford in *Sports Illustrated*.

Chapter 11

The major portion of this chapter resulted from personal interviews by a number of people mentioned elsewhere in the list of acknowledgments. The *Evening Bulletin* in an article by Bob Vetrone and Philadelphia *Inquirer* in an article by Edgar Williams also provided useful information.

Chapter 12

Helpful material for this chapter came from the following books: *Spanning the Globe: The Rise, Fall, and Return of the Harlem Globetrotters* by Ben Green, *They Cleared the Lane: The NBA's Black Pioneers* by Ron Thomas, *Tall Tales: The Glory Years of the NBA in the Words of the Men Who Played, Coached, and Built Pro Basketball* by Terry Pluto, and *Wilt, 1962: The Night of 100 Points and the Dawn of a New Era* by Gary Pomerantz, plus books cited above by Robert Peterson and John Taylor. Also used as reference material were articles by Bob McGowan in the *Daily News,* Frank Brady in the *Evening Bulletin,* and Malcolm Poindexter in the Philadelphia *Tribune.*

Chapter 13

A variety of sources are reflected in this chapter, not the least of which are books mentioned earlier by Ben Green, Robert Peterson, and the *NBA Encyclopedia.* Again, articles can be cited from the *Evening Bulletin* by Bill Dallas and Jim Heffernan. Also particularly useful was *The Wigwam,* the Warriors' game program edited by Dave Zinkoff.

Chapter 14

As before, books listed for earlier chapters by Ben Green, Terry Pluto, Gary Pomerantz, and John Taylor made significant contributions to this chapter, as did *Wilt: Larger Than Life* by Robert Cherry, and *Wilt: Just Like Any Other 7-Foot Black Millionaire Who Lives Next Door* by Wilt Chamberlain and David Shaw. Also useful were articles by Jack Kiser in the *Daily News,* and Jim Heffernan and Alan Richman in the *Evening Bulletin.*

Chapter 15

Significant information for this chapter came from the *Modern Basketball Encyclopedia,* as well as the books by Robert Cherry, Ben Green, Terry Pluto, Gary Pomerantz, and John Taylor. Other contributors included the Naismith Basketball Hall of Fame, Jack Kiser in the *Daily News,* Tom Fox, Herb Good, and Jim Heffernan in the *Evening Bulletin,* John Dell in the *Inquirer,* United Press International, and Gaeton Fonzi in *Greater Philadelphia Magazine.*

Chapter 16

Among the many helpful sources for this chapter, of particular note was material found at the Naismith Basketball Hall of Fame in Springfield, Massachusetts.

Again, books by Robert Peterson, Leonard Koppett, and Terry Pluto were important sources, as were articles in the *Inquirer* by Fred Byrod, in the *Evening Bulletin* by
Hugh Brown, in the *Daily News* by Jack Kiser, and in *Inside Basketball*.

Chapter 17

An important contribution to this chapter was made by *Hardball: The Education of a
Baseball Commissioner* by Bowie Kuhn and Marty Appel. Also, the Philadelphia City
Archives were helpful, as was material at the Naismith Basketball Hall of Fame.
Articles in the *Daily News* by Stan Hochman, in the *Inquirer* by John Dell, in *Bas-
ketball Weekly* by Jim Haughton, and in the St. Louis *Post-Dispatch* by Bob Broeg
contributed.

OTHER SOURCES

African American Museum, Philadelphia; Baseball Hall of Fame, Cooperstown,
New York; Naismith Basketball Hall of Fame, Springfield, Massachusetts; Fam-
ily History Center–Church of Jesus Christ of Latter Day Saints, Broomall, Penn-
sylvania; Free Library of Philadelphia; Golden State Warriors; National Archives;
National Basketball Association; Negro League Baseball Museum, Kansas City, Mis-
souri; Philadelphia Jewish Archives; Pennsylvania Historical Society; Philadelphia
District Court; Philadelphia City Archives; Philadelphia Jewish Sports Hall of Fame;
Springfield, Pennsylvania, Library; Temple University Urban Archives.

Index

Rich Westcott is a writer and sports historian and a veteran of more than 40 years as a working journalist. He is a leading authority on the Phillies, and for 14 years was editor and publisher of *Phillies Report*. A native Philadelphian, he is the author of 18 other books, including *Veterans Stadium, Philadelphia's Old Ballparks, The Phillies Encyclopedia* (with Frank Bilovsky), and *A Century of Philadelphia Sports*. Westcott has seen or covered all the major teams in Philadelphia, including the Warriors and 76ers.